Rosie
O'Donnell

The People to Know Series

Madeleine Albright
*First Woman
Secretary of State*
0-7660-1143-7

Neil Armstrong
*The First Man
on the Moon*
0-89490-828-6

Isaac Asimov
*Master of
Science Fiction*
0-7660-1031-7

Robert Ballard
*Oceanographer Who
Discovered the Titanic*
0-7660-1147-X

Willa Cather
Writer of the Prairie
0-89490-980-0

Bill Clinton
*United States
President*
0-89490-437-X

Hillary Rodham Clinton
Activist First Lady
0-89490-583-X

Bill Cosby
Actor and Comedian
0-89490-548-1

Walt Disney
*Creator of
Mickey Mouse*
0-89490-694-1

Bob Dole
Legendary Senator
0-89490-825-1

Marian Wright Edelman
*Fighting for
Children's Rights*
0-89490-623-2

Bill Gates
*Billionaire
Computer Genius*
0-89490-824-3

Jane Goodall
Protector of Chimpanzees
0-89490-827-8

Al Gore
*Leader for the
New Millennium*
0-7660-1232-8

Tipper Gore
*Activist, Author,
Photographer*
0-7660-1142-9

Ernest Hemingway
Writer and Adventurer
0-89490-979-7

Ron Howard
*Child Star &
Hollywood Director*
0-89490-981-9

John F. Kennedy
*President of the
New Frontier*
0-89490-693-3

Stephen King
*King of Thrillers
and Horror*
0-7660-1233-6

John Lennon
The Beatles and Beyond
0-89490-702-6

Maya Lin
Architect and Artist
0-89490-499-X

Jack London
*A Writer's
Adventurous Life*
0-7660-1144-5

Barbara McClintock
*Nobel Prize
Geneticist*
0-89490-983-5

Rosie O'Donnell
*Talk Show Host
and Comedian*
0-7660-1148-8

Christopher Reeve
*Hollywood's Man
of Courage*
0-7660-1149-6

Ann Richards
*Politician, Feminist,
Survivor*
0-89490-497-3

Sally Ride
*First American Woman
in Space*
0-89490-829-4

Will Rogers
Cowboy Philosopher
0-89490-695-X

Franklin D. Roosevelt
*The Four-Term
President*
0-89490-696-8

Steven Spielberg
Hollywood Filmmaker
0-89490-697-6

John Steinbeck
America's Author
0-7660-1150-X

Martha Stewart
*Successful
Businesswoman*
0-89490-984-3

Amy Tan
*Author of
The Joy Luck Club*
0-89490-699-2

Alice Walker
*Author of
The Color Purple*
0-89490-620-8

Simon Wiesenthal
*Tracking Down
Nazi Criminals*
0-89490-830-8

Frank Lloyd Wright
Visionary Architect
0-7660-1032-5

People to Know

Rosie O'Donnell

Talk Show Host and Comedian

Virginia Meachum

Enslow Publishers, Inc.
40 Industrial Road   PO Box 38
Box 398   Aldershot
Berkeley Heights, NJ 07922   Hants GU12 6BP
USA   UK
http://www.enslow.com

Library of Congress Cataloging-in-Publication Data

Meachum, Virginia.
    Rosie O'Donnell : talk show host and comedian / Virginia Meachum.
        p. cm. — (People to know)
    Includes bibliographical references and index.
    Summary: A biography of a popular talk show host, describing her childhood,
education, and career in comedy, the movies, on Broadway, and on television.
    ISBN 0-7660-1148-8
    1. O'Donnell, Rosie Juvenile literature. 2. Comedians—United States Biography
Juvenile literature. 3. Motion picture actors and actresses—United States
Biography Juvenile literature. 4. Television personalities—United States Biography
Juvenile literature. [1. O'Donnell, Rosie. 2. Comedians. 3. Entertainers.
4. Women Biography.] I. Title. II. Series.
PN2287.O27M43   2000
792.7'028'092—dc21
[B]   99-26875
                                               CIP

Printed in the United States of America

10 9 8 7 6 5 4 3 2 1

To Our Readers:
All Internet addresses in this book were active and appropriate when we went to press.
Any comments or suggestions can be sent by e-mail to Comments@enslow.com or to
the address on the back cover.

Illustration Credits: AP/Wide World Photos, pp. 6, 89, 92, 94; © Corel
Corporation, pp. 12, 15; Courtesy of Seth Poppel Yearbook Archives, p. 24;
Doug Curran/Everett Collection, p. 54; E.J. Camp/Everett Collection, p. 73;
Everett Collection, pp. 40, 43, 45, 49, 52, 82; George Lange/Everett
Collection, p. 64; Kimberly Wright/Everett Collection, p. 68; Mary Ellen
Matthews/Everett Collection, p. 59.

Cover Illustration: Everett Collection

Contents

Rosie O'Donnell

Something Nice

In a television studio at Rockefeller Center in New York City, a thirtyish woman sits onstage behind a desk, shooting Koosh balls into the audience. While channel surfing, you have just tuned in to *The Rosie O'Donnell Show*. This popular daytime TV show is already in progress. But look closely. The one hundred eighty audience seats are filled with children. They are cheering and waving pompoms. Off to one side of the stage, a five-piece band whips up a staccato beat as clusters of balloons dance beneath the ceiling. What is going on?

It is Monday, October 13, 1997, the national holiday celebrating the birthday of Christopher Columbus. Schools are closed for the day, and talk show host Rosie O'Donnell is doing a show especially for kids.

Now the cheery host in a bright blue pantsuit struts out into the audience, microphone in hand, seeking young talent. Each fleeting performance—a magic trick, a riddle, an imitation of a famous person— is rewarded with a furry, stuffed toy.

Returning onstage, O'Donnell, with the lively spirit of a ten-year-old, oversees the planned fun. Youngsters from the audience are invited to play games and win prizes. Next, two professional child actors are interviewed by Rosie, as she is popularly known. Singer Alea, from the sound track of Disney's *Anastasia*, performs one of the songs, along with three backup singers. The television twins Mary-Kate and Ashley Olsen (*Full House* and *Two of a Kind*) show up to talk about appearing in television commercials. Next, they are joined by eight kids from the audience to play a rousing balloon-flipping game. There are no losers. Everyone wins books and videos.

The band members, wearing funny hats, strike up a final musical number that signals the close of this wild and happy hour. Applause, applause, cheers, music, fadeout. You have just witnessed the highest-rated new talk show of the decade.[1]

The point of *The Rosie O'Donnell Show* is happy entertainment. This is totally different from the focus of the numerous talk shows that dominated daytime television in the early and mid-1990s. Personal problems had become the central theme of those shows. Drug addiction, marital infidelity, traumatic divorce, and similar topics were openly discussed by the alleged victims. Sometimes their anger erupted into foul language, hair pulling, and even fistfights—all shown on television. Clearly, a different kind of program was needed for daytime viewers.

On June 10, 1996, the ABC television network introduced *The Rosie O'Donnell Show*. The host, stand-up comic and movie actress Rosie O'Donnell, burst upon the screen with music, fascinating guests, and fun. This one-hour variety talk show aired throughout most of the nation. It was an immediate hit. Reviews of the show were highly enthusiastic. One reviewer wrote: "She's taken the trash out of talk by making nice, not nasty. And for that she should be given a Nobel Prize. . . ."[2] Another praised O'Donnell for being "animated, funny, and endearing."[3] Four weeks after the opening show, *Newsweek* featured Rosie O'Donnell on its cover and named her "The Queen of Nice."[4]

Rosie O'Donnell first rose to the attention of moviegoers with her wisecracking role as the third baseman in the movie *A League of Her Own*. Later, in the Broadway musical *Grease!*, she played bad girl Betty Rizzo, leader of the tough-talking "Pink Ladies."

How did a sassy, tough-talking Rosie O'Donnell bring about that much-needed "something nice" to daytime television?

2

Growing Up Fast

Roseann O'Donnell was born on March 21, 1962, in Commack, New York. She was the third child of Edward J. and Roseann Murtha O'Donnell. Roseann's brother Edward Jr. was then two years old, and Daniel was age one. A sister, Maureen, was born fifteen months after Roseann, followed by brother Timothy in 1966.

The children's father worked as an electrical engineer, and their mother (for whom daughter Roseann was named) was a homemaker. As a young child, Edward O'Donnell had immigrated with his parents to the United States from Donegal, Ireland. They settled on Long Island, where he eventually met his future wife. Roseann Murtha O'Donnell was also of Irish heritage, but she was born in the United States.

The O'Donnell family lived in a two-story, brick and cedar-shingled home on Rhonda Lane in Commack. This working-class community on Long Island is about fifty miles east of New York City. Rhonda Lane was a street of modest homes and wide lawns and had several other Irish Catholic families among its residents.

The O'Donnell children were brought up in the Catholic faith, and the family worshiped each Sunday at the nearby Roman Catholic Church. Their father and mother were quite opposite in personality. Edward O'Donnell was close-mouthed, very conservative, and stern. Roseann Murtha O'Donnell was outgoing, friendly, and cheerful. Dark-haired and blue-eyed, she was described by her sons as looking like actress Elizabeth Taylor.[1] She had a passion for movies, Broadway musicals, and television. She bought soundtrack albums of Broadway shows and played them regularly as she worked around the house. Also, she would rearrange the family household schedule in order to watch a television appearance by a favorite performer such as Barbra Streisand.[2] Hearing show tunes at home became a natural part of young Roseann's growing up, and she was quick to pick up the lyrics.

A tomboy, Roseann spent many hours outdoors playing kick-the-can, hide-and-seek, and other games with her siblings and the neighborhood children. When her brothers went to Little League, she tagged along. At that time, girls were not allowed to play with the boys in organized baseball. Before and after the games, however, the coach let Roseann join

The New York City theater district: Rosie's mother had a passion for Broadway musicals, and young Rosie learned the words to a variety of show tunes.

in the practice. She soon became a skilled player, particularly as a pitcher and a shortstop. "I was always the first girl picked for the neighborhood teams," she recalls.[3]

Roseann shared her mother's sunny disposition and passion for musical theater. Memorizing the lyrics from her mother's record albums, she imitated the singers, and entertained her mother in the kitchen as she cooked dinner. Her sister, Maureen, remembers, "Rosie was always telling jokes and doing imitations."[4]

"Rosie" was one of Roseann's nicknames during her growing-up years. Another was "Dolly," which began when infant Roseann was brought home from the hospital. Her toddler brothers could not say "Roseann," so they called the new baby "Dolly." From then until she was about twelve years old, the family called her Dolly.[5]

When Rosie was six years old, her mother took her to see *Funny Girl*, the movie musical starring Barbra Streisand. The singer-actress made a lasting impression on the young child. Rosie imitated Streisand's speech, sang songs from her albums, and dreamed of being the next Barbra Streisand. Mrs. O'Donnell pointed out that Roseann did not have the same kind of voice as her idol, but her starstruck daughter was confident. "I'll learn," she said.[6]

Roseann entered Rolling Hills Elementary School at the age of six, and her need to perform soon found a place. While her classmates would bring their Barbie dolls and other treasures for Show and Tell, Roseann preferred to sing "Oklahoma" or some other lively Broadway tune. In second grade, she played Glinda the Good Witch in *The Wizard of Oz*. This was her first stage appearance, and she knew then that she wanted to be an entertainer.[7]

Rosie's mother served for a time as president of the Parent-Teacher Association of Rolling Hills Elementary School. Sometimes when she visited the school, teachers came out of their classrooms to talk with her. Through the windows along the hallway, Roseann could see her mother talking and then the teachers laughing. One time she accompanied her mother to a PTA meeting. When Mrs. O'Donnell spoke in front of the group, she soon had everyone laughing.

Rosie remembers feeling that it was an amazing thing and wanting to be like her mother in that way.[8]

Mother and daughter shared their enjoyment of movies and musical theater. Occasionally, they would ride the Long Island Railroad into Manhattan and attend the stage show and movie at Radio City Music Hall. Mrs. O'Donnell bought the cheapest seats, which meant sitting high up in the theater, far from the stage. But this did not dim their appreciation of the performance. Rosie has said that her fondest childhood memory is of sitting high in the balcony of Radio City Music Hall, sharing lemon drops with her mother.[9] Television was another activity they enjoyed together. Every day after school, Rosie would hurry home to watch the afternoon talk shows with her mother. Merv Griffin and Mike Douglas were Rosie's heroes, she has said, because their talk shows "made everyone feel at home."[10]

When she was ten years old and in the fifth grade, Roseann seemed to be enjoying a happy, carefree childhood. But all of this would soon change.

In December 1972, Mrs. O'Donnell was diagnosed with cancer. The details of her illness were not discussed within the family, but Roseann noticed that her normally stocky mother was becoming very thin.[11] When Mrs. O'Donnell was hospitalized, the children were told their mother had hepatitis. Because they did not know what the word meant, Rosie looked it up in the library and found that it was a disease that came from dirty needles. Rosie thought to herself that her mother had gotten sick from sewing.[12]

Of course she wanted to visit her mother in the

Rosie's favorite childhood memory is of eating lemon drops with her mom in the highest balcony of Radio City Music Hall in New York City.

hospital. "At the time, you weren't allowed to go in if you were under twelve, so the nurses would sneak us up in the emergency-room elevator."[13]

On St. Patrick's Day, March 17, 1973, Mr. O'Donnell told his children that their mother had "passed away."[14] As before, they were given no explanation. Their questions went unanswered. This was four days before Roseann's eleventh birthday. Forever after, she would refer to the loss of her mother as "the defining moment in my life."[15]

The days that followed were very confusing. The children were not permitted to see their mother's body or to attend the funeral. The reason given was that it would be too traumatic.[16] Their grief-stricken father would not talk about their mother's death. Soon after, he arranged to have all of her possessions removed from the house.

For a time, Roseann was convinced that her mother was not actually dead. She engaged in fantasies about what might really have happened.[17] Maybe she had been kidnapped, and nobody was telling the children. Or perhaps she had run off to California to escape the responsibility of parenting five children. Sometimes, when playing in a basketball game at school, Roseann imagined that her mother was sitting in the stands, watching.[18]

Meanwhile, Edward O'Donnell, immersed in his own grief, became more and more withdrawn from the children. He was at work all day and was frequently absent in the evenings. Left to care for themselves, the five children drew together as a team. The older brothers did much of the cooking and cleaning.

Roseann became the mother figure, assigning chores, refereeing family arguments, and defending her younger sister and brother from schoolyard bullies. Too soon, her childhood had ended.

One way that she coped was to hang out at her best friend's house across the street. Jackie Ellard and Roseann had been friends since they were two years old. Jackie's mother, Bernice Ellard, was always there to provide support when needed. Several nights a week, Roseann would eat dinner at the Ellards. She began to notice how different things were at their house compared with hers. They had serving dishes and serving spoons, and real Tupperware with lids that matched. They served gravy on ordinary days, not just at Thanksgiving.[19] At Rosie's house, they did not have what she called "luxuries"—matching socks, underwear that fit, top sheets for the bed, or a hair dryer. They used a "vacuum cleaner with the hose on the turn-around side," said Rosie.[20] Someday, she wanted a home like the Ellards.[21]

Watching television was another way that Rosie coped with her family loss. She now turned to family shows: *Eight Is Enough*, *The Brady Bunch*, *The Partridge Family*. "I would watch these shows," she said, "hoping that my father would meet a Julie Andrews–type who would bring love and life back to our home."[22] But this wishful fantasy did not make it any easier to accept her loss.

In the fall of 1974, Roseann entered junior high school. At the elementary school, her mother had been well known and the teachers were aware of her death. At the junior high school, none of the teachers knew.

On the third day of school, Roseann had not done her homework, and one of the teachers said, "What's your mother's name? I'm calling your house." Roseann could not bring herself to answer. She could hear her classmates begin to whisper among themselves. When the teacher demanded, in a much louder voice, "What's her name?" a second and a third time, Roseann ran out of the school building and hid in the woods until dark.[23]

At a meeting after school, the incident was discussed, and the loss of Roseann's mother became known to her new teachers. Afterward, her seventh-grade math teacher, Pat Maravel, personally involved herself in helping Roseann cope both in school and out. She became a positive influence throughout Roseann's adolescent years.

Now, in a way, both Pat Maravel and Bernice Ellard filled in for the mom that Roseann no longer had. Their support would never be forgotten. Throughout the following years, they would each receive a card on Mother's Day from an ever-grateful Roseann. Later, she would become the godparent of Pat Maravel's two children.[24]

Building a Dream

In September 1976, Roseann entered Commack High School South. In addition to the required classes, she plunged into a full schedule of extracurricular activities. From drama club to team sports to yearbook staff, she was there, bringing abundant energy and her own kind of humor.

Roseann's humor—her constant effort to make others laugh—may not always have been appreciated by her teachers. With no parental guidelines at home, she had not learned to respect authority. Like many teenagers, she felt she knew more than her elders. "I got away with that attitude," she said later, "because I was funny."[1] Actually, her interest was more in making the teachers laugh than in entertaining the students. "I was always trying to get the teachers, who were around the age of my mother, to like me and validate me."[2] Joking and making witty remarks was her way of seeking their approval.

Roseann was not a troublemaker. "I never rebelled in traditional ways," she has said. "I didn't smoke, drink, or have sex. . . . I was rebellious in that I was always the boss. My father was not really around, and there was no mother, so I did what I wanted."[3]

As a teenager, Roseann's ultimate dream was to become an actress. It was the same dream she had as a child, when entertaining her mother in the kitchen with Barbra Streisand songs and imitations. When Edward O'Donnell removed his wife's possessions from the house immediately after her death, her Barbra Streisand records were the only things left. For Roseann, Streisand was a connection to her mom.[4]

Although Streisand may have been Roseann's first and most impressive role model, others in the entertainment arena also captured her admiration. Among them were Bette Midler, who appeared on Broadway in *Clams on the Half-Shell Revue*, which Roseann saw when she was twelve years old. In this offbeat musical, actress Midler showcased her talent for comedy as well as singing and dancing. Roseann was fascinated. "I remember watching her up there on stage and thinking, 'That's what I want to do.'"[5] She began to collect Bette Midler record albums and memorize the lyrics. Later, when the star appeared at a Manhattan bookstore to promote her book *The Saga of Baby Divine*, Roseann's brother Danny stood in line for an hour to get an autographed copy for his sister.[6]

Roseann also admired comic actresses. When she

saw actresses such as Vivian Vance playing Ethel Mertz on the *I Love Lucy Show*, and Valerie Harper playing Rhoda Morgenstern on *The Mary Tyler Moore Show*, she knew, "Now *there's* a role for me."[7]

High school for Roseann was only one of the activities that filled her days. As the mother figure to her siblings, she had a household to run. Also, there were TV shows she did not want to miss (*Ryan's Hope* had become a favorite soap opera), after-school basketball and other sports, and baby-sitting for neighborhood children. Baby-sitting earnings, along with her allowance, provided funds for her real passion—attending Broadway shows.

Roseann was always aware of the new musicals opening in New York City. It was not unusual for her to cut classes on a Wednesday and ride the train into Manhattan to see a matinee performance. Afterward, she hurried around to the stage door where fans waited for the stars to autograph their printed programs. That was how she became acquainted with Lucie Arnaz, the daughter of Lucille Ball and Desi Arnaz of the television show *I Love Lucy*.

In 1978, Lucie Arnaz costarred with Robert Klein in the musical *They're Playing Our Song*. Following the show, Roseann joined the many fans crowding around the stage door to meet Lucie Arnaz and to get her autograph. Soon after, expressing her admiration for both the Broadway star and her actress mother, Roseann sent a fan letter to Arnaz at the theater. Stars rarely reply to fan letters, but this star wrote back. Surprisingly, Arnaz and her young fan exchanged several notes during the show's New York run. These were carefully preserved by Roseann in her Lucie Arnaz scrapbook.[8] Beginning in childhood, she kept scrapbooks with photos and autographs of favorite stars. The walls of her bedroom were covered with pictures of Streisand, Midler, and other performers who caught her interest. Being surrounded by these images helped to keep her dream alive. They inspired her to believe in herself.[9]

Another of Roseann's passions was movies. Unlike most of her high school friends, she was more into moviegoing than dating. On weekends, she often attended movies alone. Later, she joined her friends' parties, eager to talk about the latest film. In general, their attitude was, "It's only a movie, who cares."[10]

But her sister, Maureen, cared. She too was a movie enthusiast. Each year, the two of them would make viewing the televised Academy Awards ceremony their special event. On that evening, a golden statuette, nicknamed Oscar, is presented to individuals for outstanding achievement in the film industry. The O'Donnell sisters both had their own ideas of who should be awarded an Oscar for Best Actor, Best Actress, Best Picture, and other categories. They would dress up for the occasion, prepare their favorite food (pigs-in-a-blanket), and watch the televised ceremony all evening, rooting for their favorite performers.[11]

One nighttime activity for sixteen-year-old Roseann and her friends was to hang out at one of the many local comedy clubs. The Ground Round Restaurant in Mineola on Long Island was a particular favorite. Famous for its hamburgers, it also had a microphone in the bar area where comics performed. Tuesdays were contest nights called "open mikes," and amateurs were invited to compete. One evening, Roseann's friends dared her to try, and she accepted their challenge. She had not prepared an act, but quickly came up with some one-liners and funny stories. Much to her surprise, she won the $50 first prize. "Wow, this is easy," she thought.[12]

Sometimes when Roseann was late getting home, her father waited by the front door and accused her of smoking marijuana. "You're taking pot, aren't ya!" he would shout. "Oh, ye bunch of pot takers."[13] He was mistaken, though. Roseann never smoked.

Roseann continued to have trouble accepting her mother's death. It would be several years before she could actually say that her mother had died. When someone called and asked if her mother was home, Roseann would say, "She's in the shower, can you call back?"[14] The loss of her mother had never been discussed in their house. Roseann was sixteen years old when she found out that the cause of her mother's death was cancer. A neighbor revealed the truth during an American Cancer Society bike-a-thon.[15]

Despite her many activities both in and out of school, Roseann managed to maintain a B average. She credited this to "a great memory," rather than to her study habits.[16] At age seventeen, five feet seven inches tall, Roseann was physically fit. She was on both the varsity tennis and junior varsity volleyball teams, and she played baseball, field hockey, and other sports.

Throughout her high school years, Roseann served on various committees and on the Executive Board of

At Commack High School South, Rosie won the award for Most School Spirit and was voted Class Clown. She was also elected senior class president and prom queen.

the Student Council. As a Drama Club member, she appeared in almost every school play, and she played the drums in a school rock group. Her outgoing nature and sense of humor made her popular among the other students. One school friend remembers that it was fun having her around. "She was . . . a very funny, happy, warm person." Said another, "The guys liked Rosie because . . . she was more than a match for them. She could throw a football, catch a baseball and curse with the best of the boys."[17]

Roseann's popularity was evident in the titles she was awarded by her peers—Most School Spirit, Class Clown, Personality Plus, and Homecoming Queen. As a senior, Roseann was elected class president and also prom queen.

One event that would influence Roseann's future occurred during her appearance in the Senior Follies. This annual student production was made up of original comedy skits about the teachers at Commack High School South. With her talent for mimicry, Roseann gave a convincing impersonation of Roseanne Roseannadanna, a character created by actress Gilda Radner on the popular television show *Saturday Night Live.*

Afterward, a man in the audience invited Roseann to do stand-up comedy at his club nearby, the Eastside Comedy Club in Huntington, Long Island. She really wanted to be an actress, not a comic, but this would be an opportunity to perform before an audience. She agreed to give it a try.[18]

Roseann graduated from Commack High School South in June 1980 and entered the world of professional entertainment.

A Shaky Start

Roseann O'Donnell's first performance as a stand-up comic was an eye-opening experience for her. As the lone entertainer onstage in the spotlight, she was expected to keep the audience amused for a certain number of minutes, with no breaks. It turned out that her series of one-liner jokes, celebrity impressions, and personal anecdotes were not enough to fill her time slot. The audience response was far from enthusiastic.

At first, O'Donnell blamed the audience. "I was seventeen . . . and I had a very big ego. When people didn't laugh, I thought *they* were stupid. My adolescent arrogance carried me right through. I had that 'try anything' attitude. But I had to *learn* to be funny onstage."[1]

O'Donnell tried padding her performance with

wisecracks to individuals in the audience, such as "Nice shirt. Where'd you get it, Kmart?" But she soon realized that she needed to be better prepared. She needed to work up a real act.

The problem was solved one day when she watched a young comic on *The Merv Griffin Show*. In a soft-spoken, unhurried style, he made witty observations about daily events. His act brought instant laughter from the studio audience and from O'Donnell. With her gift for memory and mimicry, she easily memorized his dialogue and manner of speaking. The comic was Jerry Seinfeld. On her next appearance at the comedy club, she presented his routine. The audience responded enthusiastically.

O'Donnell felt triumphant, but not for long. As she left the stage, the other comics descended upon her and demanded to know where she got those jokes. When she told them from Jerry Seinfeld on TV, they said, "You can't do that!" They told her she would have to write her own jokes. "I was totally devastated," recalls O'Donnell. "I went home thinking, 'How am I going to do this if I have to make up my own jokes?'"[2]

What O'Donnell had not known was that some jokes have been around for such a long time, they are in the public domain. That is, those jokes may be used by anyone. However, no professional comic would intentionally perform another person's act.[3]

How do comics come up with fresh, original material for their routines? They hire a gag writer or they write their own jokes. Since O'Donnell could not afford to hire someone, she began to write her own material. She exaggerated her experiences from daily life, and from her Irish Catholic background, to make them into a funny act. Once she had developed a comedy routine, she could perform it at several different clubs in the area.

O'Donnell also visited comedy clubs as a member of the audience. While her friends were out partying, she would be sitting in the back of places like the Eastside Comedy Club, taking notes, trying to see how the comics presented a joke and how they made a smooth transition from one topic to another.[4]

It was during her early years of stand-up comedy that O'Donnell acquired her stage name. When Roseann O'Donnell was introduced by an emcee (master of ceremonies), her name sounded somewhat like "Roseannadanna." When Gilda Radner, creator of that popular *Saturday Night Live* character, did not appear onstage, the disappointed audience reacted by booing O'Donnell. To prevent this from happening again, the emcee introduced her as "Rosie" O'Donnell. That became her name both onstage and off.[5]

During this period of learning how to be a comic, O'Donnell also observed the person acting as master of ceremonies. An emcee does not do a lengthy act. The emcee's gags and anecdotes are scattered throughout the show between the acts of other performers. An emcee's major duty is to introduce the other comedians on the program. Also, at that time, an emcee earned $15 a night, whereas a comic earned only $10. Occasionally, O'Donnell had the opportunity to be the emcee at an area comedy club. Standing offstage, she studied each performer, noting how a comic would take an experience from life that people could relate to. By giving it a humorous slant, the audience would feel, "Oh, yeah, I've done that," and would respond with laughter.[6]

In the fall of 1980, O'Donnell shifted her attention back to her education. With prodding from her father, she had made plans to enter college. Edward O'Donnell believed a college education would be important to her future.[7]

In September, O'Donnell entered Dickinson College in Carlisle, Pennsylvania. A coed school, with an enrollment of about seventeen hundred students, it is located about 230 miles from Commack. This was the first time O'Donnell had lived away from home. Her older brothers were already away, following their own career paths, and Maureen and Timothy were still at home with their father.

O'Donnell lived in a women's dormitory and worked in the administration office as part of a work-study requirement that provided her with a student loan. She did well in gym classes and all sports activities, but not as well in academic classes. "It was a school for people much smarter than me," she said.[8]

O'Donnell got along well with her fellow students and office coworkers. Her thoughts, however, were more focused on pursuing a show business career. It was about this time that she finally came to terms with her deep personal loss—the death of her mother. One day her college roommate asked, "Why do you always talk about your father, and never your mother?" As O'Donnell recalls, "I stopped for a moment, and I remember having to choke the words out: 'Well, she died.' That was the first time I ever said it."[9] When her mother died, O'Donnell says that she herself "just shut down emotionally. You're angry, you're wounded. You use coping mechanism after coping mechanism."[10]

Apparently, O'Donnell's coping mechanism was to zero in on her goal of becoming an actress and a Broadway star. Stand-up comedy might lead the way. Even while she was in college, O'Donnell tried to learn more about the business. Often, on weekends, she and a dorm mate rode two hours by bus to Philadelphia, where they hung out at some of the city's comedy clubs.

Since studying had not been a high priority for O'Donnell, her freshman year ended with a disappointing D average. There was no point in returning to Dickinson the following year.

Her interest now turned to Boston University, known for its theater arts department. In the summer of 1981, O'Donnell auditioned for admittance to the department with a scene from the Broadway musical *Hello, Dolly!* Having watched the Barbra Streisand film version many times, and learned each word and gesture, O'Donnell gave a performance that earned her an acting scholarship.

At that time, Boston University had an enrollment of about fourteen thousand undergraduate students. The campus, within the busy, metropolitan area of Boston, Massachusetts, provided easy access to theaters and comedy clubs. Despite classwork, O'Donnell found time to see all the new movies and plays and to visit many of the numerous comedy clubs in the city. She even accepted a few stand-up comedy engagements, or "gigs."

O'Donnell's student life took an unexpected turn during her second semester at Boston University. In one of her drama classes, the professor made some sarcastic remarks about her work. In front of the entire class, he told her that the part of Rhoda Morgenstern had already been cast, and that she would never make it as an actress.[11] He was referring to the character Rhoda Morgenstern from *The Mary Tyler Moore Show*, one of O'Donnell's favorite television sitcoms.

O'Donnell was so humiliated and angered by the professor's nasty comment that she dropped out of college, never to return.[12]

A Lucky Star

Rosie O'Donnell returned to her family home on Rhonda Lane. The harsh judgment of her drama professor fueled her determination to work even harder at becoming an actress.

To provide a steady income, she found a daytime job in the catalog department at Sears. At night, she began accepting gigs as an emcee in various comedy clubs throughout Long Island. Meanwhile, she worked at creating a comedy act of her own.

In planning her act, she set one important guideline for herself. As an emcee, she had sometimes heard comics make hurtful comments about well-known people in order to get a laugh. In her own act, she determined never to say anything about another individual that she would not say to him or her in person. As in her open-mike days, she drew upon family humor, accenting her father's faint Irish brogue, and upon funny incidents from her working-class background. Also, as a skillful mimic, she created brief skits using the speech and mannerisms of women comics she admired—Carol Burnett, Whoopi Goldberg, Lily Tomlin, and others.

O'Donnell first performed her new routine at several Long Island clubs. Then she decided to sign on with a booking agent and take her act on the road. A booking agent decides the best way to market a comic's special brand of humor. After a contract is agreed upon and signed, the agent finds places for the comic to perform. These might include a supper club, business convention, casino, pop concert (as the warm-up act), or other places where an audience has gathered for entertainment.

At the age of twenty, Rosie O'Donnell was now a professional stand-up comic, performing in cities all across the country. From Boston, Detroit, and Atlanta, to as far west as Newport Beach, California, she traveled by bus, car, train, or plane on the comedy-club circuit. It was not an easy life. Arriving in an unfamiliar town, she would be driven to a condominium apartment owned by the comedy club. That was where the comics stayed. Most of the other comedians were older men who liked to drink, do drugs, and throw wild parties. None of this appealed to O'Donnell. She often pushed furniture up against the door to her room before going to bed. Looking back on that experience, she recalls how she felt. "I was just this little girl on the road, scared in her room."[1]

Despite the concern of family and friends, O'Donnell refused to give up. "Time and time again, people told me to quit, that I was too tough, I was too New York, I was too heavy. But I didn't listen to them. I thought, 'You're all idiots!'"[2] She always performed with the hope that someone would see her act and put her in a sitcom, a movie, or a Broadway show.

Fortunately for a young comic like O'Donnell, who was just starting out, the 1980s was like a golden age of stand-up comedy. Almost every small town had at least one comedy club, and at the height of its popularity, comedy was featured in more than fifteen hundred nightclubs.[3] At times, there were not enough comics to meet the demand. Female comics were especially rare. When O'Donnell started out, only about six women were working the comedy circuit. This was an advantage for her. A female comic performing in a comedy club was so unusual that it made her more noticeable. Some female comics were even jealous of one another. Their thinking was that if one of them became a guest on the *Tonight Show*, the others could not. O'Donnell's philosophy was "If she did, we can, too. Success breeds success."[4]

Back on Long Island in 1982, an improvisational group was being formed at the Eastside Comedy Club. The group was to be called the Laughter Company and would perform on Monday nights, when most clubs were traditionally closed. Auditions were being scheduled. Between her bookings, O'Donnell joined the many performers who were trying out.

Improv—short for improvisation—is a performance

without a written script. A situation is presented, and it can lead to a series of unexpected events. The odd responses of the performers to these predicaments are usually what brings laughter. The actors say and do whatever pops into their heads.

When the auditions were over, Rosie O'Donnell and four other performers were chosen for the improv group. Rehearsals would be on Monday afternoons to rough out some sketches for a two-hour show on Monday nights. Meanwhile, they all had their individual nightly and weekend gigs to perform.

At first, the improv shows did not always run smoothly, but they provided much-needed acting experience for O'Donnell. Eventually, with practice and creativity, the Laughter Company players became a popular attraction on Long Island.

O'Donnell's sharpened comedic skills were now drawing some favorable attention. One night in 1984, after her stand-up act, she was approached by a young woman in the audience who asked if she would like to be on *Star Search*. This nationally syndicated television show was a talent contest for hopeful singers, dancers, actors, and comics. It was hosted by Ed McMahon, Johnny Carson's sidekick on the late-night talk show *The Tonight Show*.

O'Donnell was skeptical at first, but then the young woman introduced herself. She was Claudia McMahon, the daughter of Ed McMahon and a talent scout for *Star Search*. This weekly television show featured competition in eight categories: male actor, female actor, male vocalist, female vocalist, vocal group, dancer, comic, and model/spokesperson. Each week, two contestants competed in each category. The winning contestant, selected by a panel of judges, returned the following week to compete with a new challenger. The winning contestants received cash prizes. The longest-reigning champions in each category were to return in the spring to compete for Best New Star of the Year.[5]

Appearing on national television would be an opportunity for O'Donnell to be seen across the country. She agreed to make a performance tape to send to the Los Angeles auditions. Her taped audition won her a contestant spot, and she was flown to Los Angeles to compete on the show. Once again, this was against the advice of family and friends, but she went anyway.[6]

In the fall of 1984, Rosie O'Donnell made her first appearance on *Star Search*. She became the first woman to win in the comic category. The prize was $3,500. While waiting to be challenged in the next week's competition, she stayed at an inexpensive hotel in Hollywood near the TV studio where the show was taped. She continued to win for the next four weeks. Later, in the semifinals, she lost to the challenging male comedian, but was awarded a $1,500 consolation prize. Her winnings for her weeks on *Star Search* totaled nearly $20,000.[7]

When O'Donnell returned to Long Island, she was greeted as if she were a celebrity. Her nationwide television appearances on *Star Search* had brought recognition. When she went to the mall, people she did not know smiled and offered congratulations. Perhaps, someday, she really would become a star.

A Break—At Last

With her winnings from *Star Search*, Rosie O'Donnell decided to move to Los Angeles to find an acting job. "If you want to surf, you have to go to the water," she explained.[1] She believed that by living where movies were being produced, she would be readily available for an audition.

O'Donnell rented a furnished studio apartment in Hollywood. Next, she had her teeth crowned, ready for close-up photos when needed. Then, she contacted a booking agent for the local comedy clubs. O'Donnell soon learned that the Los Angeles area was so flooded with young male comedians that few female comics were given a chance to perform. She also learned that *Star Search* winners were of no special interest to Hollywood movie producers or booking agents.

As her savings dwindled, O'Donnell was forced to go back on the road with her stand-up act. In other parts of the country, her *Star Search* fame was more valued, and it earned her engagements at comedy clubs in Detroit, Atlantic City, and San Francisco. All the while, O'Donnell was constantly polishing her act and adding new material. As she gained recognition on the circuit, she often appeared as the opening act for celebrity performers. At Caesar's Palace in Las Vegas, she opened for magician David Copperfield. On another engagement, she was the opening act on tour with country music singer Dolly Parton. The star performed nightly in concert in many different cities. Parton recalls that her fans loved O'Donnell because "she was so real and so down-home and they understood her comedy. We made a good team."[2]

Finally, in 1986, Rosie O'Donnell had an opportunity to perform near her new home, at Igby's Comedy Cabaret in West Los Angeles. It was a popular club, and O'Donnell soon became a frequent attraction. One night it was rumored that NBC president Brandon Tartikoff and *Saturday Night Live* producer Lorne Michaels would be in the audience. They were coming to view the act of comic Dana Carvey. O'Donnell was also performing later that evening. Right after Carvey's performance, the executives prepared to leave, but they were delayed by a cocktail waitress whom O'Donnell had befriended. She refused to give them their check until they had seen O'Donnell's act.[3] They liked what they saw. At Tartikoff's request, O'Donnell came to his office the next day, and he offered her a role in the TV comedy series *Gimme a Break*. She signed a contract for the 1986–1987 television season. Rosie O'Donnell would soon appear in her first role as a television actress.

Gimme a Break, a half-hour situation comedy, had been launched in October 1981. The story was about a black housekeeper employed by a white widower with three young daughters. It starred Nell Carter, Tony Award winner from the Broadway musical *Ain't Misbehavin'* and Emmy winner for her performance on a television special. Costarring with Carter was actor Dolph Sweet from such daytime soap operas as *The Edge of Night* and *Another World*.

The sitcom was based on laughable incidents in the daily life of this fictional family, aided by its caring and witty housekeeper. In 1985, upon the sudden death of actor Sweet, the story line underwent a major revision. Another male character was added, and the setting was changed from California to a New York City apartment. O'Donnell was to play Maggie O'Brien, a spunky, smart-talking upstairs neighbor.

On November 19, 1986, Rosie O'Donnell made her first appearance on the revised *Gimme A Break*. Although her character added some much-needed humor to the show, the overall experience for her was not satisfactory. From years of working together, the cast had become a tight-knit group. As a newcomer, O'Donnell never felt part of that group. Meanwhile, viewer ratings for the show were rapidly declining. At the end of the season in May 1987, the network canceled the series. O'Donnell called the experience "the most crushing blow of my career." In an interview for *US* magazine, she said, "My goal was to be on a

In 1986, O'Donnell appeared in the television sitcom Gimme a Break. *She played Maggie O'Brien, a spunky, smart-mouthed neighbor.*

sitcom; then I got on this show in its last year and people weren't real happy to be there. I thought, I've climbed this mountain and there's nothing there."[4]

Being in a television series that flopped was a big letdown for the hardworking O'Donnell, still intent on becoming a movie actress. Acting for a longer time in the sitcom might have been a step in that direction.

O'Donnell's disappointment over *Gimme a Break* stirred up a personal problem that could have become a threat to her future success. In her early comedy-circuit days, to ease the pain of loneliness she often stayed on after a show, talking and having a few beers with the waitresses. She had developed a habit of frequently drinking too much. Luckily, a therapist friend cautioned her that if the habit continued, she could become an alcoholic. This suggestion so angered O'Donnell that she stopped drinking totally for five years just to prove that she could. Years later, O'Donnell said, "I think it's good that I did, because if I had continued . . . I seriously feel that it would have become a problem for me."[5]

With the end of her short-lived television career, O'Donnell returned to doing stand-up comedy. One good result from appearing in *Gimme a Break* was the recognition. Appearing week after week in the series, she had become visible to many more viewers than she could reach in the average two-hundred-seat comedy club. Her name now brought her acceptance in major comedy clubs like the LA Improv, and her club performances were sometimes taped to be shown on Showtime and other cable networks.

When O'Donnell learned that MTV was seeking a

female comic to become a veejay (video jockey) on its cable music network, she immediately arranged for an audition. A veejay is the host who comments between each music video.

Before long, O'Donnell learned that her taped audition had been rejected by MTV. Although she was disappointed, O'Donnell wrote a note to the producer. This gesture so impressed him that it paved the way to another job. In a meeting with MTV executives, O'Donnell was told that their other cable channel, VH-1 (Video Hits One), might have an opening for her. Once again, she auditioned. This time, she was hired. "A thank-you note got me that job," she said.[6]

In April 1988, at age twenty-six, Rosie O'Donnell became a veejay on the VH-1 cable channel. Her job was to introduce a series of Top 40 rock music videos. Along with introducing each video, she had to fill the two minutes between videos with amusing remarks to keep the viewer tuned in. "I had to make my humor conversational, as opposed to presentational," she said. She further explained that in stand-up comedy, you tell planned jokes. In veejay segments, you talk about what happened in your day. "We had to fill eight segments an hour, two minutes a segment," said O'Donnell. "That's a lot of just banter. . . . It's a lot of stuff to make up."[7]

The work was not easy, but it gave O'Donnell a potential viewing audience far greater than any comedy club could. VH-1 reached close to 30 million homes throughout the United States.

She had been working for two years when MTV reviewed VH-1's programming and decided to phase

O'Donnell's popularity as a stand-up comic led to a job as a veejay on the VH-1 cable music channel.

out the veejays. Instead, the network would present thirty-minute specials featuring popular singers.

O'Donnell's contract had not expired, so she requested a meeting with MTV executives and came up with a new idea. She suggested a weekly thirty-minute comedy show called *Stand-up Spotlight*. It would feature established stand-up comics as well as new talent. MTV seemed interested and agreed to consider her idea. Finally, after some time had gone by, they agreed to accept the *Spotlight* show with O'Donnell as both host and executive producer.

Stand-up Spotlight first appeared on VH-1, on a Sunday night in November 1989. The thirty-minute show was taped before an audience in a comedy club. The Ice House in Pasadena, California, with seating for two hundred, was chosen as the ideal setting. Tapes of *Spotlight* were aired and then repeated throughout the cable network season. As emcee, O'Donnell opened each show with a snappy new monologue, followed by three acts—two by experienced comedians and one by a new comedian.

Stand-up Spotlight proved to be popular with viewers, and it brought Rosie O'Donnell two award nominations—one for an American Comedy Award and another for a Cable Ace Award. The show gave O'Donnell an opportunity to audition unknown comics from all over the country and to showcase their talent. It also provided an opportunity to display her own talent as well as to develop her skill as a host.

Pleased with O'Donnell's work, executives from MTV's parent company also signed her up to appear in a half-hour cable television special on their other

Comedians Rosie O'Donnell and Bill Engvall appear as "A Pair of Jokers," on Showtime's Comedy Club All Stars *in 1990.*

network. *Showtime's Comedy Club All Stars* featured O'Donnell and comic Bill Engvall as "A Pair of Jokers." The performance was taped at the Comedy and Magic Club in Hermosa Beach, California, and was shown on June 2, 1990.

For three years, O'Donnell's work first as a veejay and then as the producer of *Spotlight* had enabled her to spend less time performing on the road in comedy clubs. With regular working hours and a steady income, she could now spend more time at home. Ever since moving to California, "home" for O'Donnell had been furnished apartments or condos. In 1990 she decided to buy her first home. She chose a modest two-bedroom house with a two-car garage. It was located in the Studio City area of Los Angeles, near the San Fernando Valley. She described the neighborhood as being like the street she grew up on: "Kids on Big Wheels and dogs barking at all hours."[8] It is like "the house I wish I had when I was a child," she explained.[9]

O'Donnell's decor included a vast collection of plastic figurines. She had begun collecting McDonald's Happy Meal toys while touring the country as a stand-up comic. "They reminded me of my childhood," she said.[10] Through the years, the collection would expand to include traditional dolls, figures from classic television shows, and a variety of miniature toys.

Rosie O'Donnell had settled into a real home and a more balanced life. She now lived only minutes away from some of the leading movie and television studios. She was ready for her next big break.

Movieland

In August 1990, O'Donnell worked on her first movie. She had a small part in *Car 54, Where Are You?*, based on an old television series about the comic adventures of two Bronx policemen. O'Donnell was cast as Lucille Toody, the loving wife of one of the officers. The filming lasted only two months, but the movie was not released until 1994 because of financial problems at the film company.

In the spring of 1991, O'Donnell's agent informed her that director Penny Marshall was planning to do a movie about women in baseball. Marshall sent out a casting call for actresses who looked experienced at playing the game. This immediately appealed to O'Donnell, who had spent much of her childhood playing baseball on neighborhood teams. She read the script for *A League of Their Own* and thought, "If I don't get this part, I'll quit show business. If there's one thing I can do better than Meryl Streep and Glenn Close, it's play baseball."[1]

The producers hired University of Southern California coach Rod Dedeaux to conduct auditions on the university ball field in Los Angeles. About two hundred actresses showed up. Under the watchful eyes of Coach Dedeaux and his staff, they were videotaped and graded on throwing, catching, hitting, and running.

O'Donnell easily survived the initial tryouts. Then she auditioned for Penny Marshall. The two had never met, but Marshall was familiar with O'Donnell's stand-up comedy work. Marshall hired O'Donnell for the role of Doris Murphy, a wisecracking, soft-hearted third baseman. "The part was originally for a hot, sexy girl, but I liked Rosie so much we changed the story to suit her," said Marshall. "She can make anything funny."[2]

A League of Their Own is a comedy based on the All-American Girls Professional Baseball League. The league was created in 1943, when most professional players had left baseball to fight in World War II. Costarring in the movie were Tom Hanks, as a one-time baseball great, Geena Davis, Lori Petty, Jon Lovitz, Megan Cavanaugh, and Madonna.

Meeting for the first time, Rosie and Madonna were cast as best buddies in the movie. Between filming sessions, they talked about their lives and discovered many similarities. Both were raised in Catholic families, both were named after their mothers, and both were young children when they lost their mothers. O'Donnell

Rosie O'Donnell plays the role of a wisecracking, soft-hearted third baseman in A League of Their Own.

later said that this created a "sort of sisterly-like relationship that has continued since we met."[3]

The story line of *League* involves a skillful catcher/ hitter (Geena Davis) who is caught in a dispute with her sister/pitcher (Lori Petty) and the team's hard-drinking coach (Tom Hanks). Comic relief is provided by O'Donnell, Megan Cavanaugh, and Jon Lovitz.

The shooting began in July 1991. It was done on location, partly at Chicago's Wrigley Field and partly in Evansville, Indiana. Long hours of playing baseball in the sun, in hundred-degree temperatures, was difficult. But O'Donnell said she loved Evansville: "There was a movie theater, a mall, and a McDonald's. That's all I need to be happy."[4] Filming ended on October 30.

O'Donnell later said that working on *A League of Their Own* was "the best experience that you could have as a debut film. It really was great. And we got to play ball every day and we got paid for it. . . . And to be around that many women . . . who were all supportive of each other . . . and also to celebrate the women, who did have the All-American League."[5]

During the months that *League* was being readied for release, O'Donnell agreed to accept a costarring role in a new Fox network sitcom, *Stand by Your Man*. Taped before a live studio audience, the comedy series featured two sisters—O'Donnell as cynical Lorraine, a stockroom clerk in a discount store, and Melissa Gilbert as a flighty housewife. Both had husbands imprisoned in the state penitentiary. Each week's episode revolved around the comic complication of their daily lives. *Stand by Your Man* debuted April 5, 1992, on the Fox network. The series was never well received by television critics, though O'Donnell was praised for bringing fun, energy, and credibility to the show. *Stand by Your Man* was canceled on May 17, 1992, after airing only seven episodes.

Now with no long-term commitment, O'Donnell accepted some stand-up comedy engagements, and made guest appearances on numerous TV shows to promote the soon-to-be-released baseball story, *A League of Their Own*. On *CBS This Morning, NBC Today, The Tonight Show with Jay Leno,* and other shows, Rosie O'Donnell enthusiastically told millions of television viewers about the movie.

A League of Their Own opened in movie theaters in June 1992 and became a major hit. Critic Leonard Maltin called the film "good-natured fiction that sheds light on a neglected chapter of real-life sports history."[6] Steve Wulf of *Sports Illustrated* wrote that the movie deserved a wide audience, "if only because the actors' joy in making the film comes through."[7]

Rosie O'Donnell's dream of becoming a movie actress had finally come true. At thirty years of age, she had costarred in a big hit film. This would boost her image as an actress in the film community.

When screenwriter/director Nora Ephron began casting for the movie *Sleepless in Seattle*, O'Donnell auditioned. It was the first that Ephron had heard of her. Ephron's children, however, were familiar with O'Donnell from watching VH-1. "She's funny, Mom, you should cast her," urged Ephron's thirteen-year-old son.[8] O'Donnell won the role of Becky, the best friend of Annie, played by Meg Ryan.

The romantic comedy centers on the grief of a

widower (Tom Hanks) who talks about his departed wife on a call-in radio show. Annie feels destined to meet him, and with help from the widower's young son, Jonah (Ross Maliger)—who has adjusted to grief better than his father—a romance blooms.

The film, released in June 1993, was enormously popular with moviegoers. It received mixed reviews, but O'Donnell's characterization of Becky was liked by most critics. Jack Matthews, reviewer for *New York Newsday*, wrote, "Rosie O'Donnell . . . has the bulk of the best one-liners, and her performance is a joy."[9]

In the popular romantic comedy Sleepless in Seattle, *Rosie O'Donnell plays the best friend of Meg Ryan, right, who falls in love with a man she has heard talking on the radio.*

O'Donnell's performance in that supporting role brought her a nomination for an American Comedy Award. Her two screen roles as a likable, easygoing best friend reinforced viewers' image of her. Rosie O'Donnell was now a recognizable name in the movies.

Along with her success came many requests for guest appearances and charity performances. In October 1992, O'Donnell taped a segment on singer Gloria Estefan's Hurricane Relief show—a benefit for Florida's disaster victims. She made guest appearances on television's *Beverly Hills 90210*, *Celebrity Jeopardy*, and the CBS *Back to School '92* special. On August 30, 1992, Rosie O'Donnell was a celebrity presenter at the forty-fourth annual prime-time Emmy Awards. These awards, given by the Academy of Television Arts and Sciences, honor excellence in various categories of prime-time television shows.

In 1993, she accepted a cameo role in *Fatal Instinct*, directed by Carl Reiner. O'Donnell was cast as an eccentric bird-shop owner. This film is a comedy-spoof combining features from such dark-themed films as *Fatal Attraction* and *Basic Instinct*. That same year, O'Donnell appeared briefly, in the role of a makeup artist, in director James L. Brooks's film *I'll Do Anything*.

Meanwhile, Jeffrey Katzenberg, then chairman of the Walt Disney Studios, was involved in the planning of *Another Stakeout*, a comedy-thriller film. Actors Richard Dreyfuss and Emilio Estevez had already been cast as undercover cops. The role of Gina Garrett, an assistant district attorney, was yet to be cast. At a meeting, Katzenberg mentioned Rosie

O'Donnell's name. She was called in for an audition and immediately chosen for the part.

In shooting the film, the three costars often strayed from the script, improvising their actions and dialogue. This pleased O'Donnell, who later said, ". . . those times ended up being the funny parts of the film."[10] She was not as pleased, however, with another cast member—Archie, a Rottweiler. This large, powerful dog was cast as an inseparable companion of O'Donnell's character, Gina Garrett. O'Donnell described him as "very big, very wild, very young and

In Another Stakeout, *assistant district attorney Gina Garrett (Rosie O'Donnell) helps a pair of undercover police officers—played by Emilio Estevez, left, and Richard Dreyfuss, center—search for a key witness in a mob trial.*

not well-trained," and she was afraid of him. In one scene, Gina has been shot and the dog is supposed to lick her. To entice him, O'Donnell has to put steak all over her face. "Yechh!" she said. "It was the most difficult part of the film, without a doubt."[11]

In the spring of 1993, O'Donnell's agent informed her that director Steven Spielberg was planning a new film and wanted her to come in for a reading. The film was *The Flintstones*, a live-action movie of the cartoon classic. She was to audition for the part of Betty Rubble.

At the audition, O'Donnell impressed the casting staff with her knowledge of the original animated series, and with her mimicry of Betty Rubble's distinctive laugh. To accomplish this, she raised her voice an octave while laughing, "Heee-heee-heee."[12] Even though she looked nothing like the petite cartoon character, O'Donnell won the part. When the director, Brian Levant, was asked about their difference in size, he replied, "We only wanted the funniest person for the role, not necessarily someone who physically resembled the cartoon character."[13] Costarring with Rosie O'Donnell were John Goodman (Fred Flintstone), Elizabeth Perkins (Wilma Flintstone), Rick Moranis (Barney Rubble), and Elizabeth Taylor (Pearl Slaghoople) as Fred's overbearing mother-in-law.

To prepare for her role, O'Donnell went to the library and researched the prehistoric Stone Age, when the story of *The Flintstones* takes place.[14] The people of this era lived outdoors or in caves. They used stone and bone as tools and weapons and wore animal skins for clothing. For her role in the film,

O'Donnell wore a blue suede dress, a blue hair bow, and bone earrings.

The shooting was done from May to August 1993, mostly in Santa Clarita Valley, about forty miles northeast of Los Angeles. The area's Vasquez Park, with its natural rock formations, provided a realistic Stone Age look. The temperature was extremely hot, and each day thousands of tourists came to watch the outdoor filming.

Next, director Garry Marshall persuaded O'Donnell to accept a costarring role in his film *Exit to Eden*. Marshall is the brother of director Penny Marshall, and O'Donnell has said, "I have tremendous respect for him."[15] The film is loosely based on a best-selling novel of the same name by Anne Rice, known for her series of books about vampires.

The filming of *Exit to Eden* ran from mid-September to December 1993. O'Donnell plays an undercover agent. She and fellow agent Dan Aykroyd are sent to investigate a murder at a fantasy camp. The comical role required O'Donnell to wear a skimpy black leather costume. The scenes took place in various parts of Los Angeles and New Orleans and on the island of Lanai in Hawaii.

Swept up in a whirlwind of moviemaking, television appearances, and charity benefits, O'Donnell found one event particularly satisfying. In her years of watching television while growing up, O'Donnell had imagined herself on *Saturday Night Live*. She was invited to appear on the November 13, 1993, show. That night, she was the guest host of the show, as well as performing in some of the comedy sketches.

Hello, Broadway!

During the filming of *The Flintstones*, O'Donnell learned that director-choreographer Tommy Tune was casting for a 1994 revival of the 1970s Broadway musical *Grease!* She had seen the movie version of the show, and the part of tough-talking, heart-of-gold Betty Rizzo had intrigued her. *Grease!* is a musical about a 1950s high school romance between a tough boy and a sensitive girl. At Rydell High School, Rizzo is the leather-jacketed leader of the tough-talking Pink Ladies. O'Donnell wanted to play that part. It would be her long-desired chance to appear on Broadway.

In June 1993, during a scheduled break in filming, O'Donnell flew to New York for an audition with Tommy Tune. Trying out on a New York stage was a new experience for her. Appearing onstage in front of the celebrated Tommy Tune "was the most thrilling thing I've ever done," she said.[1]

Busy with producing his musicals, Tune had not heard of Rosie O'Donnell before. She had to show him and his staff that she was right for the part of Betty Rizzo. She sang two songs and then was asked, "You can dance, right?"

O'Donnell took a deep breath and replied untruthfully, "Oh, yeah, I can dance."[2]

Determined to persuade Tune and his staff that he should hire her, she explained about her past two movie hits, about her current role in *The Flintstones*, and about how her name would help to sell tickets to *Grease!*

Apparently, she was convincing. A few weeks later, O'Donnell was awarded the part of Rizzo, and she signed a ten-month contract. This included a rehearsal period in New York City, a three-month try-out tour around the country, and a return for the show's Broadway opening in May 1994.

Back in Hollywood, O'Donnell's decision to take time away from moviemaking was met with strong opposition. "More people see you in one movie than will ever see you in a two-year run of a Broadway show," said her agent. Her actor friend Tom Hanks said, "You'll get so bored you're going to want to kill yourself after two weeks."[3]

But O'Donnell knew what she wanted; her decision was made. O'Donnell also wanted a break from filmmaking to think about her career path. She thought that after her run in *Grease!* and after the

A childhood dream come true: O'Donnell was invited to host Saturday Night Live in November 1993.

release of her two latest films (*The Flintstones* and *Exit to Eden*), she would be in a better position to make decisions and maybe get into directing.[4]

O'Donnell moved to New York City early in 1994 and shared an Upper West Side apartment with another member of the cast. On the first day of rehearsals, the truth about her dancing ability was revealed. Associate choreographer Jerry Mitchell announced the first dance routine. "We're going to do step-touch, step-touch, hip, hip together, back and up. And two and three and go."[5] Everyone went into action except O'Donnell. Having had no formal dance training, she had to be taken aside and tutored in the basic steps. It soon became clear to her that all the cast members were far more experienced dancers, as well as singers, than she. But O'Donnell was friendly and funny, and the cast members were very supportive.

Although O'Donnell took private voice lessons to prepare for her role, her singing still needed some work. For her two solos, "Look at Me, I'm Sandra Dee" and "There Are Worse Things I Could Do," director Jeff Calhoun arranged for her to be backed up by a rousing chorus of singers. The dialogue scenes had to be smoothed out, too. The character of Rizzo was supposed to smoke cigarettes, but O'Donnell flatly refused. "I've never tried a cigarette," she said. "I'm repulsed by it."[6] At the next day's rehearsal, she replaced Rizzo's cigarette-smoking habit with another one. O'Donnell brought in a shocking-pink yo-yo, which she expertly manipulated during act one. That activity, along with the chewing and snapping of bubble gum, seemed right to portray Betty Rizzo.

O'Donnell found that daily rehearsals, with only a five-minute break each hour, were far more hectic than the usually slow-paced moviemaking. There was always work to be done—dance routines to practice, singing to rehearse, and dialogue to learn. She got along well with the cast, including music director John McDaniel. He shared her sense of humor, and their friendship would continue into future show business projects.

In February, the entire company of *Grease!* began a twelve-week tryout tour, which took them to cities from coast to coast. Rosie O'Donnell's drawing power, the natural audience appeal of *Grease!*, and an intensive promotion campaign—with media advertising and posters announcing the coming of *Grease!* in each city—all helped to make the road trip a financial success. Finally, returning to New York, the show opened on May 11, 1994, at Broadway's Eugene O'Neill Theatre.

The opening night audience was warmly receptive to the 1950s humor, and the entire performance brought rousing applause. In general, the show received only lukewarm reviews from the critics. *New Yorker* critic Nancy Franklin, however, wrote that "Rosie O'Donnell . . . as the tough-talking Rizzo, is the very soul of likability; she's so game and seems so happy to be part of this enterprise, that even though she doesn't project very well, and doesn't have much of a singing voice, you're on her side."[7]

For O'Donnell, one of the joys of being in *Grease!*

was the youngsters waiting at the stage door, as she had done years ago, "with that shiny Playbill in their hands and their eyes all wide and full of wonder. That's why you do it!" she said.[8]

O'Donnell has admitted that she was less than enthusiastic about certain parts of the show. "In *Grease* there are a lot of offensive lines. . . . I don't even like the message of the play: If you're a nice, normal girl, change yourself into a trampy, slutty girl to be accepted by the cool boy." When she saw little girls in the audience, she wanted to shout at the end of the show, "Don't believe it!"[9]

As time went on, six months of performing in eight shows a week became a tedious routine. During that time, a CD was made with the songs performed by O'Donnell and the other cast members. When her contract expired at the end of October, she left the show.

In an interview about her Broadway experience, O'Donnell was asked if she was beyond tough reviews. Some of the reviews of her performance had been harsh and insensitive. Wrote one New York critic: "My only problem is with Rosie O'Donnell! She delivers her lines with the proper deadpan hauteur, but a fat Rizzo?"[10]

O'Donnell replied that she knew her performance in *Grease!* was not Tony Award–winning material. "Believe me, I don't have any illusions that it was a powerfully brilliant performance. But it hurts when they say things about my physique. . . . It hurts when they take swipes at something I think is quite obviously an issue I'm struggling with."[11]

Weight became a problem for O'Donnell during her stand-up comedy days on the road. Dining on fast-food meals and snacking on treats high in calories soon added extra pounds. Before the shooting of *A League of Their Own*, director Marshall had asked O'Donnell to lose twenty pounds. And she replied, "Penny, if I *could* lose twenty pounds, I *would*. I don't walk around going, 'I like to be a little overweight.'"[12] She is five feet seven inches tall, and her weight has varied from 140 to 170 pounds on a regular basis. During the run of *Grease!*, her changing weight made it difficult to get into the tight-fitting hourglass costume worn in one scene.[13] "But I don't think that I'm less of a person because I'm bigger than some people," she has said, "nor do I think I'm better when I'm thinner."[14]

Living in New York while performing in *Grease!* enabled O'Donnell to spend time with her family. Her oldest brother, Edward, is an accountant who lives in New Jersey with his wife and two sons. Her brother Daniel, an attorney, is single and a New York City resident. Her sister, Maureen Crimmins, lives in New Jersey with her husband and young daughters. Maureen served as O'Donnell's business manager. She would do so until the birth of her third child in 1996, when she chose to stay at home full-time.

O'Donnell's younger brother, Timothy, and his wife and two children live in Florida but keep in close touch. By this time, their father had remarried, retired, and moved to North Carolina. Although Rosie and her father spoke occasionally by phone, their relations remained strained.

The O'Donnell siblings are close, and many were

at the Eugene O'Neill Theatre on the opening night of *Grease!* During the curtain calls that night, Rosie O'Donnell stepped forward on the stage and spoke to the audience. "This is such a wonderful night; it's a dream come true. The only sad part is that my mother didn't see it." Her words brought tears to her eyes, and another huge round of applause.[15]

During the months of O'Donnell's appearances in *Grease!*, her two latest films were released. *The Flintstones* opened in May 1994. O'Donnell attended the Hollywood premiere, and partied afterward at

The Flintstones *starred Rosie O'Donnell and Rick Moranis as Betty and Barney Rubble, with John Goodman and Elizabeth Perkins as Fred and Wilma Flintstone.*

Planet Hollywood with her costars. The film, which appealed to both children and adults, was an immediate box-office success. Wrote critic Richard Schickel in *Time* magazine: "*The Flintstones* doesn't feel overcalculated, overproduced or overthought. Nor, however, is it aimed solely at 'the young and the thumbless' (to borrow the name of Bedrock's favorite soap opera)."[16] Critic Leonard Maltin called it "a bouncy concoction with an enthusiastic (and well-chosen) cast. . . . Mainly for kids, who should understandably lap it up."[17] Not only did kids "lap it up," *The Flintstones* became a major hit as a family movie.

When *Exit to Eden* was released in October 1994, the film was not well received by either critics or moviegoers. A *People* magazine reviewer called it "draggy and repulsive." O'Donnell was described as overdoing everything, "blaring her lines . . . and throwing in lots of upstaging stage business even when she has only mundane lines."[18] One critic, however, disagreed, saying that O'Donnell's bright performance was the one justification for the film's existence.[19]

Exit to Eden was not popular at the box office, and it disappeared from theaters after only a few weeks. O'Donnell herself called it "the worst film I've ever made and probably one of the worst I've ever seen."[20]

9

Time for a Change

The year 1994 was a busy one for Rosie O'Donnell. Besides her performance in *Grease!* she appeared in several other entertainment areas.

On March 21, 1994, she was invited to be one of the presenters at the sixty-sixth Annual Academy Awards ceremony in Los Angeles. Hosted that year by Whoopi Goldberg, this televised event was watched by an estimated one billion viewers worldwide. Also in 1994, she appeared on *The Late Show with David Letterman* and as a celebrity contestant on *Jeopardy*.

In November 1994, at the end of her Broadway run and after a brief vacation in Hawaii, O'Donnell accepted some stand-up comedy engagements. She had expanded her act to include observations and hilarious anecdotes from both her movie and her

Broadway experiences. Thanksgiving weekend she performed her fresher, longer routine for three nights in the Superstar Theatre at Resorts Casino Hotel in Atlantic City, New Jersey. O'Donnell's act was well received and brought her a contract for future appearances at this Merv Griffin resort.

O'Donnell keeps returning to stand-up comedy as an outlet for expressing herself and for making others laugh. She finds it more flexible than working in movies, which requires going away on location for several months, or acting onstage in a Broadway show with the same lines repeated every night. She has said, "I prefer stand-up comedy because you're the one who is in control of what you say and when you say it, and also how much you work."[1]

Returning to Hollywood, O'Donnell was given many more opportunities for movie roles. The first role she accepted was in *Now and Then*. In this tale of four female friends, O'Donnell was cast as the hometown physician. Her adult costars were Demi Moore, Rita Wilson, and Melanie Griffith. The shooting was done on location in the Savannah, Georgia, area. Set in a small Midwestern town in 1970, four teenage friends vow always to be there for one another. The story covers the various challenges in their lives. Twenty years later, they reunite for the birth of the first child of one of the friends. In her role as Dr. Roberta Martin, O'Donnell delivers the baby girl. Four teenage actresses portray the friends during their adolescent years. *Now and Then* was released in 1995 and received only lukewarm reviews.

In her next film, *Beautiful Girls*, O'Donnell was

From left: Demi Moore, Rosie O'Donnell, Rita Wilson, and Melanie Griffith play best friends in the 1995 movie Now and Then.

cast as Gina, the smart-mouthed owner of a beauty salon. The story revolves around a tenth high school reunion and the relationships between men and women. O'Donnell appears only briefly but gives an attention-grabbing lecture to two of the high school buddies (played by Timothy Hutton and Matt Dillon) about the difference between *Penthouse* models and real women. The lecture is explosively delivered as the two young men follow Gina on a fast-moving walk across the street to a drugstore magazine rack.

"Rosie O'Donnell's speech," wrote a *Glamour* magazine reviewer, ". . . is enough to make this movie worth recommending."[2]

By now, *The Flintstones* had become a true blockbuster success. O'Donnell as Betty Rubble had acquired an impressive number of loyal fans. In May 1995, based on 26 million call-in votes to the cable channel, Rosie O'Donnell won Nickelodeon's annual Kids' Choice Award for her role as Betty Rubble. Recipients of these awards are chosen by children, who phone a toll-free number or use the Internet to vote for their top movie, TV, music, and sports stars.[3]

O'Donnell usually autographs any award that she receives and then gives it to a charity to auction off as a fund-raiser. She appreciates winning the award, and she will remember the experience, but she would also like it to benefit others. She made an exception and kept the Kids' Choice Award.

"It means so much to me," she explained, "when a kid stops me and says, 'I recognize you.'"[4] As a child, O'Donnell used TV and movies to imagine a life better than the one she was living. Those fantasies helped drive her toward her goals. "I think if you inspire a kid or spark some creativity in a child's life, it's very valuable," she said.[5]

During the early days of struggling to build a career, Rosie O'Donnell was totally focused on her work. All her energy and talent were centered on becoming a movie actress and a Broadway star. Now it was time to focus on her personal life. Rosie O'Donnell had always wanted to have children. "The same way I knew that I would be an entertainer, I knew that I would be a mother," she said.[6]

Her desire to raise a child was so great that she could hardly watch holiday television programs that featured orphans. When she saw all those kids who need to be adopted, she told a magazine reporter, "I'm hysterical thinking, I can put bunk beds in the spare room!"[7]

So at the age of thirty-two, O'Donnell began to take steps toward adopting a baby. Through her attorney, she started the procedure of interviews and counseling that was required for adoption. The process could take at least a year. She had no preference about gender—boy or girl, either would be welcome.

Meanwhile, for months O'Donnell had been preparing for her first one-woman TV special to be shown on HBO in April 1995. She had been trying out new material in her various engagements on the road, studying the audience reactions. Some of her humor now targeted certain issues in the news, such as the O. J. Simpson trial, but even her topical humor was something her audience could relate to.

Rosie O'Donnell's TV special was taped at a club familiar to her, the Comedy Connection in Boston. It was then aired on HBO on the night of April 29, 1995. Her first hour-long stand-up comedy performance on TV was a hit with both viewers and critics. It brought her an Emmy nomination for Outstanding Individual Performance in a Variety or Music Program. When the winners were announced, however, at the September 1995 Emmy Awards, O'Donnell's idol, Barbra Streisand, had won for her own TV special.[8]

Earlier, when O'Donnell had seen the positive response her role as Betty Rubble had on youngsters, she told her agent she would like to do a movie for children. Before long, Nickelodeon announced that it would produce a feature film. Besides being popular with kids, this successful cable television channel also appealed to parents because of its evening showing of classic sitcom reruns on *Nick at Night*.

Nickelodeon Movies (a branch of the Nickelodeon channel) wanted to do a feature film based on the children's book *Harriet the Spy*, by Louise Fitzhugh. The story tells of an eleven-year-old girl who wants to become a writer. Her nanny, Golly, suggests she keep a journal to record her observations and feelings. Harriet carries the project a bit too far. She begins spying on her neighbors, family, and friends and then writes unkind comments about them. When the journal is discovered by her friends, they become angry and banish her.

The book *Harriet the Spy* was published in 1964, and O'Donnell remembered reading it as a child. Although the role of Golly was a small one, it was an important one. With guidance from her nanny, Harriet learns to respect individual differences and is inspired to keep on writing. The role of the nanny appealed to O'Donnell, and she signed a contract with Nickelodeon to play that part. Shooting the film would take place during the summer of 1995 on location in Toronto, Canada.

On May 25, 1995, O'Donnell received the good news that her son-to-be had been born. His birth took place in Florida. Two days later, Rosie O'Donnell signed the adoption papers and carried her new baby home. She named him Parker Jaren. "As I held him in my arms the first night," she later said, "everything just naturally fell into place. It completed me in a way that nothing else could have."[9]

The new mother and son were immediately the center of attention among friends and the media. They were showered with gifts and good wishes and parenting advice. Rita Wilson (who is married to actor Tom Hanks) came over with her own mother to reassure and instruct Parker's mom in her new role. Kate Capshaw (who is married to director Steven Spielberg) was there to provide whatever help was needed "in any way, shape or form," said O'Donnell.[10] Meg Ryan, costar of *Sleepless in Seattle*, gave a baby shower, attended by many of O'Donnell's celebrity friends and fellow entertainers.

O'Donnell was celebrating and adjusting to a new way of life. She felt that parenthood was the best thing that ever happened to her, and she wished she had done it sooner. O'Donnell had no doubts about adopting as a single parent. "If I had married and had a biological family that would be great," she said. "It didn't happen. I didn't make the choice not to include a father—there just wasn't one."[11]

O'Donnell knew she wanted more children, too. "I have a big and loving family, so Parker has aunts and uncles and many nieces and nephews who are all very supportive. . . . I don't think there's one ideal situation in which a child can or should be raised—except that there be love and security."[12]

When Parker was only a few months old, O'Donnell flew with him to Toronto, Canada, for the filming of *Harriet the Spy*. The role of Harriet would be played by eleven-year-old Michelle Trachtenberg. A

In Harriet the Spy, *O'Donnell plays Golly, the wise and witty nanny of Harriet (Michelle Trachtenberg), whose spying gets her into trouble.*

veteran actress, Trachtenberg appeared as a regular on ABC-TV's *All My Children* and in numerous commercials. The filming for *Harriet the Spy* lasted twenty-three days.

During that time, O'Donnell saw her infant son only between takes, about one hour a day. This was not her idea of parenthood. One day, Parker had not seen his mom for so long, he seemed not to recognize her. The next day, O'Donnell called her agent and said that *Harriet the Spy* would be her last movie.[13]

She wanted to be a hands-on mother, and she wanted stability for Parker. If she continued in movies, it meant he would need to be with her on location, living in various parts of the country for long stretches of time. O'Donnell wanted her little boy to be able to sleep in his own bed every night. She said, "My sister and her children, my brother and his kids, all live right in the New York area. I wanted him to grow up knowing his cousins. I wanted him to have his own toys, his own play group and a routine."[14]

It is easy to see why Rosie O'Donnell would soon be moving to New York City. She was focusing now on her son's growing-up years, and on a career change for herself. O'Donnell sold her home in Los Angeles. Late in 1995, she and Parker moved into a three-bedroom apartment on the twelfth floor of a Manhattan high-rise.

She had once told her friend Madonna, "I miss New York City. I miss the whole feeling of New York City."[15] Her decision to move there would prove to be a wise one.

"And Now, Here's Rosie!"

In seeking a change from moviemaking, Rosie O'Donnell knew exactly what she wanted to do. She wanted to host a viewer-friendly talk show. That is the kind of show she enjoyed watching after school as a child—the shows hosted by Merv Griffin, Dinah Shore, and Mike Douglas. O'Donnell wanted to revive the style of those earlier talks shows, to do a show with no bickering or conflict. With that in mind, her agent, Risa Shapiro, agreed to present O'Donnell's concept to various television producers.

The idea of a positive daytime talk show did not immediately appeal to studio executives. O'Donnell was told repeatedly that her concept would not work. Finally, Warner Brothers Television decided to take a chance on a new talk show. In November 1995, Warner Brothers signed her to a one-year contract reportedly worth $4.5 million. O'Donnell now had what she wanted—her own show, with regular hours, and a location close to her Manhattan apartment.[1]

With a debut date of June 10, 1996, a staff had to be quickly assembled. Assisting with this procedure would be Jim Paratore, president of Telepictures Productions, a division of Warner Brothers.[2] As executive producer, O'Donnell would be in control of her show, but to produce the one-hour show five days a week, she needed an experienced production staff. For her coexecutive producer, O'Donnell chose Daniel Kellison, who had been a segment producer on *The David Letterman Show*. He would manage the daily operations, assisted by a thirty-person staff. Randy Cohen, also from the *Letterman* show, would be her head writer, working with a staff of five. The syndicated program would be taped before an audience, each weekday morning, in a studio at Manhattan's Rockefeller Center.

In an interview for *People* magazine, O'Donnell said, "This is not going to be a show where we combat guests or humiliate and embarrass them." She planned to mix stand-up comedy with friendly interviews, and . . . cooking segments. "That will be my biggest challenge," she said. "I live in New York City. I'm only good at ordering out."[3]

During the time that preparations were being made for the new show, Rosie O'Donnell was also involved in other professional activities. In the fall of 1995, she teamed up with Penny Marshall to make a series of ten commercials for the Kmart store chain. These brief humorous skits, written by O'Donnell, began appearing nationally on television in November 1995. The series was so well received that another series was filmed for the following summer.

Ever since Marshall had directed O'Donnell in *A League of Their Own*, the two had been good friends. Talking about Rosie O'Donnell, another friend—Nora Ephron, director of *Sleepless in Seattle*—has said, "She feels like someone who you have known all your life—or wish you had. She is completely up-front. If she thinks something is baloney, she will say so, and she is genuinely interested in other people."[4]

In January 1996, O'Donnell substituted for comedian George Burns for his one hundredth birthday celebration at Caesar's Palace in Las Vegas, Nevada. Burns was too frail to attend, so O'Donnell was asked to take his place.

Following that stellar evening, O'Donnell had another mission in Las Vegas. The annual NATPE (National Association of Television Program Executives) convention was meeting there at that time. O'Donnell went right to work, meeting the participants and promoting her upcoming talk show to possible markets throughout the country.

Shortly after, she spent several days playing a small role in the movie *Wide Awake*. In this story about a small boy's spiritual search after the death of his grandfather, O'Donnell is cast as Sister Terry, a baseball-loving nun and teacher. She had taken the role because the boy, Joshua Beal (played by Joseph Cross), loses his grandfather at the same age she was when her mother died. "I think it's an important movie for kids to see with their parents," she said. "It opens up a whole line of communication about spirituality and the topic of death."[5]

In February 1996, O'Donnell appeared in a cameo role on the TV sitcom *The Nanny*, playing a New York cab driver. Later, as a guest on the soap opera *All My Children*, she portrayed a tough-talking, gum-snapping uniformed maid. For this appearance, O'Donnell later won the award for Best Guest Appearance from *Soap Opera Digest*.[6]

By March 1, 1996, preparations for *The Rosie O'Donnell Show* were under way. As the host and executive producer, O'Donnell had the final word on selecting the content of each show, the guests to be invited, the jokes to be used, and numerous other details. Energetic staff workers bustled in and out of her office, but she still managed to be a hands-on mom. Parker, barely one year old, cooed happily from his playpen next to her desk. During the show's taping, Parker would be cared for by a friend in the nursery provided by Warner Brothers, next to his mother's office.

Despite O'Donnell's busy professional life, she was planning a permanent home for Parker and herself. Early in March 1996, she purchased a twenty-two-room mansion once owned by Broadway actress Helen Hayes and her husband, playwright Charles MacArthur. This 1880 estate, overlooking the Hudson River, is in Nyack, New York, about twenty miles north of Manhattan. O'Donnell planned extensive renovations to be completed before she and Parker moved in. Occupancy would not be possible for at least a year. Meanwhile, the O'Donnells continued to live in their Manhattan apartment.

On Monday morning, June 10, 1996, audience members filed into Studio 8G at Rockefeller Center. They soon filled the twelve tiered rows of 180 seats. On each seat was a snack—a package of Drake's cakes, a half-pint of low-fat milk, a napkin, and a straw. Onstage, before a colorful background, were a large desk and chair for the host, and three side-by-side chairs for guests.

While the audience members munched on their treats, comic Joey Kola, a staff member, came out to warm up the group and assure them that this is Rosieville—a show about fun. Here, for one hour, they could forget their problems and be entertained. He instructed them to clap only when the APPLAUSE signs flashed, and explained that no photos were to be taken during the show. Kola also cautioned the audience not to yell to Rosie or her guests during the show. Music director John McDaniel, O'Donnell's friend from *Grease!*, led his five-piece band, the McDLTs, in a lively rock number. Then silence reigned as the countdown began.

The cameras started to roll, panning the audience. A preselected audience member rose from the front row and announced the day's guests. Animated graphics of Rosie O'Donnell filled the TV screen, accompanied by taped music. Then the announcer shouted, *"And Now, He-E-E-Re's Rosie!!"* The band began to play, and the beaming host stepped through the curtains, met by thunderous applause from the wildly enthusiastic audience. The first *Rosie O'Donnell Show* had begun.

The format of each *Rosie O'Donnell Show* is structured to provide variety and fun. Although changes in the format might take place in the future, certain elements would remain the same. Emerging from the stage curtain, O'Donnell dance-steps a few feet forward, greets the audience, and thanks the guest announcer. Then, sitting behind her desk, scattered with miniature toys, Koosh balls, and "flingshots," she chats informally with bandleader John McDaniel. Seated at the piano in a niche near the stage, McDaniel and O'Donnell have a casual conversation about whatever is new—and often humorous—in their lives at the moment. Then, after the first break for commercials, an impressive lineup of celebrities and musical acts follows.

O'Donnell welcomes her guests warmly and quickly engages them in easy conversation. Sometimes clips are shown from an actor's movies, or, in the case of a singer, O'Donnell may impulsively break out into the guest's trademark song. Guest Jane Pauley once described her as a "human jukebox," for O'Donnell appears to know the lyrics to every song written in the 1970s.[7]

The first week of *The Rosie O'Donnell Show* brought rave reviews and great ratings. "Comic actress Rosie O'Donnell promised hers would be a nice talk show, à la Merv Griffin's," wrote critic Ken Tucker in *Entertainment Weekly*. "What she delivers is a refreshing dose of spunk, fire, and genuine fun."[8]

Her show averaged a 3.2 Nielsen rating in its first

week. (Each Nielsen rating point stands for 960,000 homes tuned in to a particular channel.) This was the highest debut rating for a daytime talk show since *The Oprah Winfrey Show* ten years earlier, and it held steady in the second week.[9] Four weeks later, in a *Newsweek* cover story on Rosie O'Donnell, the magazine reported, "Her new show is a hit—and she never bashes anyone."[10]

The incredible popularity of O'Donnell's show was soon credited with changing the direction of television's daytime "trash" talk shows from nasty to nice. Echoing the sentiments of many others, O'Donnell said, "I think the American public, myself included, was sick of those shows." Calling them a "humiliation festival," she felt that *The Rosie O'Donnell Show* was benefiting because viewers saw it as such a sharp contrast.[11]

O'Donnell's show continued to do well. Within two months, it had an estimated audience of 4.5 million viewers daily. Four months after it was launched, Warner Brothers renewed the show's one-year contract until the year 2000 with a fee increase reported to be the largest in television history.[12]

Viewers of *The Rosie O'Donnell Show* can expect a lighthearted hour of the unexpected. Guests range from celebrities in the entertainment world to outstanding personalities in other areas. Barbra Streisand, Whoopi Goldberg, Isabella Rosselini, Elton John, George Clooney, Michael Douglas, and Tom Cruise are only a few of the performers who have appeared as guests.

Many of O'Donnell's guests have a special personal

significance to her. She often jokes about her crush on Tom Cruise, for example, and speaks of her life-long admiration for Barbra Streisand. In an emotional moment on her show, she told Barbra Streisand, "You were a constant source of light in an often dark child-hood."[13]

In other areas, outstanding guests have included First Lady Hillary Rodham Clinton, who discussed the need for quality child care. The first lady and O'Donnell joined a group of six- and seven-year-old

Audiences love the celebrity interviews on The Rosie O'Donnell Show. *This Muppet from* Sesame Street *is dressed just like Rosie.*

children to demonstrate the craft of handprinting. Children and their welfare are major interests of O'Donnell. After the taping of each show, kids under age sixteen are invited to come onstage to meet O'Donnell and receive a personally autographed photo.

Journalist Walter Cronkite observed his eightieth birthday on *The Rosie O'Donnell Show*. Culinary expert Julia Child engaged O'Donnell—a self-described noncook—in an entertaining cooking session.

Not all of the show's guests are widely known, but all are interesting to know. On National Secretary's Day, the attendance secretary for Commack Public Schools did the show's opening *"He-E-E-Re's Rosie"* introduction. To the delight of the audience, she also revealed the less than perfect attendance record of the former Commack High School South student. O'Donnell listened with a look of mock surprise.

Youngsters, too, have occupied the guest chair on the show. One was a seven-year-old girl who wants to be a talk show host and had sent in a tape of her version of *The Rosie O'Donnell Show*. Another was an eight-year-old Little League player who delivered his favorite snack food (bagels) to the host and reported on the wins (4) and losses (0) of his team.

Between segments, the McDLTs, led by McDaniel, fill the studio with upbeat music. Music is a frequent part of the agenda, often showcasing guest singers, bands, and acts in full costume from Broadway shows: *The Lion King, Cabaret, The Sound of Music,* and others. Because of this focus on Broadway, O'Donnell has become a major power in the Broadway world. "Nothing quite excites me like a Broadway musical," she has said.[14] On her show, O'Donnell loves to promote Broadway productions. Her effect on theater has been compared with Oprah Winfrey's influence on books and reading. When O'Donnell talks about a Broadway musical or play—or features cast members on her show—ticket sales immediately rise. "The impact of her personal opinion was phenomenal," said one producer.[15]

Still, on *The Rosie O'Donnell Show*, no matter how entertaining the program may be, the main attraction is the host herself. Rosie O'Donnell has been described as "animated, funny, and endearing."[16] One day, while warming up the audience before the show's taping, Joey Kola asked one woman if she knew Rosie. "No," the woman replied, "but I feel like she's a friend."[17]

In 1996, *Glamour* magazine honored O'Donnell as one of its ten Women of the Year "for giving us talk without trash."[18] In January 1997, she was among seven Women of the Year honored by *Ms.* magazine for inspiring us to continue to strive for a better world. O'Donnell was praised "for bringing respect and feminist values to talk TV."[19] And how does Merv Griffin, O'Donnell's role model, feel about all this? "Rosie was born to do a talk show," he says.[20]

Amid all of this praise, O'Donnell was once asked if she had any bad qualities. "It depends on who you ask," she replied. "Some people could say I'm bossy; I probably am."[21] According to some accounts, Rosie O'Donnell is a demanding boss. Says one former director, who left the show after four months, "She was always saying she wanted a big show. . . . And if it didn't come out the way she saw it in her mind, she would get frustrated."[22]

"I would close the door and yell and scream," O'Donnell says matter-of-factly.[23]

The show's comedy producer, Janette Barber, says that in the early days, this kind of show was a new experience for this younger generation of television people, and the staff had a lot of turnover. Many producers, writers, and directors left during the show's first year.[24]

About O'Donnell, Barber thinks the title 'The Queen of Nice' diminishes who she is. "She's not nice because she's sweet all the time. She's nice because she's honest and loyal. She's the most honest person I've ever known."[25]

O'Donnell's friend Rita Wilson agrees. "Not only is she always honest, but she makes other people come up to her level. She requires you to be a better person, a more decent person."[26]

Less than a year after the debut of *The Rosie O'Donnell Show*, its host had also gained the respect of her peers in the television establishment. At the twenty-fourth annual Daytime Emmy Award ceremonies in 1997, O'Donnell won the award for Outstanding Talk Show Host. The Daytime Emmy Award winners are selected in various categories by members of the National Academy of Television Arts & Sciences, and the Academy of Television Arts & Sciences.

11

A League of Her Own

Early in 1997, Rosie and Parker O'Donnell moved into their newly renovated home in Nyack. The three-story house and large property are surrounded by a brick wall high enough to provide family privacy. The veranda overlooks a rose garden, numerous bird feeders, play equipment, and a swimming pool. O'Donnell remarked that her friends who have babies (including Madonna and Kate Capshaw) could visit without having to be concerned about photographers.[1]

At the same time, O'Donnell changed her living quarters in Manhattan, moving from her apartment into a penthouse suite leased to her by Warner Brothers. The building is located on Manhattan's Upper West Side about a mile from her previous apartment, with access to the Hudson River. This gave O'Donnell a place to dock her twenty-seven-foot power boat. She considered the boat an investment in privacy. After a day of taping the show, O'Donnell and Parker could don life jackets and cruise around the island of Manhattan. Living in the spotlight is not easy, and this allowed them to get away from everyone for a few hours.

Although O'Donnell and her son often stayed in Manhattan during the week, weekends and summer breaks were spent in Nyack. There they could go for walks into town for ice cream, ride the mechanical horse at the local market, and play in the park with neighborhood children. When asked by children to sign autographs, O'Donnell always does—but for children only, not parents. From the time they moved to Nyack, O'Donnell tried to minimize her celebrity there. "I'm not gonna be Rosie O'Donnell in this town," she told the youngsters. "I'm just gonna be Rosie, Parker's mommy, okay?" And she felt they always understood. As she walked past, she heard them telling each other, "She's not a star here, she's just Parker's mommy."[2]

By October 1997, O'Donnell, along with Warner Brothers, had established a day-care center down the hall from her office. The center was created to accommodate Parker as well as some of the staffers' children. "I didn't think it was right that I had my kid here every day and nobody else could," said O'Donnell.[3] The spacious, soundproof area includes a gym, a small library, art equipment, a kitchen, and a bathroom. Staffed by two full-time teachers, it is also a preschool.[4]

Rosie O'Donnell tries to keep her private life separate from her public life, but she does not always succeed. She adopted a baby girl shortly after the infant's birth on September 20, 1997. O'Donnell named her daughter Chelsea Belle. The name Chelsea was suggested by her sister, Maureen. Belle comes from Parker's favorite character in *Beauty and the Beast*. O'Donnell had wanted to keep the adoption a secret until Thanksgiving, so the family could have some time alone without publicity. The news had to be announced earlier, however, after two-year-old Parker started telling people that he had a new baby sister. "I kept saying, 'He means baby-sitter,'" O'Donnell recalls, laughing. "But I couldn't go on lying to everyone."[5] She made the announcement on her November 12, 1997, show. While still an infant, Chelsea would be cared for at home by a family friend. "I want her face out of the press until she's at least two years old," said her mom.[6]

During the second season, Rosie O'Donnell continued to receive praise and awards. Appearing on *Time* magazine's list of "The 25 Most Influential Americans," O'Donnell was selected as "the chatterbox whose cheer is influential."[7] This was a surprise to her. Doing *The Rosie O'Donnell Show*, she said, is like doing stand-up comedy—as if she is performing only for the two hundred people in the studio audience. Those are the faces she tries to make laugh. "I don't have a consciousness that it's going out to millions of people," she says. "It is a little surprising that

Rosie O'Donnell holds the Emmy she won for Outstanding Talk Show Host at the Daytime Emmy Awards for 1996–1997.

it reaches that many people, and that that many people watch it."[8]

At the twenty-fifth annual Daytime Emmy Award ceremonies on May 15, 1998, O'Donnell won her first award for Outstanding Talk Show. In accepting this award, she paid tribute to fellow talk show host Oprah Winfrey, who, O'Donnell said, "sets the standard for excellence in daytime television, a level we strive to maintain."[9] Winfrey's show had won the Emmy for Outstanding Talk Show for several years in a row.

When the winners for Outstanding Talk Show Host were announced, O'Donnell and Oprah Winfrey were tied. It was the first time there had been a tie in that category. O'Donnell and Winfrey embraced as they accepted their awards.[10]

O'Donnell has expressed great respect for Winfrey, calling her "a great lady" who helped pave the way for O'Donnell's career. When Rosie O'Donnell was not yet well known, Winfrey invited her to be a guest on *The Oprah Winfrey Show*. "She's inspired millions of women," says O'Donnell, "and I'm one of the women that she inspired."[11]

O'Donnell works tirelessly as a fund-raiser for children's charities. She often plugs products—such items as toys, books, and household objects—on *The Rosie O'Donnell Show*. In return, a company whose product appears is asked to donate two hundred of that product as a giveaway to the studio audience. Also, the company is asked to donate an equal number to a charity of its choice or to O'Donnell's staff, who will arrange for distribution to a charity.[12]

O'Donnell uses her celebrity status to raise money for less fortunate kids in numerous ways. In her show's first year she created the For All Kids Foundation. The foundation awards grants to non-profit organizations that support programs for disadvantaged children throughout the United States. By the end of its first fiscal year, the foundation had awarded grants totaling $1.5 million to help support such programs as child care, tutoring and mentoring for underperforming students, health care for low-income children, treatment and cure of serious illnesses afflicting children, and intervention and shelter for families at risk of domestic violence.[13]

That same year, O'Donnell collected many of the jokes, riddles, and drawings sent by children to her show, and compiled them into a book. Titled *Kids Are Punny*, it was published by Warner Books and became an immediate best-seller. All profits from the book go into the For All Kids Foundation. An all new collection, *Kids Are Punny 2*, was published in 1998. Its profits, too, go into the foundation.

During the 1997 holiday season, O'Donnell introduced a Rosie O'Donnell doll to her audience. This soft-bodied doll, created by Tyco Toys, Inc., resembled its namesake. Five hundred thousand dolls were available at Kmart and Toys "R" Us through March 31, 1998. Ten dollars from the sale of each doll, priced at $24.99, was donated to the For All Kids Foundation. Also, Warner-Lambert (the maker of Listerine mouthwash) promised to donate $1,000 for each kiss O'Donnell received from guests on *The Rosie O'Donnell Show* between February 1997 and the

O'Donnell and Parker attend a Women's National Basketball Association game at Madison Square Garden in New York City. When she is out with her son, Rosie is not a star—she is "just Parker's mommy."

end of the show's first season. Five hundred kisses later, Warner-Lambert donated $500,000 to the foundation. This, along with the sales of the Rosie O'Donnell doll, the *Kids Are Punny* books, and other donations, brought more than $3 million to the For All Kids Foundation during its first year.[14]

The year 1999 also marked the release of the Rosie O'Donnell celebrity doll by Mattel, Inc. O'Donnell says the doll does not have an "hourglass type" figure, but she is still "very glamorous." Some of these profits, too, will go into the foundation.[15]

O'Donnell's support for children's welfare is ongoing. She is a spokesperson and member of the board of directors of the Children's Defense Fund. Founded by its president, Marian Wright Edelman, the organization focuses on bringing the needs of the nation's children to the attention of local, state, and federal lawmakers. The Children's Defense Fund emphasizes such issues as foster care, teen pregnancy, and child care.[16]

"What drives you to give everything you can to help children?" O'Donnell was asked in a *Good Housekeeping* magazine interview. "I'm haunted by the faces of children in need," she replied. She spoke of the child abuse stories in newspapers, and of the children with cancer who come on her show. "I see these kids' faces in my head every day. . . . I feel a moral obligation to try to do something."[17]

She also feels that her strong empathy for children can be traced to her own childhood. "I definitely think it comes from a childhood that was quite neglectful.

Rosie O'Donnell as a guest on The Oprah Winfrey Show. O'Donnell calls Winfrey a "great lady who has inspired millions of women."

You learn compassion if you're a child who has suffered."[18]

O'Donnell has become a leader in promoting breast cancer awareness and in raising funds for breast cancer research. During October, which is National Breast Cancer Awareness Month, she repeatedly urges women to get an annual mammogram for early detection of breast cancer. In 1997, to help raise funds for research, she provided the voice in two commercials for the California Prune Board in exchange for a $350,000 donation to the National Breast Cancer Coalition.[19]

This project is of personal interest to O'Donnell because of her mother's early death due to cancer. When their mother died at the age of thirty-nine, the children were told she died of hepatitis. Later, they were told it was cancer of the liver and pancreas. In September 1997, O'Donnell learned that her mother actually died of breast cancer.[20]

And what about Rosie O'Donnell, who seems to be caring for everyone else? "Who takes care of you these days?" she was asked. O'Donnell explained that other women throughout her life have found her and mothered her. "My friend Jackie, who lived across the street from me my whole life, her mother mothered me. Teachers mothered me. . . . Everyone in my life who is old enough to be my mom takes that sort of role."[21] And, of course, there is her sister, Maureen, with whom she talks every day. "My sister and I are very close—we always were."[22] O'Donnell also has a strong bond with childhood friend Jackie Ellard, who helps manage her fan mail, and high school friend

Jeanne Davis, a speech therapist who lives on Long Island. "Rosie had to be her own parent," recalls Davis. "She threw herself into everything and became a take-charge person. . . . Today Rosie takes care of everyone."[23]

These days, weight for O'Donnell is still a problem, but she deals with it. "I don't have an accurate perception of what size I am. When I'm between 150 and 200 pounds, I never can gauge where I am. . . . I just want to be healthy." She goes to a nutritionist because she is always tired and wants more energy. "But," she says, "I'll never be thin."[24]

O'Donnell thinks that she may identify getting thin with her mother's death. Her mother got very thin before she died. "I was a child, and I didn't really understand this," said O'Donnell. "But I associated getting thin with getting sick and going away."[25]

A longtime snack-food eater, Rosie O'Donnell often discusses favorite snacks with her television guests. This prompted *Self* magazine to list her among the Top Twenty-five Food Influentials. That is, "people who currently most influence what we eat, how we eat, and how we think about food." O'Donnell's title was "Snack-Food Queen."[26]

On *The Rosie O'Donnell Show*, January 4, 1999, O'Donnell launched into an effort to lose weight. She announced the formation of "Rosie's Chub Club," and invited viewers to join her. Judy Molnar, an advertising executive from St. Joseph, Michigan, was introduced as the coach. By eating less at every meal and exercising a little each day, Molnar managed to lose 120 pounds, and now competes in Ironman triathlons (swimming, biking, and running). The club motto is "Eat Less, Move More."[27]

Rosie O'Donnell's weight and choice of wardrobe led *People* magazine to choose her as one of the Top 10 Trendsetters of 1998. The tailored pantsuits O'Donnell wears on her talk show have given many plus-size women a new attitude toward fashion. Fashion director Monique Keegan of Lane Bryant—a chain specializing in women's fashions in sizes 14 to 28—said about O'Donnell, "She has validated that large-size women don't have to wear sloppy, loose-fitting clothes."[28]

O'Donnell does wear more casual clothes when she is not on camera. Most often she can be seen in a T-shirt, sweatpants or bicycle shorts, and sneakers.

By her midthirties, it seemed that everything Rosie O'Donnell dreamed about as a child had come true. Is there anything she wants to do that she has not done?

O'Donnell would like to play Totie Fields in a future ABC-TV movie about this stand-up comic's life.[29] A popular performer in the 1960s and 1970s in nightclubs and on the Ed Sullivan and the Merv Griffin television shows, Fields died in 1978 at the age of forty-eight. The filming of this movie could take place during the summer break of O'Donnell's daytime show.

Another of her interests is directing. "I would love to direct films," she told CNN's Larry King. ". . . I think it's the most creative part of the film making process . . . to be involved in something from conception to finished project and the editing."[30]

In another interview, she spoke again of her future plans. "I want to direct and produce movies . . . put a movie together from start to finish—direct, edit, score—that's much more interesting to me than performing."[31]

With her natural talent and determination, millions of fans may one day know her as "Director O'Donnell." As a stand-up comic, Hollywood actress, Broadway star, talk show host, and mother, Rosie O'Donnell is truly in a league of her own.

Chronology

1962— Roseann O'Donnell born March 21 in Commack, Long Island, New York.

1973— Death of Roseann's mother on March 17.

1978— Wins first prize in weekly amateur contest at Ground Round Restaurant in Mineola, Long Island.

1980— Graduates from Commack High School South; attends Dickinson College in Carlisle, Pennsylvania.

1981— Attends Boston University in Boston, Massachusetts.

1982— Performs as emcee and stand-up comic in local nightclubs; begins touring across the country as a stand-up comic.

1984— Five-time comedy champion on television show *Star Search*; moves to Los Angeles.

1986— Appears in NBC television series *Gimme a Break*.

1988— Veejay on cable music channel VH-1.

1989— Host and producer of *Stand-up Spotlight* on VH-1.

1990— Appears on *Showtime's Comedy Club All Stars* with costar Bill Engvall in "A Pair of Jokers"; films small role in *Car 54, Where Are You?* (released in 1994).

1992— Film career launched in *A League of Their Own*; costars in Fox TV sitcom *Stand by Your Man*.

1993— Supporting role in films *Sleepless in Seattle* and *Another Stakeout*; appears in *Fatal Instinct*, and *I'll Do Anything*; guest host on *Saturday Night Live*.

1994— Costars in film version of cartoon classic *The Flintstones* and in *Exit to Eden*; debuts on Broadway in musical revival of *Grease!*

1995— Costars in film *Now and Then*; appears in *Beautiful Girls*; adopts infant son Parker Jaren, born May 25, 1995; wins Nickelodeon's Kids' Choice Award; costars in film *Harriet the Spy*; moves from Los Angeles to New York City.

1996— Host and coexecutive producer of *The Rosie O'Donnell Show*; establishes the For All Kids Foundation; spokesperson for the Children's Defense Fund; named "Queen of Nice" by *Newsweek*; chosen one of *Glamour* magazine's "Women of the Year."

1997— Chosen one of *Ms.* magazine's "Women of the Year"; hosts the fifty-first Annual Tony Awards; wins Emmy Award for Outstanding Talk Show Host; compiles book *Kids Are Punny*; adopts infant daughter Chelsea Belle, born September 20, 1997; selected by *Time* as one of "The 25 Most Influential Americans."

1998— Hosts fifty-second Annual Tony Awards; wins Emmy Award for Outstanding Talk Show; wins Emmy Award, in a tie with Oprah Winfrey, for Outstanding Talk Show Host; compiles book *Kids Are Punny 2*.

1999— Provides the voice of Terk in the Disney animated film *Tarzan*.

Chapter Notes

Chapter 1. Something Nice

1. Kristen Golden, "Rosie O'Donnell," *Ms.*, January/February 1997, p. 53.

2. Rick Marin, "Coming Up Roses," *Newsweek*, July 15, 1996, p. 45.

3. Golden, p. 53.

4. "Queen of Nice," *Newsweek*, July 15, 1996, cover.

Chapter 2. Growing Up Fast

1. Hilary de Vries, "It Looks Like Everything's Comin' Up Rosie's," *Chicago Tribune*, May 29, 1994, arts sec., p. 7.

2. Patrick Pacheco, "Wondrous Rosie O'Donnell!" *Cosmopolitan*, June 1994, p. 74.

3. Marjorie Rosen and Craig Tomashoff, "On Base With a Hit," *People*, July 20, 1992, p. 65.

4. Ibid., p. 66.

5. *The Rosie O'Donnell Show*, April 2, 1998.

6. Martha Frankel, "Rosie's Big (and Little) New Plans," *Redbook*, October 1997, p. 106.

7. "Rosie O'Donnell," *Biography Today* (Detroit: Omnigraphics, April 1997), p. 64.

8. Liz Smith, "Really Rosie," *Good Housekeeping*, June 1997, p. 170.

9. Allison Adato, "Love Ya (Kiss, Kiss) Don't Change," *Life*, July 1996, p. 49.

10. Rick Marin, "Coming Up Roses," *Newsweek*, July 15, 1996, p. 47.

11. Rosie O'Donnell interview, *The Oprah Winfrey Show*, May 20, 1997, transcript, p. 19.

12. Sheryl Altman, "Everything's Coming Up Rosie," *Biography*, August 1998, p. 34.

13. Jeff Giles with Mark Miller, "Playing in a League of Her Own," *Newsweek*, August 16, 1993, p. 60.

14. *The Oprah Winfrey Show*, transcript, p. 14.

15. Margy Rochlin, "Rosie O'Donnell," *US*, June 1996, p. 52.

16. Frankel, p. 106.

17. Rosen and Tomashoff, p. 66.

18. Pacheco, p. 74

19. Joan Gelman, "Home Is Where Her Heart Is," *McCall's*, February 1998, p. 21.

20. Rochlin, p. 112.

21. Gelman, p. 21.

22. Melina Gerosa, "Miss Congeniality," *Ladies' Home Journal*, February 1997, p. 106.

23. Rochlin, p. 52.

24. Ibid.

Chapter 3. Building a Dream

1. Patrick Pacheco, "Wondrous Rosie O'Donnell!" *Cosmopolitan*, June 1994, p. 74.

2. Gail Buchalter, "You Have to Dream It to Live It," *Parade*, July 13, 1997, p. 4.

3. Nancy Mills, "Major League," *Chicago Tribune*, August 22, 1993, Womanews sec., p. 1.

4. Melina Gerosa, "Miss Congeniality," *Ladies' Home Journal*, February 1997, p. 156.

5. Rosie O'Donnell, "The Best Friends' Club," *McCall's*, May 1997, p. 38.

6. Ibid.

7. Gerosa, p. 106.

8. Frank DeCaro, "Really Rosie," *TV Guide*, April 5–11, 1997, p. 24.

9. Kristen Golden, "Rosie O'Donnell," *Ms.*, January/ February 1997, p. 55.

10. James Robert Parish, *Rosie: Rosie O'Donnell's Biography* (New York: Carroll & Graf, 1997), p. 26.

11. DeCaro, p. 27.

12. Parish, p. 31.

13. Mary Murphy, "Rosie . . . Really," *TV Guide*, June 15, 1996, p. 30.

14. Joan Gelman, "Home Is Where Her Heart Is," *McCall's*, February 1998, p. 23.

15. Murphy, p. 28.
16. George Mair and Anna Green, *Rosie O'Donnell: Her True Story* (Secaucus, N.J.: Carol Publishing, 1997), p. 19.
17. Parish, p. 26.
18. Mair and Green, p. 21.

Chapter 4. A Shaky Start

1. Liz Smith, "Really Rosie," *Good Housekeeping*, June 1997, p. 174.
2. Jeff Giles and Mark Miller, "Playing in a League of Her Own," *Newsweek*, August 16, 1993, p. 60.
3. Ken Berryhill, *Funny Business* (Englewood Cliffs, N.J.: Prentice-Hall, 1985), p. 35.
4. Smith, p. 174.
5. James Robert Parish, *Rosie: Rosie O'Donnell's Biography* (New York: Carroll & Graf), 1997, p. 45.
6. Ibid., p. 34.
7. George Mair and Anna Green, *Rosie O'Donnell: Her True Story* (Secaucus, N.J.: Carol Publishing, 1997), p. 23.
8. Ibid.
9. Joan Gelman, "Home Is Where Her Heart Is," *McCall's*, February 1998, p. 23.
10. Ibid.
11. Parish, p. 38.
12. Ibid.

Chapter 5. A Lucky Star

1. "Rosie O'Donnell," *Current Biography Yearbook 1995* (New York: H. W. Wilson, 1995), p. 448.
2. Nancy Mills, "Major League," *Chicago Tribune*, August 22, 1993, Womanews sec., p. 4.
3. George Mair and Anna Green, *Rosie O'Donnell: Her True Story* (Secaucus, N.J.: Carol Publishing, 1997), p. 27.
4. Ibid., p. 29.
5. Alex McNeil, *Total Television* (New York: Penguin Books, 1996), p. 785.
6. Trish Deitch Rohrer, "Rosie O'Donnell," *Mirabella*, June 1993, p. 51.

7. Gloria Goodman, *The Life and Humor of Rosie O'Donnell* (New York: William Morrow, 1998), p. 38.

Chapter 6. A Break—At Last

1. Jeff Giles and Mark Miller, "Playing in a League of Her Own," *Newsweek*, August 16, 1993, p. 60.

2. George Mair and Anna Green, *Rosie O'Donnell: Her True Story* (Secaucus, N.J.: Carol Publishing, 1997), p. 36.

3. Melina Gerosa, "Miss Congeniality," *Ladies' Home Journal*, February 1997, p. 107.

4. Mark Morrison, "Rosie Days," *US*, July 1993, p. 82.

5. Patrick Spreng, *Everything Rosie* (Secaucus, N.J.: Carol Publishing, 1998), p. 30.

6. Gerosa, p. 107.

7. Rosie O'Donnell interview, CNN's *Larry King Live*, May 28, 1997, transcript, p. 2.

8. Morrison, p. 82.

9. Chantel Westerman, "Comic Strip: Rosie O'Donnell Bares All," *Elle*, October 1994, p. 82.

10. Rosie O'Donnell, "My Favorite Room," *People*, April 21, 1997, p. 68.

Chapter 7. Movieland

1. Marjorie Rosen and Craig Tomashoff, "On Base with a Hit," *People*, July 20, 1992, p. 65.

2. Ibid.

3. Gloria Goodman, *The Life and Humor of Rosie O'Donnell* (New York: William Morrow, 1998), p. 69.

4. Rosen and Tomashoff, p. 66.

5. Rosie O'Donnell interview, CNN's *Larry King Live*, May 28, 1997, transcript, p. 4.

6. Leonard Maltin, *Leonard Maltin's 1998 Movie and Video Guide* (New York: Penguin, 1997), p. 754.

7. Steve Wulf, "Field of Dames," *Sports Illustrated*, July 6, 1992, p. 4.

8. George Mair and Anna Green, *Rosie O'Donnell: Her True Story* (Secaucus, N.J.: Carol Publishers, 1997), p. 82.

9. Jack Matthews, "Sleepless in Seattle," *New York Newsday*, June 25, 1993.

10. Nancy Mills, "Major League," *Chicago Tribune*, August 22, 1993, Womanews sec., p. 4.

11. Ibid.

12. Hilary de Vries, "It Looks Like Everything's Comin' Up Rosie's," *Chicago Tribune*, May 29, 1994, arts sec., p. 7.

13. James Robert Parish, *Rosie: Rosie O'Donnell's Biography* (New York: Carroll and Graf, 1997), p. 146.

14. Madonna, "Coming Up Rosie," *Mademoiselle*, August 1993, p. 163.

15. Chantel Westerman, "Comic Strip: Rosie O'Donnell Bares All," *Elle*, October 1994, p. 82.

Chapter 8. Hello, Broadway!

1. Hilary de Vries, "It Looks Like Everything's Comin' Up Rosie's," *Chicago Tribune*, May 29, 1994, arts section, p. 7.

2. William Norwich, "Rosie's Turn," *Vogue*, June 1994, p. 92.

3. Ibid.

4. de Vries, p. 7.

5. Norwich, p. 92.

6. James Robert Parish, *Rosie: Rosie O'Donnell Biography* (New York: Carroll & Graf, 1997), p. 177.

7. Nancy Franklin, "Camping Out," *New Yorker*, May 30, 1994, p. 101.

8. Parish, p. 179.

9. George Mair and Anna Green, *Rosie O'Donnell: Her True Story* (Secaucus, N.J.: Carol Publishing, 1997), pp. 105–106.

10. John Simon, "Wall-to-Wall Musicals," *New York*, May 23, 1994, p. 71.

11. Chantel Westerman, "Comic Strip: Rosie O'Donnell Bares All," *Elle*, October 1994, p. 80.

12. Liz Smith, "Really Rosie," *Good Housekeeping*, June 1997, p. 170.

13. Norwich, p. 92.

14. Kristen Golden, "Rosie O'Donnell," *Ms.*, January/February 1997, p. 54.

15. Mair and Green, p. 105.

16. Richard Schickel, "Maverick Is Painless; The Flintstones Is Fun," *Time*, May 30, 1994, p. 60.

17. Leonard Maltin, *Leonard Maltin's 1998 Movie and Video Guide* (New York: Penguin, 1997), p. 452.

18. Ralph Novak, "Exit to Eden," *People*, October 31, 1994, p. 19.

19. Maltin, p. 410.

20. Parish, p. 167.

Chapter 9. Time for a Change

1. George Mair and Anna Green, *Rosie O'Donnell: Her True Story* (Secaucus, N.J.: Carol Publishing, 1997), p. 115.

2. Juliann Garey, "Beautiful Girls," *Glamour,* February 1996, p. 120.

3. Stephanie Williams, "Kidding Around," *TV Guide*, April 5–11, 1997, pp. 24–25.

4. Frank DeCaro, "Really Rosie," *TV Guide*, April 5–11, 1997, pp. 26–27.

5. Ibid., p. 27.

6. Melina Gerosa, "Miss Congeniality," *Ladies' Home Journal*, February 1997, pp. 106–107.

7. Patrick Pacheco, "Wondrous Rosie O'Donnell," *Cosmopolitan*, June 1994, p. 71.

8. James Robert Parish, *Rosie: Rosie O'Donnell's Biography* (New York: Carroll & Graf, 1997), p. 207.

9. Margy Rochlin, "Rosie O'Donnell," *US*, June 1996, p. 50.

10. Ibid.

11. Gail Buchalter, "You Have to Dream It to Live It," *Parade*, July 13, 1997, p. 5.

12. Ibid.

13. Gerosa, p. 107.

14. Rosie O'Donnell interview, CNN's *Larry King Live*, May 28, 1997, transcript, p. 3.

15. Madonna, "Coming Up Rosie," *Mademoiselle*, August 1993, p. 217.

Chapter 10. "And Now, Here's Rosie!"

1. Allison Adato, "Love Ya (Kiss, Kiss) Don't Change," *Life*, July 1996, p. 49.

2. George Mair and Anna Green, *Rosie O'Donnell: Her True Story* (Secaucus, N.J.: Carol Publishing, 1997), p. 179.

3. Kim Cunningham, "Mix Master," *People*, June 17, 1996, p. 180.

4. Mary Murphy, "Rosie . . . Really," *TV Guide*, June 15, 1996, p. 29.

5. David Bauder, "Rosie O'Donnell Kicks Back for a While," *The News-Gazette* (Champaign, Ill.), April 5, 1998, p. F-1.

6. Patrick Spreng, *Everything Rosie* (Secaucus, N.J.: Carol Publishing, 1998), p. 44.

7. Kristen Golden, "Rosie O'Donnell," *Ms.*, January/February 1997, p. 54.

8. Ken Tucker, "Rosie's Baby," *Entertainment Weekly*, June 28, 1996, p. 89.

9. Gloria Goodman, *The Life and Humor of Rosie O'Donnell* (New York: William Morrow, 1998), p. 155.

10. Rick Marin, "Coming Up Roses," *Newsweek*, July 15, 1996, p. 3.

11. David Wild, "Television Whole Lotta Rosie," *Rolling Stone*, August 2, 1996, p. 107.

12. Melina Gerosa, "Miss Congeniality," *Ladies' Home Journal*, February 1997, p. 156.

13. Victoria Kohn Michels, "A Host Who's Silly, Passionate, Gushing, Glad," *The New York Times*, June 20, 1999, sec. 2, p. 31.

14. Janny Scott, "Rosie Speaks, and Broadway Ticket Sellers Cheer," *The New York Times*, May 3, 1998, p. A1.

15. Ibid.

16. Golden, p. 53.

17. Marin, p. 46.

18. "Women of the Year 1996," *Glamour*, December 1996, p. 91.

19. Golden, p. 53.

20. "Women of the Year 1996," p. 91.

21. Liz Smith, "Really Rosie," *Good Housekeeping*, June 1997, p. 172.

22. Johanna Schneller, "Rosie O'Donnell," *US*, February 1998, p. 43.

23. Ibid.

24. Ibid.

25. Ibid., p. 42.

26. Ibid.

Chapter 11. A League of Her Own

1. Joan Gelman, "Home Is Where Her Heart Is," *McCall's*, February 1998, p. 22.

2. Martha Frankel, "Rosie's Big (and Little) New Plans," *Redbook*, October 1997, p. 144.

3. Joanna Powell, "Rosie's Devotion," *Good Housekeeping*, June 1998, pp. 101–102.

4. Ibid., p. 101.

5. Gelman, p. 20.

6. Ibid.

7. "Time's 25 Most Influential Americans," *Time*, April 21, 1997, p. 48.

8. Rosie O'Donnell interview, CNN's *Larry King Live*, May 28, 1997, transcript, p. 2.

9. "O'Donnell's Emmy Ends Winfrey's Four-Year Streak," *Chicago Tribune*, May 16, 1998, section 1, p. 2.

10. "O'Donnell, Winfrey Tie for Emmy," *The News-Gazette* (Champaign, Ill.), May 16, 1998, p. A7.

11. *Larry King Live*, transcript, p. 4.

12. Sharon Maughan, "Children's Books Get a 'Rosie' Reception on TV," *Publishers Weekly*, June 2, 1997, p. 33.

13. "Mission and Background Statement," For All Kids Foundation, Inc., P.O. Box 225, Allendale, N.J. 07401, <http://www.rosieodonnell.com/cmp/allkids/mission.htm>.

14. Powell, p. 102.

15. Melina Gerosa, "Rosie Revealed," *Ladies' Home Journal*, February 1999, p. 118.

16. Cathleen Collins Lee, "Marian Wright Edelman," *Newsmakers* (Detroit: Gale Research, 1990), p. 119.

17. Powell, p. 101.

18. Ibid.

19. Patrick Spreng, *Everything Rosie* (Secaucus, N.J.: Carol Publishing, 1998), p. 184.

20. Ibid., p. 4.

21. Powell, p. 158.

22. Liz Smith, "Really Rosie," *Good Housekeeping*, June 1997, p. 170.

23. Gelman, p. 23.

24. Ibid., pp. 22–23.

25. Chantel Westerman, "Comic Strip: Rosie O'Donnell Bares All," *Elle*, October 1994, p. 80.

26. John Gallagher, "Snack-Food Queen," *Self*, February 1998, p. 114.

27. Rosemarie Lennon, "Get in Shape with Rosie," *Star*, January 22, 1999, p. 20.

28. "Top 10 Trendsetters '98," *People*, February 16, 1998, p. 67.

29. Spreng, p. 71.

30. *Larry King Live*, transcript, p. 6.

31. Hilary De Vries, "Everything's Coming Up Rosie," *Chicago Tribune*, June 7, 1998, sec. 7, p. 10.

Further Reading

Books

Golden, Gloria. *The Life and Humor of Rosie O'Donnell.* New York: William Morrow, 1998.

Krohn, Katherine. *Rosie O'Donnell.* Minneapolis: Lerner Publications, 1999.

Mair, George, and Anna Green. *Rosie O'Donnell: Her True Story.* Secaucus, N.J.: Carol Publishing, 1997.

Parish, James Robert. *Rosie: Rosie O'Donnell's Biography.* New York: Carroll & Graf, 1997.

Spreng, Patrick. *Everything's Rosie.* Secaucus, N.J.: Carol Publishing, 1998.

Internet Addresses

Warner Bros. official Rosie Web site
<http://rosieo.warnerbros.com/>

The ACME Rosie Page
<http://maikon.net/spreng/rosie/index.html>

ROMonky's Rosie O'Donnell Fan Page
<http://www.geocities.com/Hollywood/Makeup/5215/index.html>

Rosie Page
<http://www.geocities.com/Hollywood/Boulevard/6516/index/html>

Index

Coherence in Natural Language

Coherence in Natural Language

Data Structures and Applications

Florian Wolf and Edward Gibson

A Bradford Book
The MIT Press
Cambridge, Massachusetts
London, England

MIT Press books may be purchased at special quantity discounts for business or sales promotional use. For information, please e-mail special_sales@mitpress.mit.edu or write to Special Sales Department, The MIT Press, 55 Hayward Street, Cambridge, MA 02142.

This book was set in Sabon by Graphic Composition, Inc., Athens, Georgia, and was printed and bound in the United States of America.

Library of Congress Cataloging-in-Publication Data

Wolf, Florian.
Coherence in natural language : data structures and applications / Florian Wolf and Edward Gibson.
    p.   cm.
Includes bibliographical references and index.
ISBN 0-262-23251-0 (alk. paper)
1. Cohesion (Linguistics) 2. Discourse analysis. 3. Computational linguistics. I. Gibson, Edward, 1962– II. Title.
P302.2.W65   2006
401'.41–dc22

                                                           2005058025

10 9 8 7 6 5 4 3 2 1

Contents

Acknowledgments

First and foremost, we would like to thank the people in our lab and our visitors over the last several years for great discussions and for asking really good questions: Emmanuel Bellengier, Mara Breen, Evan Chen, Evelina Fedorenko, Dan Grodner, John Hale, Barbara Hemforth, Doug Rohde, Tessa Warren, and Duane Watson. One member of our lab deserves special mention: Timmy Desmet, who collaborated with us on psycholinguistic experiments. No screw-up in experimental designs or hypotheses could escape him.

Several undergraduate students in our lab contributed to the work reported in this book. In particular, Amy Fisher and Meredith Knight annotated text after text, and are now busy developing a version of Trivial Pursuit based on what they have learned from 1986–1989 news texts.

A number of other people contributed strongly to the ideas presented here. After every meeting with Regina Barzilay, we always came away with many new ideas to explore. The same is true for Michael Collins, Andy Kehler, Neal Pearlmutter, Whitman Richards, Pawan Sinha, and Josh Tenenbaum. It would be nice if our days had significantly more than 24 hours so that we could explore all their great suggestions and ideas.

The (wider) MIT community in general and the audiences at the CogLunch seminars in the Department of Brain and Cognitive Sciences in particular have provided constructive criticism in the true sense of these words. In particular, we would like to thank David Caplan, Phil Holcomb, Nancy Kanwisher, Steve Pinker, Molly Potter, Anthony Wagner, Gloria Waters, and Ken Wexler, as well as Doug Jones, Doug Reynolds, and Marc Zissman from Lincoln Laboratories.

On the home front, the first author would like to thank his parents and his brother for their support. The second author would like to thank his sons, Peter and Mitchell, for keeping him away from work a lot of the time.

Coherence in Natural Language

1 | Introduction

Consider the following two texts

(1) *Coherent example text*

    a. The weather at the rocket launch site in Kourou was good yesterday.

    b. Therefore, the launch of the new Ariane rocket could take place as scheduled.

    c. The rocket carried two test satellites into orbit.

(2) *Incoherent example text*

    a. A new communications satellite was launched.

    b. Therefore, Mary likes spinach.

    c. John stayed home in bed.

The text in (1) makes sense; that is, it is coherent. It is easy to infer informational relations between the sentences in (1): sentences (1a) and (1b) stand in a causal relation (the weather for a rocket launch generally has to be good; because the weather was good, the launch could take place as scheduled). The sentence in (1c) provides additional details about the Ariane rocket mentioned in (1b), so (1c) and (1b) are in an elaborative relation.

    By contrast, it is much harder to infer such informational relations between the sentences in (2). For example, the coordinating conjunction *therefore* in (2b) indicates that there should be a causal relation between (2a) and (2b). However, without any further context, it is not clear how that causal relation should be interpreted; it is not obvious what liking spinach has to do with the launch of a communications satellite. Furthermore, the relationship between (2c) (John's staying home in bed) and the other two sentences is also unclear. It is possible, however, to construct a context which makes (2) coherent. It could be that Mary worked on the satellite and ate spinach on the day the satellite was launched. The fact that the satellite launch was successful made her happy (because she had worked on the satellite), and now, everytime she sees spinach, it reminds her of the day of the successful satellite launch. Thus, the additional context makes it possible to construct a causal relation between (2a) and (2b). A further causal relation might even be possible between

(2a) and (2c). Perhaps John wanted to see the satellite launch, and his TV is in his bedroom. Therefore, in order to watch the satellite launch on his TV, he stayed in bed.

The text in (2) can be made coherent only by providing context in addition to that available in the text itself or as part of general background knowledge. That is, it would probably be unreasonable to assume as general knowledge that Mary had worked on the satellite launch, had spinach for lunch on the day of the successful launch, and now has a positive association with eating spinach; or that John has his TV in his bedroom, wanted to see the satellite launch on TV, and therefore stayed in bed to watch TV. By contrast, it is easy to infer a coherence structure for (1),[1] given the information provided by the text and a reasonable amount of general background knowledge (i.e., that rocket launches usually require good weather and that rockets can carry satellites into orbit).

In this book, we examine coherence structures that are inferable solely from the information provided by the text and by a reasonable amount of general background knowledge. For example, we assume that it is part of general background knowledge that New York is, among other things, a place where stocks are traded. However, we do not assume that it is generally known how the stock of a particular company performed at a particular point or during a particular period in time. In the research reported here, we wished to determine whether a consensus generally exists about what inferable coherence relations are possible between segments in a discourse. To do so, we had two independent annotators code for coherence structure 135 texts from the *Wall Street Journal* and the *AP Newswire*. They achieved high interannotator agreement, which we take as an indication that people can usually agree on the inferable coherence structures for given discourses.

Our first goal for this book is to develop a descriptively adequate representation for discourse structure. Our second goal is to test the influence of discourse structure on psycholinguistic processes, in particular, on pronoun processing. Our final goal is to test the influence of coherence structures on the relative saliency of discourse segments. The following three sections will describe these goals in detail. We conclude the chapter with comments on how different areas of research (cognitive science, natural language engineering, information extraction) might be informed by the issues we address.

1.1 Representations and Data Structures for Discourse Coherence

Our first goal is to specify a descriptively adequate data structure for representing discourse coherence. In particular, we will evaluate whether trees are descriptively adequate or whether more powerful data structures are needed. Most accounts of discourse coherence assume trees as a data structure (e.g., Carlson, Marcu, and Okurowski 2002; Corston-Oliver 1998; Grosz and Sidner 1986; Mann and Thompson 1988; Marcu 2000; Polanyi

1996). Some accounts are primarily tree based and do not allow crossed dependencies; however, they allow nodes with multiple parents (e.g., Lascarides and Asher 1993; Webber et al. 1999). Other accounts assume more general graphs that allow both nodes with multiple parents and crossed dependencies (e.g., Danlos 2004; Hobbs 1985; McKeown 1985).

So far, the issue of descriptively adequate data structures for representing coherence has not been empirically evaluated. To do so, we examined discourse structures of naturally occurring coherent texts to determine whether they contain violations of tree structure constraints, that is, nodes with multiple parents or crossed dependencies. Our results indicate that they do, suggesting that more powerful data structures than trees are needed to represent discourse coherence. However, another empirical question is how frequently crossed dependencies and nodes with multiple parents occur. If they are rare, one could retain a tree-based representation and accept a certain (low) error rate. If, however, they are common, they clearly must not be ignored.

A final empirical question is whether there are any constraints on where crossed dependencies and nodes with multiple parents can occur. If such constraints exist, an augmented tree structure could accommodate certain well-specified violations. If there are no obvious constraints, however, there is a clear need for data structures more powerful than trees.

In order to address the questions of how frequently tree structure violations occur and whether there are any constraints on their occurrence, we collected a database of 135 texts from the *Wall Street Journal* and the *AP Newswire* and had them hand-annotated for coherence structures. Our results indicate that crossed dependencies and nodes with multiple parents occur frequently, and that there are no obvious constraints that would allow maintaining even an augmented tree structure (Wolf and Gibson 2005; Wolf et al. 2003).

On this basis, we propose the use of connected, labeled chain graphs instead of trees as a data structure for representing discourse coherence.[2] In labeled coherence chain graphs, an ordered array of nodes represents the discourse segments; the order in which the nodes occur reflects the temporal sequencing of the discourse segments. Labeled directed or undirected arcs represent coherence relations that hold among the discourse segments. In chapter 2, we will discuss in detail what kinds of coherence relations we use and how they are represented by directed and undirected arcs.

Using chain graphs instead of tree-based coherence criteria allows the representation of a far greater number of possible coherent discourse structures: given the same number of nodes, it is possible to draw a far greater number of connected chain graphs than trees. The number of these coherent discourse structures may well be limited, however, by constraints other than those applicable to chain graphs. For instance, certain graphs or subgraphs might occur more frequently than others: our database of 135 texts, for example, contains no coherence graph that is fully connected. It is possible that fully connected graphs and other (sub)graphs are part of a set of graphs that rarely, or never, occur. Furthermore, text genres might differ in how often they exhibit certain (sub)graphs. Questions regarding constraints such as these should be addressed in future research.

1.2 Discourse Coherence and Psycholinguistic Processing

Our second goal in this book is to determine whether processes underlying the establishment of coherence structure can influence psycholinguistic processes, one of which is pronoun processing. The use of pronouns and other referring expressions is a critical means for connecting clauses and phrases and establishing coherence (Garnham 2001; Haliday and Hassan 1976; van Dijk and Kintsch 1983). Pronoun processing is thus an important part of discourse comprehension.

One hypothesis about how pronoun processing works is that it is based on principles or heuristics that are specific to pronoun processing. There might also be principles involved in pronoun processing that are specific to language in general. Alternatively, pronoun processing may be part of more general cognitive mechanisms underlying the establishment of coherence. If so, the investigation of pronoun processing could also shed light on the operation of these cognitive mechanisms.

Most accounts of pronoun processing are based on sentence-level syntactic or semantic principles (e.g., Chambers and Smyth 1998). One such account is Centering Theory, a general approach to discourse processing with implications for pronominal resolution (Grosz, Joshi, and Weinstein 1995; cf. Wundt 1911). For two-clause sentences such as the ones to be investigated in chapter 3, Centering Theory predicts that pronouns prefer referents in the subject position of a sentence over referents in object position. A different, pronoun-specific account, Parallel Preference (Chambers and Smyth 1998), predicts that subject pronouns preferentially pick out subject referents, whereas object pronouns prefer referents in object position (but see chapter 3 for important qualifications of this statement).

In contrast to these pronoun-specific accounts, coherence-based accounts treat pronoun processing as a by-product of more general inference processes that are used when establishing coherence in a discourse (e.g., Hobbs 1979; Kehler 2002). These accounts argue that people use different pronoun resolution strategies under different coherence relations. If this hypothesis is correct, that is, if coherence relations can influence pronominal processing, it would also constitute evidence that coherence relations have psychological validity. We tested pronoun-specific and coherence-based accounts in an online comprehension study and in an off-line production study. As chapter 3 will show, the results from both studies support accounts based on general inference processes, rather than on pronoun-specific structures.

Although there is no direct evidence yet linking specific cognitive processing mechanisms with specific coherence relations, we believe that these results support the idea that coherence relations can influence other cognitive processes. In a similar vein, Kintsch (1998; Kintsch and van Dijk 1978) has shown in text comprehension experiments that people remember information conveyed in a text better if that text involves causal coherence relations than if it involves elaborating coherence relations.

1.3   Discourse Coherence and the Importance of Document Segments

Due to the internet and inexpensive data storage space, an ever-increasing amount of text is becoming available. This creates a need for information extraction and text summarization systems that can manage and utilize the vast amount of information available in these documents. An important subcomponent of information extraction and text summarization systems are algorithms that can determine the relative importance of segments in a text (e.g., Brandow, Mitze, and Rau 1995; Mitra, Singhal, and Buckley 1997). *Relative importance* refers to how significant the content of a text segment is relative to the content of the text as a whole. Determining the relative saliency of a text segment is crucial to information extraction because it aims to recover the essential information from a text; similarly, in text summarization, only the key information in a text should be included. Because of these practical needs, the automatic ranking of text segments for their importance is a natural language engineering problem that has received considerable attention.

A number of approaches have been proposed to determine automatically the relative saliency of discourse segments in a text. We tested the performance of different discourse segment ranking algorithms by comparing the algorithm output to human rankings obtained in a psycholinguistic experiment. The algorithms we tested were either word-, layout-, or coherence-based.

The basic idea behind word-based approaches is that the saliency of a discourse segment in a text increases with the importance of the words it contains. Different word-based approaches vary in their definitions of what makes a word important. For example, an algorithm described by Luhn (1958) has a "stoplist" of nonimportant words (i.e., words that do not help to distinguish the informational content of one text from that of another, such as *and, of, is,* etc.). In each discourse segment, the important words (i.e., those words that are not on the stoplist) form clusters. The more clusters a discourse segment has and the bigger they are, the more important the discourse segment is. Another example of a word-based algorithm is described by Salton and Buckley (1988). This algorithm determines the importance of a word according to the ratio of its frequency within a document to its frequency in a whole set of documents. The higher that ratio, the more important that word is. The importance of a discourse segment can then be determined by adding the importance rankings of each word in that discourse segment.

Layout-based approaches contend that layout information makes discourse segments more or less important. For instance, information conveyed in headlines or titles is usually assumed to be more important than information conveyed in the text itself, which in turn is held to be more important than information conveyed in footnotes. Furthermore, writers are often encouraged to place the most important information at the beginning of a paragraph (e.g., Eden and Mitchell 1986). In our test of a simple version of the layout-based approach, for example, we ranked the first sentences of the first four paragraphs in a document as important and the other sentences in the document as not important.

Coherence-based approaches maintain that the saliency of a discourse segment is based on its position in the informational structure of a discourse. The positions that make a discourse segment more or less salient depend on the data structure used for representing discourse coherence. Tree-based approaches assume that the importance of a discourse segment is greater the higher it occurs in the tree (e.g., Marcu 2000). Chain graph approaches are based on the idea that a discourse segment is more important the more other discourse segments relate to it (e.g., Sparck-Jones 1993).

The experimental results reported in chapter 4 indicate that coherence-based methods that operate on chain graphs performed better than those operating on trees (see also Wolf and Gibson 2004). We suggest that errors in estimating discourse segment salience may be caused by the fact that trees cannot represent nodes with multiple parents. Thus, the choice of data structure for representing discourse coherence might not be only a question of descriptive adequacy. Our results suggest that having more descriptively adequate data structures for representing discourse coherence might also be more useful for natural language engineering tasks such as discourse segment ranking.

1.4 Cognitive Science and Natural Language Engineering

The issues we address in this book pertain to areas of cognitive science as well as to natural language engineering and information extraction applications, especially in the realm of coherence structures. For example, in cognitive science, an important question regarding human language processing is whether people prefer certain kinds of data structures over others (e.g., those that are easier to produce or comprehend). In natural language engineering, the kind of data structure used for representing discourse coherence partly determines what kinds of algorithms could be used for parsing coherence structures (e.g., whether context-free parsers can be used).

Chapter 3, which discusses the relation between coherence and pronoun resolution, is primarily aimed at a cognitive science audience. Our aim there is to determine whether coherence can influence preferences in human pronoun comprehension and production. We believe that this also tests the psychological plausibility of the coherence relations we investigated: if varying the kind of coherence relation between the clause containing the antecedent and the clause containing the pronoun has an effect on pronoun processing, it suggests that these kinds of coherence relations play a role in cognitive processing.

Chapter 4, which investigates discourse segment ranking, is relevant to understanding certain aspects of human document understanding, as well as to problems in natural language engineering and information extraction. With respect to human document understanding, we examine what properties of a document (i.e., layout, distribution of words, or informational structure) correlate best with human rankings of what is important in a text. We also believe that a better understanding of the factors that make some parts of a document more important than others is crucial to the success of engineering applications in the area of document analysis and understanding.

2 | Representing Discourse Coherence: Corpus-Based Analysis

2.1 Introduction

This chapter presents a set of discourse structure relations and develops criteria for an appropriate data structure to represent these relations.

2.1.1 Claims about the Taxonomies of Coherence Relations

Different accounts of discourse coherence have proposed a range of taxonomies of coherence relations. Some accounts propose taxonomies of intentional coherence relations (e.g., Grosz and Sidner 1986), others argue for informational coherence relations (e.g., Hobbs 1985; Kehler 2002), and some assume a mixture of intentional and informational relations (e.g., Mann and Thompson 1988; Carlson, Marcu, and Okurowski 2002).

In intentional-level accounts, coherence relations reflect how the role played by one discourse segment (i.e., its *purpose*) relates to the role played by another segment with respect to the interlocutors' intentions (e.g., Grosz and Sidner 1986; Nakatani, Grosz, and Ahn 1995). Consider example (3):

(3) *Example discourse with intentional-level annotation (adapted from Nakatani, Grosz, and Ahn 1995)*

   I. *Teach new cook how to make stuffed sole*
     We're going to be making sole, stuffed with shrimp mousse.

     i. *Identify ingredients*
       In the small bag are the sole and the shrimp. And there are ten small sole fillets and there's a half a pound of medium shrimp.

     ii. *Instruct new cook to get equipment ready*
       Okay, and you're going to need a blender to make the mousse. So you should get your blender out.

In example (3), the *discourse segment purposes* (term from Grosz and Sidner 1986) are identified by Roman numerals. Thus, the purpose of segment I has two subpurposes, (i) and (ii). However, the definitions of the discourse segment purposes in example (3) are specific to discourses with a certain topic (cooking). It is hard to see how these definitions would generalize, for example, to discourses about soccer games or stock market developments. Note also that it still needs to be investigated in future research how exactly discourse segment purpose and coherence relations relate to each other.

In contrast with intentional-level approaches, informational-level accounts aim to represent how the meaning conveyed by one discourse segment relates to the meaning conveyed by another discourse segment (e.g., Hobbs 1985; Webber et al. 2003). More specifically, discourse segments can be in a causal relation as in example (4), where discourse segment (4a) states the cause for the effect stated in (4b). Another example of an informational coherence relation is the similarity relation illustrated in (5), where what is stated in (5a) is similar to what is stated in (5b).

(4) *Causal relation between discourse segments*
    a. There was bad weather at the airport
    b. and so our flight got delayed.

(5) *Similarity relation between discourse segments*
    a. There is a train on platform A.
    b. There is another train on platform B.

Taxonomies of informational coherence relations vary greatly with respect to how many kinds of relations they employ. For example, Grosz and Sidner (1986) assume only two coherence relations in their informational-level representation, *causal* and *not-causal*. In contrast, Hovy and Maier (1995) report variations of Rhetorical Structure Theory (RST; cf. Mann and Thompson 1988) with over 400 kinds of coherence relations. However, Hovy and Maier (1995) argue that at least for informational-level accounts, taxonomies with more relations represent subtypes of taxonomies with fewer relations. This means that different taxonomies can be compatible with each other; they differ with respect to the detail in which they represent informational structures of texts. For example, a more detailed taxonomy might differentiate between volitional and nonvolitional causal relations (e.g., Marcu 2000). This difference is illustrated by examples (6) and (7).

(6) *Volitional causal relation*
John dropped a glass because he wanted to see how it shattered.

(7) *Nonvolitional causal relation*
John dropped a glass because he had slippery hands.

In example (6), John intentionally dropped a glass (because he wanted to see how it shattered). By contrast, in example (7), John did not intend to drop a glass; he had slippery hands, and the glass slipped between his fingers and fell. However, in both examples, John is the agent that caused the glass to be dropped. Less fine-grained coherence relation taxonomies might not distinguish volitional and nonvolitional causal relations, labeling both examples as causal relations (e.g., Hobbs 1985).

Another example of a more detailed taxonomy is proposed by Martin (1992), who also distinguishes different kinds of causal relations, as illustrated in examples (8) and (9).

(8)   We arrived late, so we didn't have much time to prepare.

(9)   The new software has to work. Otherwise everyone will be upset.

Example (8) describes something that already took place: a consequence (not having much time to prepare) of a cause (arriving late). On the other hand, example (9) describes a condition that has to be met (the new software working) in order to avoid an undesirable consequence (everyone being upset).

In Mann and Thompson's (1988) account, intentional and informational coherence relations are represented in one discourse structure. Mann and Thompson argue in addition that only one coherence relation can hold between any two discourse segments. However, Moser and Moore (1996) argue that intentional and informational relations may determine legitimate but incompatible structures for the same discourse segments. Consider example (10).

(10)   *Example text (from Moser and Moore 1996)*
    a.   Come home by 5:00.
    b.   Then we can go to the store before it closes.

Moser and Moore maintain that there are two ways in which (10) may be annotated. Figure 2.1 shows an annotation with an intentional coherence relation from Mann and Thompson (1988), *motivation;* wanting to go to the store before it closes is the motivation for the speaker to utter discourse segment (10a). Figure 2.2 shows an annotation with a *condition* relation, which is an informational coherence relation (Mann and Thompson 1988; cf. Hobbs 1985; Kehler 2002); coming home by 5:00 is the condition for being able to go to the store before it closes.

The two annotations shown in figures 2.1 and 2.2 are incompatible under Mann and Thompson's (1988) account, which allows only one coherence relation between any two discourse segments. The direction of the motivation relation is from discourse segment (10b) to discourse segment (10a) (the second discourse segment states the motivation for the first). By contrast, the direction of the condition relation is from (10a) to (10b) (the first discourse segment states the condition for the second). Moser and Moore (1996) argue that both kinds of coherence relations would be appropriate for annotating (10), and that it is hard to see why one of the relations should be preferred over the other. Thus Moser

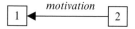

Figure 2.1
Annotating with intentional structure

Figure 2.2
Annotating with informational structure

and Moore conclude that legitimate intentional and informational coherence relations may not always be representable if only one kind of coherence relation can hold between any two discourse segments.

2.1.2 Claims about Data Structures for Representing Discourse Coherence

Most accounts employ tree structures to represent the coherence relations between discourse segments in a text (e.g., Mann and Thompson 1988; Marcu 2000; Polanyi and Scha 1984). Tree structures do not allow crossed dependencies or nodes with multiple parents. Figure 2.3 shows a tree with both crossed dependencies and nodes with multiple parents. The relation between nodes 1 and 3 crosses with the relation between nodes 1 and 2 and with the relation between nodes 2 and 3. Furthermore, nodes 1, 2, and 3 have multiple parents: node 1 is dominated by nodes A and D; node 2 by nodes A and E; and node 3 by nodes D, E, and B. Note that a well-formed tree without crossed dependencies or nodes with multiple parents would result from removing nodes D and E as well as the edges adjacent to (i.e., the branches off of) these nodes.

Some accounts of coherence do not allow crossed dependencies but appear to allow nodes with multiple parents (e.g., Webber, Knott, Stone et al. 1999). For example, in figure 2.3, if node D and the edges adjacent to it were removed, the resulting data structure would have no crossed dependencies, but it would have two nodes with multiple parents: node 2 would be dominated by nodes A and E, and node 3 would be dominated by nodes E and B.

Other accounts assume less constrained graphs allowing both crossed dependencies and multiple parents (e.g., Danlos 2004; Hobbs 1985; for dialogue structure, see Penstein Rose et al. 1995). An example of such a graph is given in figure 2.4, which shows the same underlying dependency structure as figure 2.3.

For representing discourse coherence, both tree structures and more general graphs have an ordered array of terminal nodes (nodes 1, 2, 3, and 4 in figures 2.3 and 2.4), which rep-

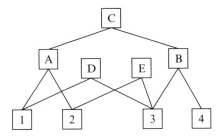

Figure 2.3
Crossed dependencies and nodes with multiple parents in a tree

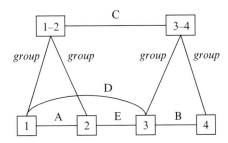

Figure 2.4
The relations in figure 2.3 represented in a more general graph

resent discourse segments. The ordering of the nodes reflects the order of the discourse segments in the text. Furthermore, both tree- and graph-based representations of discourse coherence have a set of intermediate nodes. In tree-based representations, these intermediate nodes represent the result of applying coherence relations to terminal nodes (nodes A, B, D, and E in figure 2.3) or to other intermediate nodes (node C in figure 2.3); for example, node A in figure 2.3 represents the result of applying coherence relation A to the content of nodes 1 and 2. By contrast, intermediate nodes in more general graphs represent the content of topically related, contiguous discourse segments (nodes 1-2 and 3-4 in figure 2.4). We will discuss in section 2.3.2 how the content of terminal nodes can be grouped in order to form the content of intermediate nodes.

As noted above, tree-based representations use intermediate nodes to signal coherence relations in a discourse. By contrast, in representations that are based on more general graphs, coherence relations are represented by labeled arcs (the arcs labeled A, B, C, D, and E in Figure 2.4). In more general graphs, there are also arcs between terminal nodes and intermediate nodes, which can be labeled (e.g., the arcs labeled *group* in figure 2.4).

Tree-based and graph-based representations of discourse structure also differ in the criteria they use for distinguishing coherent from incoherent discourses. For trees, a discourse is coherent if its structure can be represented in a well-formed tree (cf. Marcu 2000), that is, a tree with no crossed dependencies and no nodes with multiple parents (although Webber et al. 2003 allow the latter). By contrast, a discourse represented by more general graphs is coherent if its structure forms a connected graph. In a connected graph, every node relates to (i.e., is connected to) some other node in the graph; this differs from a fully connected graph, where every node relates to every other node in the graph. This distinction is important in that if a coherence graph is not connected (i.e., if there is at least one node that does not relate to any other node in the graph), it implies that there is at least one discourse segment for which no coherence relation with any other discourse segment can be inferred.

The choice of data structure for representing discourse coherence also has implications on how discourse structures can be determined for a text. Context-free parsers can be used to derive discourse trees (Marcu 2000). By contrast, at least some context sensitivity is necessary to represent more general graphs. However, the extent to which parsers for more general graphs have to be context sensitive it is an open research question.

The rest of this chapter is organized as follows. Section 2.2 reviews current approaches to discourse structure. Section 2.3 describes the procedure we used to collect a database of 135 texts annotated with coherence relations. Section 2.4 describes in detail the descriptional inadequacy of tree structures for representing discourse coherence, and section 2.5 provides statistical evidence from our database that supports these claims. Section 2.6 provides some concluding remarks.

2.2   Current Approaches to Representing Discourse Structure

This section reviews current approaches to discourse structure. For each approach, we discuss its central features and identify its relevance to the approach that we propose. Some of the issues raised in this section, particularly the question of whether trees are descriptively adequate for representing discourse structures, will be discussed at length in subsequent sections.

Section 2.2.1 reviews issues addressed by an account that employs tree structures allowing nodes with multiple parents, Discourse Lexicalized Tree-Adjoining Grammar. In section 2.2.2, we discuss mechanisms for inferring coherence structures that were developed in the context of Segmented Discourse Representation Theory. Although our book focuses on the informational structure of discourse, we will briefly discuss in section 2.2.3 Grosz and Sidner's (1986) representation of intentional structure in their three-layered approach to discourse structures. Sections 2.2.4 and 2.2.5 present Mann and Thompson's (1988) and

Hobbs's (1985) accounts, respectively. Both accounts focus on representing informational discourse structure, although Mann and Thompson also include intentional structure in their descriptions of discourse structure and use tree structures to represent discourse coherence.

2.2.1 Two Levels of Representation for Discourse Structure: Discourse Lexicalized Tree-Adjoining Grammar (D-LTAG)

Webber, Knott, and Joshi (1999), Webber, Knott, Stone et al. (1999), and Webber et al. (2003) aim to develop a representation of discourse structure within the formalism of tree-adjoining grammars (e.g., Joshi and Schabes 1997). They note that a single discourse segment often relates to more than one other discourse segment. An example is given in (11). Webber et al. (2003) observe that discourse segment 3 has two parents: a *succession* and a *manner* relation (see figure 2.5).[3]

(11) *Example text (from Webber et al. 2003); S stands for* segment
   a.   S1: The first to do that were the German jewelers,
   b.   S2: in particular Klaus Burie.
   c.   S3: And Morris followed very quickly after,
   d.   S4: using a lacquetry technique to make the brooch.

But whereas Webber et al. (2003) allow nodes with multiple parents in a discourse "backbone" structure, they hypothesize that crossed dependencies are allowed only in a secondary level of representation. Consider example (12), which we adapt from Webber, Knott, Stone et al. (1999).

(12) *Example text (adapted from Webber, Knott, Stone et al. 1999)*
   a.   S1: I wanted to drive through many states
   b.   S2: and I also wanted to see as many mountain ranges as possible.
   c.   S3: When I got to Arkansas,
   d.   S4: I stopped in the Ozarks.

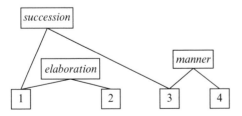

Figure 2.5
Discourse structure for (11)

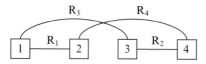

Figure 2.6
Possible discourse structure for (12)

There is a relation R_1 between discourse segments 1 and 2;[4] both state a desire of the subject of the sentences (i.e., to see states and mountain ranges). Discourse segments 3 and 4 are related by R_2; what is stated in by segment 4 takes place under the circumstances described by segment 3. R_3 relates discourse segments 1 and 3; both refer to states (Arkansas is a state in the United States). Finally, R_4 relates discourse segments 2 and 4; both refer to mountain ranges (the Ozarks are a mountain range in Arkansas). Figure 2.6 illustrates a possible discourse structure for (12).

As Figure 2.6 shows, the discourse structure for (12) contains a crossed dependency between R_3 and R_4. But Webber, Knott, and Joshi (1999) and Webber et al. (2003) maintain that R_3 and R_4 are in a different level of representation than R_1 and R_2. R_1 and R_2 are part of what these researchers call structural or nonanaphoric discourse structure (i.e., the discourse "backbone" structure mentioned above). They suggest that the relations R_3 and R_2, on the other hand, are part of a secondary representation which they refer to as anaphoric or nonstructural discourse structure. Anaphoric relations are the basis of this level of representation. For example, Webber, Knott, Stone et al. (1999) argue that in (12), R_3 is based on an anaphoric relation between *states* in segment 1 and *Arkansas* in segment 3. R_4 is based on an anaphoric relation between *mountain ranges* in segment 2 and *Ozarks* in segment 4. Note that without these two relations, the remaining discourse structure includes no crossed dependencies.

The analyses proposed by Webber, Knott, Stone et al. (1999) and Webber et al. (2003) raise two important questions. First, why do they not allow crossed dependencies in structural representations? Second, how can one distinguish what parts of a discourse structure should be represented by the structural versus the nonstructural discourse structure? With respect to the first question, Webber, Knott, Stone et al. (1999) and Webber et al. (2003) maintain that allowing crossed dependencies in the structural layer of representation would be too costly (Webber et al. 2003, 547), although, they do not explain whether it would be too costly for natural language engineering applications or too costly for humans to process.

In natural language engineering applications such as discourse parsing, it could be more costly to allow crossed dependencies because this could increase the search space for possible discourse structures. However, there might be constraints that could limit the search space for general graphs in ways distinct from tree constraints. Furthermore, accounts like

Webber et al.'s (2003) do not guarantee a smaller search space for possible coherence structures than accounts assuming more general graphs. In particular, it is not known how costly it is to develop a unification mechanism for what is represented by the tree and what is represented by the augmented structure (cf. a similar argument for sentence structures proposed by Skut et al. 1997). Finally, crossed dependencies might also be too costly for humans to process. While this seems to be the case for English sentence syntax (Gibson and Breen 2003), we do not yet know whether this also holds for discourse structures.

With respect to the second question above, Webber et al. (2003) define the difference between structural and nonstructural discourse structure in terms of coordinating conjunctions (e.g., *because, then, also, otherwise, instead,* etc.). That is, the particular coordinating conjunction used signals whether a relation is structural or nonstructural. An example of a structural coordinating conjunction (also termed *adverbial*) is *because;* nonstructural (or discourse) adverbials include *then, also, otherwise, nevertheless,* and *instead.* One problem with Webber et al.'s (2003) proposal is that their list of discourse adverbials seems to be open ended. Furthermore, it is unclear how their account could generalize to cases where there is a coherence relation between two discourse segments but no discourse adverbial. This might in fact be the case for the majority of coherence relations; for example, Schauer (2000) argues that only 15–20 percent of all coherence relations in a discourse are signaled by discourse adverbials.

Knott (1996) might provide a means to formalize in an empirically testable way claims that seem to be very similar to those of Webber et al. (2003). Although it is possible to identify characteristic cue phrases for some relations (e.g., *because* would be a characteristic cue phrase for a cause-effect relation), Knott notes that he cannot do so for elaboration relations. These, he argues, are more permissive than other types of coherence relations (e.g., cause-effect, parallel, contrast). As a consequence, he proposes that elaboration relations would better be described in terms of focus structures (Grosz and Sidner 1986), which Knott argues are less constrained, than in terms of rhetorical relations (Hobbs 1985; Mann and Thompson 1988), which Knott argues are more constrained. This hypothesis makes testable empirical claims: elaboration relations should in some way pattern differently from other coherence relations. We will return to this issue in sections 2.5.1 and 2.5.2 and to Webber et al.'s (2003) account in sections 2.4, 2.5.1.2, and 2.5.2.2. In particular, we will discuss the issue of distinguishing anaphoric from nonanaphoric coherence relations.

2.2.2 Mechanisms for Determining Discourse Structures: Segmented Discourse Representation Theory (SDRT)

The goal of Lascarides and Asher (1993) is to provide an account of how coherence relations between discourse segments can be determined, based on a theory of semantics such as Dowty (1986). Coherence relations in their account refer to informational relations between discourse segments, as in Hobbs (1985), not to communicative goals and intentions, as in Grosz and Sidner (1986).

Lascarides and Asher (1993) describe mechanics for determining coherence relations that include the following:

- *Penguin Principle*[5]   prefer a more specific coherence relation over a less specific one. For example, if two events are in a temporal sequence relation and there is also a causal relation between the events, prefer cause-effect over temporal sequence (both cause-effect and temporal sequence entail a temporal order of events, but only cause-effect also entails a causal relation between these events; therefore cause-effect is more specific than temporal sequence).

- *Narration Principle*   by default, events should be described in the order in which they happened. Lascarides and Asher (1993) argue that this principle is a manifestation of Grice's (1975) Maxim of Manner.

- *Causal Law*   for a causal coherence relation to hold between the events described by two discourse segments, the event that is the cause has to precede completely the event that is the effect.

The Narration Principle is an empirical claim that remains to be tested; we used these three principles to determine coherence relations in our database of 135 texts. However, for practical considerations, our versions of the Causal Law and the Narration Principle were defined less strictly. To understand our motivation for this, consider the following example from Bateman and Rondhuis (1994):

(13)   The film was boring. John yawned.

Most people would agree that there is a causal relation between the two sentences in (13)—John yawned because he was bored by the film. However, the film event does not necessarily conclude before the yawning event; it is possible that John yawned after seeing the film, but perhaps more likely that he yawned while watching it. For a causal relation between the two sentences to be established, however, the Causal Law as stated above demands that the film end before John yawns. Therefore, if John yawned while watching the film, no causal relation can be established between the two sentences in (13). The same issue arises regarding the Narration Principle and keeps a temporal sequence relation from applying. Following Lascarides and Asher (1993), the sentences in (13) would be in a *background-elaboration* relation. Bateman and Rondhuis (1994) show that in the style of analysis proposed by Lascarides and Asher (1993), almost all coherence relations end up being background-elaboration, because the mechanisms for determining coherence relations, in particular the Causal Law, are formulated so strictly.

Lascarides and Asher (1993) also argue for structural constraints on building discourse structures. They maintain that only the right frontier of a discourse structure graph is open for attachment of new discourse segments. This means that they do not allow crossed dependencies. However, like Webber, Knott, and Joshi (1999), they appear to allow nodes with multiple parents (Lascarides and Asher 1991).

2.2.3 Intentional Discourse Structure: Grosz and Sidner (1986)

Grosz and Sidner's (1986) approach is based on the hypothesis that speaker intentions determine discourse structure. Their account is intended primarily as an account of multi-speaker dialogues, and it assumes three levels of structure: linguistic, intentional, and attentional.

Grosz and Sidner argue that linguistic structure is determined by cue words (*but, first, now, back to,* etc.). They also contend that the linguistic structure is isomorphic to the intentional structure of a discourse, and that determining the intentional structure should therefore help determine the linguistic structure. However, they provide no details for implementing these ideas (e.g., how to determine intentional structure, or linguistic structure in the absence of cue phrases, see Schauer 2000).

For Grosz and Sidner (1986), intentional discourse structure describes how the role played by one discourse segment with respect to the interlocutors' intentions—the *discourse segment purpose*—relates to the role played by another discourse segment. Discourse segment purposes can form a hierarchical structure. Consider example (14).

(14) *Example with discourse segment purpose annotation (from Nakatani, Grosz, and Ahn 1995)*

  I. *Teach new cook how to make stuffed sole*
      We're going to be making sole, stuffed with shrimp mousse.
      A. *Explain steps of initial preparation of ingredients and equipment*
          1. *Identify ingredients*
              In the small bag are the sole and the shrimp. And there are ten small sole fillets and there's a half a pound of medium shrimp.
          2. *Instruct new cook to get equipment ready*
              Okay, and you're going to need a blender to make the mousse. So you should get your blender out.

Figure 2.7 shows the hierarchical discourse structure for (14). The discourse segment purposes in (14) (the lines introduced by I, A, 1, 2) seem to be rather idiosyncratic to that example, or at least to the text domain of cooking instructions. For instance, it is hard to see how the discourse segment purposes in (14) could be used to describe the intentional

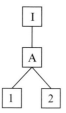

Figure 2.7
Intentional discourse structure for (14)

structure of a text about investment strategies. However, Grosz and Sidner (1986) do not discuss how a more general taxonomy of discourse segment purposes may be constructed.

Nakatani, Grosz, and Ahn (1995) also discuss the possibility of "out-of-order segments." These segments do not relate to immediately surrounding elements but to some other segment in the discourse, and can be joined in a tree structure only by allowing crossed dependencies and nodes with multiple parents. Thus, Grosz and Sidner (1986), or at least Nakatani, Grosz, and Ahn (1995), appear to allow these tree violations in intentional discourse structures.

Grosz and Sidner (1986) also discuss a third layer of discourse structure, attentional structure. This structure involves a stack containing the discourse elements on which participants focus their attention at a given point in the discourse. This stack also forms the basis of a pronoun resolution mechanism in Centering Theory (Joshi and Kuhn 1979; Grosz, Joshi, and Weinstein 1995); the entities on top of the attentional stack are assumed to be more easily accessible for pronominal reference than entities further down (see also Ariel 1990).

2.2.4   Discourse Trees: Rhetorical Structure Theory (RST)

RST (Mann and Thompson 1988; Marcu 2000) is intended to be a descriptive account of the organization of a discourse. The organization of a discourse is held to be a function of informational and intentional relations between discourse segments. The number of relations proposed varies greatly across different versions of RST, ranging from twenty-five (Mann and Thompson 1988) to over four hundred (Marcu 2000).[6] Researchers often use *cause-effect* (one discourse segment states the cause for the effect expressed by another segment), *elaboration* (one segment elaborates on another segment), and *contrast* (one discourse segment contrasts with another discourse segment). In some versions of RST, cause-effect has subcategories that can be differentiated by underlying intentions—causes can be *volitional* ("I dropped the glass because I wanted to see how it shattered on the ground") or *nonvolitional* ("I dropped the glass because I fell down").

A central feature of RST is the intuition that some coherence relations are symmetrical and others are asymmetrical. Coherence relations are symmetrical if the discourse segments between which the coherence relation holds are equally important; this is true for similarity and contrast relations, illustrated in (15) and (16).

(15) *Similarity*
   a. There is a train on platform A.
   b. There is another train on platform B.

(16) *Contrast*
   a. John supported Schwarzenegger during the campaign,
   b. but Susan opposed him.

In asymmetrical coherence relations, one participating segment is more important than the other; this is true, for example, for elaboration relations, where the elaborating discourse segment (the *satellite*) is less important than the elaborated segment (the *nucleus*) (Mann and Thompson 1988). An example of an elaboration relation is (17), where (17b) is less important than (17a).

(17) *Elaboration*
   a. A probe to Mars was launched from Ukraine last week.
   b. The European-built *Mars Express* is scheduled to reach Mars by late December.

As mentioned in section 2.1.1, Mann and Thompson (1988) also aim to represent intentional coherence relations.

2.2.5 More General Discourse Graphs: Hobbs (1985)

In Hobbs's (1985) account, discourse coherence is closely related to more general inference mechanisms (see also Hobbs et al. 1993). Similar to Lascarides and Asher (1993), Mann and Thompson (1988), and Marcu (2000), Hobbs aims to account for informational relations that hold between discourse segments. In contrast to the others, however, Hobbs does not use trees for representing discourse structures. Instead, he employs labeled directed graphs, where the nodes represent discourse segments, and the labeled directed arcs represent the coherence relations that hold between the discourse segments. Furthermore, Hobbs proposes a smaller number of coherence relations than Mann and Thompson (1988) and Marcu (2000). For the account of discourse structure that we will present in subsequent chapters, we also assume a smaller set of coherence relations because they are easier to code and allow for a more abstract representation of discourse structure.

2.3 Collecting a Database of Texts Annotated with Coherence Relations

This section describes in detail the set of coherence relations we use, which are mostly based on Hobbs (1985). We try to make as few a priori theoretical assumptions about representational data structures as possible, and the assumptions we do make are outlined below. Importantly, however, we do not use a tree data structure to represent discourse coherence structures. In fact, a major result of the discussion in chapter 2 is that trees do not seem adequate to represent discourse structures. This section describes (1) how we define discourse segments, (2) which coherence relations we used to connect the discourse segments, and (3) how the annotation procedure worked.

2.3.1 Discourse Segments

Discourse segments are generally defined as nonoverlapping, contiguous spans of text (Marcu 2000). But different accounts of discourse structure offer different definitions of discourse segment boundaries. For example, Grosz and Sidner (1986) argue that discourse is segmented into intentional units. Consider part of example (14), repeated below as (18). It consists of two discourse segments, 1 and 2. Hirschberg and Nakatani (1996) argue that in such examples, segment boundaries can be defined by prosodic features such as pauses or by a change in the speaker's fundamental frequency (f_0).

(18) *Example with discourse segment purpose annotation (from Nakatani, Grosz, and Ahn 1995)*
  1. *Identify ingredients*
     In the small bag are the sole and the shrimp. And there are ten small sole fillets and there's a half a pound of medium shrimp.
  2. *Instruct new cook to get equipment ready*
     Okay, and you're going to need a blender to make the mousse. So you should get your blender out.

Other accounts use phrasal units as discourse segments (Lascarides and Asher 1993; Longacre 1983; Webber, Knott, Stone et al. 1999). An example of such a segmentation is given in (11) above.

A less fine-grained definition of discourse segment is assumed by Hobbs (1985). There, discourses are segmented into sentences as in example (19).

(19) *Example, modified from Hobbs (1985), with discourse segmentation into sentences*
  a. I started out in Renaissance studies.
  b. But I didn't like any of the people I was working with.

For our database, we adopted a clause unit-based definition of discourse segments, with the exception of restrictive relative clauses. We originally considered using a sentence unit-based definition of discourse segments, following Hobbs (1985). However, it turned out that newspaper texts often have very long sentences containing several clauses that are in some kind of coherence relation with one another and across sentences. In order not to lose this information, we use a more fine-grained, clause unit-based definition of discourse segments. We also assume that contentful coordinating and subordinating conjunctions (see table 2.1) can delimit discourse segments.

Notice that *and* is ambiguous. It can indicate discourse segments in many different coherence relations. In addition, *and* can also be used to conjoin nouns, like *dairy plants and dealers* in (20), and verbs, like *snowed and rained* in (21):

(20) Milk sold to the nation's dairy plants and dealers averaged $14.50 for each hundred pounds. (Harman and Liberman 1993, wsj-0306)

(21) It snowed and rained all day long.

If *and* was used in one of the latter ways, we did not classify it as delimiting discourse segments.

We classified periods, semicolons, and commas as delimiting discourse segments, except in cases like (22), where they conjoin nouns in a complex noun phrase (NP).

(22) John bought bananas, apples, and strawberries.

We furthermore treat attributions ("John said that . . .") as discourse segments. This is because the texts we annotated are taken from news corpora, in which attributions can be

Table 2.1
Contentful conjunctions that illustrate coherence relations

Relation	Conjunction
Cause-effect	because, and so
Violated expectation	although, but, while
Condition	if . . . (then), as long as, while
Similarity	and, (and) similarly
Contrast	by contrast, but
Temporal sequence	(and) then; first, second, . . . ; before; after; while
Attribution	according to . . . , . . . said, claim that . . . , maintain that . . . , stated that . . .
Example	For example, for instance
Elaboration	also, furthermore, in addition, notice (furthermore) that, (for, in, on, against, with, . . .) which, who, (for, in, on, against, with, . . .) whom
Generalization	in general

important carriers of coherence structures. For instance, consider a case where source A and source B both comment on some event X. It is necessary to distinguish between a situation where A and B make basically the same statement about X, and a situation where A and B make contrasting comments about X. Note, however, that we treated cases like (23) as one discourse segment rather than two (. . . *cited* and *transaction costs* . . .). We separated attributions only if the attributed material was an embedded clause, a sentence, or a group of sentences. This is not the case in (23)—the attributed material is a complex NP (*transaction costs from its 1988 recapitalization*).

(23)   The restaurant operator cited transaction costs from its 1988 recapitalization.
       (Harman and Lieberman 1993; wsj-0667)

2.3.2   Discourse Segment Groupings

Many naturally occurring discourses consist of topics and subtopics, and thus have a (partially) hierarchical structure. This structure may be represented by discourse segment groupings. For example, discourse segments may be grouped if their content can be attributed to the same source (see section 2.3.3 for a definition of attribution coherence relations). An example of such a grouping is given in (24), where discourse segments 2 and 3 are grouped because they can be attributed to the same source, which is stated in segment 1 (i.e., *John*). The grouping in (24) is illustrated in figure 2.8.

(24)   *Grouping of segments attributed to the same source*
       a.   S1: John said that
       b.   S2: the weather would be nice tomorrow,
       c.   S3: and that he would go swimming then.

Furthermore, discourse segments were grouped if they were topically related. For example, if a text discusses inventions in information technology, there could be groups of discourse segments each concerning inventions by specific companies. There might also be subgroups consisting of discourse segments concerning specific inventions at specific companies. Thus, marking groups can determine a partially hierarchical structure for the text (for more discussion, see section 2.3.5).

Other examples of discourse segment groupings included cases where discourse segments describe an event or a group of events that all occur before another event or group of events. In that case, the content of the first group of discourse segments is in a temporal sequence relation with the content of the second. In cases where one topic requires one grouping and a following topic requires another, both groupings were annotated.

In contrast to approaches such as the TextTiling algorithm (Hearst 1997), we allow partially overlapping groups of discourse segments in order to capture situations in which a

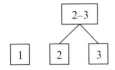

Figure 2.8
Partial discourse structure for (24) after discourse segment groupings

transition discourse segment belongs to the previous as well as the following group. However, this type of segment group did not occur in our database. This might be seen as evidence for the approach taken by the TextTiling algorithm. However, an alternative hypothesis is that nonoverlapping groups of discourse segments are a feature of news texts and that overlapping groups might occur in other kinds of texts.

2.3.3 Coherence Relations

There are a number of different informational coherence relations, dating in their basic definitions back to Aristotle (Nestle 1977) and Hume (1748) (see Hobbs 1985; Hobbs et al. 1993; Kehler 2002). The coherence relations we used are based mostly on Hobbs (1985); we will describe below each coherence relation we use and note any differences between our versions and Hobbs's (1985) set. Table 2.2 presents an overview of how the two sets compare.

One type of coherence relation we used is cause-effect, illustrated in (25). Discourse segment (25a) states the cause for the effect given in (25b).

(25) *Cause-effect*
    a.   There was bad weather at the airport
    b.   and so our flight got delayed.

Our cause-effect relation subsumes the cause and the explanation relations in Hobbs (1985). Hobbs's *cause* relation holds if a discourse segment stating a cause occurs before a discourse segment stating an effect; an *explanation* relation holds if a discourse segment stating an effect occurs before a discourse segment stating a cause. We encoded this distinction by adding direction to the cause-effect relation. In a graph, this can be represented by a directed arc going from cause to effect.

Another kind of causal relation is *condition*. Hobbs (1985) does not distinguish condition relations from either cause or explanation. However, we felt that it might be important to distinguish between a causal relation describing an actual causal event (cause-effect) on the one hand and a causal relation describing a possible causal event (condition) on the other hand. In (26), (26b) states an event that will occur only if the event described by (26a) also occurs.

Table 2.2
Correspondence between the set of coherence relations in Hobbs (1985) and our set of coherence relations

Hobbs (1985)	Current annotation scheme
Occasion	Temporal sequence
Cause	Cause-effect: cause stated first, then effect; directionality indicated by directed arcs in a coherence graph
Explanation	Cause-effect: effect stated first, then cause; directionality indicated by directed arcs in a coherence graph
—	Condition
Evaluation	Elaboration
Background	Elaboration
Exemplification: example stated first, then general case; directionality indicated by directed arcs in a coherence graph	Example
Exemplification: general case stated first, then example; directionality indicated by directed arcs in a coherence graph	Generalization
Elaboration	Elaboration
Parallel	Similarity
Contrast	Contrast
Violated expectation	Violated expectation
—	Attribution
—	Same-segment

(26) *Condition*
    a. If the new software works,
    b. everyone should be happy.

In the *violated expectation* relation (also used by Hobbs), a causal relation that would normally exist between two discourse segments is absent. For example, (27a) would normally be a cause for everyone to be happy, but this expectation is violated by the content of (27b).

(27) *Violated Expectation*
    a. The new software worked great,
    b. but nobody was happy.

Other coherence relations that we used include *similarity* (termed *parallel* in Hobbs 1985) and *contrast* relations (present also in Hobbs), where similarities and contrasts are determined between corresponding sets of entities or events. These are illustrated in (15) and (16), repeated here as (28) and (29), respectively.

(28) *Similarity*
    a. There is a train on Platform A.
    b. There is another train on Platform B.

(29) *Contrast*
    a. John supported Schwarzenegger during the campaign,
    b. but Susan opposed him.

Discourse segments can also stand in an elaboration relation (also used by Hobbs 1985). For example, (30b) elaborates on (30a).

(30) *Elaboration*
    a. A probe to Mars was launched from Ukraine this week.
    b. The European-built *Mars Express* is scheduled to reach Mars by late December.

Discourse segments can provide examples for another discourse segment (*exemplification* in Hobbs 1985). The example relation is illustrated in (31), where (31b) provides an example for what is stated in (31a).

(31) *Example*
    a. There have been many previous missions to Mars.
    b. A famous example is the Pathfinder mission.

Hobbs (1985) also includes an *evaluation* relation, as in (32), where (32b) states an evaluation of (32a). We decided to call such relations *elaborations*, since we found it too difficult in practice to reliably distinguish elaborations from evaluations; in our annotation scheme, what is stated in (32b) elaborates on what is stated in (32a).

(32) *Elaboration (from Hobbs 1985)*
    a. (A story.)
    b. It was funny at the time.

We also differ from Hobbs (1985) in not having a separate *background* relation, as in (33), where what is stated in (33a) provides the background for (33b). Similarly to the evaluation relation, we found the background relation too difficult to reliably distinguish from elaboration relations; in our annotation scheme, (33a) elaborates on (33b).

(33) *Elaboration (modified from Hobbs 1985)*
    a. T is the pointer to the root of a binary tree.
    b. Initialize T.

In a *generalization* relation, as in (34), one discourse segment states a generalization, (34b), for the content of another, (34a).

(34)   *Generalization*
    a.   Two missions to Mars in 1999 failed.
    b.   There are many missions to Mars that have failed.

Discourse segments can also be in an *attribution* relation, as in (35), where (35a) states the source for the content of (35b) (see Bergler 1991 for a more detailed semantic analysis of attribution relations).

(35)   *Attribution*
    a.   John said that
    b.   the weather would be nice tomorrow.

In a *temporal sequence* relation, as in (36), one discourse segment, (36a), states an event that takes place before another event expressed by another discourse segment, (36b). In contrast to cause-effect relations, there is no causal relation between the events described by the two discourse segments. The temporal sequence relation is equivalent to the occasion relation in Hobbs (1985).

(36)   *Temporal Sequence*
    a.   First, John went grocery shopping.
    b.   Then he disappeared in a liquor store.

The *same-segment* relation is not an actual coherence relation but an epiphenomenon resulting from assuming contiguous distinct elements of text (Hobbs 1985 does not include this relation). A same-segment relation holds if a subject NP is separated from its predicate by an intervening discourse segment. For example, in (37), (37a) is the subject NP of a predicate in (37c), so there is a same-segment relation between (37a) and (37c). In addition, (37a) is the first and (37c) the second segment of what is actually one single discourse segment, separated by the intervening discourse segment (37b). An attribution relation holds between (37a) and (37b), and therefore also between (37b) and (37c), since (37a) and (37c) are actually one single discourse segment.

(37)   *Same-segment*
    a.   The economy,
    b.   according to some analysts,
    c.   is expected to improve by early next year.

In our set of coherence relations, we distinguish between asymmetrical or directed relations on the one hand and symmetrical or undirected relations on the other (Mann and Thompson 1988; Marcu 2000; see section 2.2.4). Cause-effect, condition, violated expectation, elaboration, example, generalization, and attribution are asymmetrical or directed relations, whereas similarity, contrast, and same-segment are symmetrical or undirected relations. The directions of relations in asymmetrical or directed relations are as follows:

- *cause-effect* from the discourse segment stating the cause to the discourse segment stating the effect
- *condition* from the discourse segment stating the condition to the discourse segment stating the consequence
- *violated expectation* from the discourse segment stating the cause to the discourse segment describing the absent effect
- *elaboration* from the elaborating discourse segment to the elaborated discourse segment
- *example* from the discourse segment stating the example to the discourse segment stating the exemplified
- *generalization* from the discourse segment stating the special case to the discourse segment stating the general case
- *attribution* from the discourse segment stating the source to the discourse segment containing the attributed material
- *temporal sequence* from the discourse segment stating the event that happened first to the discourse segment stating the event that happened second

This definition of directionality is related to Mann and Thompson's (1988) notion of nucleus and satellite nodes (where the nodes can represent segments or groups of segments): for asymmetrical or directed relations, the directionality is from satellite to nucleus node; by contrast, symmetrical or undirected relations hold between two nuclei.

Note also that we decided to annotate a coherence relation if it held between the entire content of two discourse segments, or if it held between parts of the content of two discourse segments. Consider the following example from the *AP Newswire*:

(38) a. [Difficulties have arisen][in enacting the accord for the independence of Namibia]
     b. for which SWAPO has fought many years, (Harman and Liberman 1993, ap90104-0003)

For this example, we would annotate an elaboration relation from (38b) to (38a) the former provides additional details about the accord mentioned in the latter, although the relation actually holds only between (38b) and the second bracketed part of (38a). While it is beyond the scope of the current project to do so, future research should investigate annotations allowing relations only between parts of discourse segments that are directly involved in establishing a coherence relation. For example, consider (39), where brackets indicate how a more fine-grained analysis of discourse segments might be marked:

(39)   a.   [for which][SWAPO][has fought many years,]

    b.   referring to the acronym of the South West Africa People's Organization nationalist movement. (Harman and Liberman 1993, ap890104-0003)

In our current project, we annotated an elaboration relation from (39b) to (39a), because (39b) provides additional details, the full name for SWAPO, which is mentioned in (39a). A future, more detailed, annotation of coherence relations would annotate this elaboration relation to hold only between (39b) and the word *SWAPO* in (39a).

2.3.4   Coding Procedure

In coding the coherence relations of a text, we used a procedure consisting of three steps. First, a text is segmented into discourse segments (see section 2.3.1). Second, adjacent discourse segments that are topically related are grouped together as described in section 2.3.2. Third, coherence relations between discourse segments and groups of discourse segments are identified (see section 2.3.3). Finally, each previously unconnected segment or group of segments is tested for connections to any of the already-connected segments in the representation.

To help determine the coherence relation between particular (groups of) discourse segments, we asked the annotators which, if any, of the contentful coordinating conjunctions in table 2.1 could be inserted acceptably into the passage (see Hobbs 1985; Kehler 2002). When such an insertion would have been possible, we took this as evidence that the coherence relation corresponding to the conjunction did indeed hold between the two (groups of) discourse segments under consideration. We used this procedure only if a contentful coordinating conjunction that disambiguated the coherence relation was not already present.

The following list used by the annotators shows in more detail how the annotations were performed.

A. Segment the text.

1. Insert segment boundaries at every period that marks a sentence boundary (i.e., not at periods such as those in *Mrs.* or in *Dr.*).

2. Insert segment boundaries at every semicolon that marks a sentence or clause boundary.

3. Insert segment boundaries at every colon that marks a sentence or clause boundary.

4. Insert segment boundaries at every comma that marks a sentence, clause, or modifying prepositional phrase (PP) boundary (modifying PPs are an important part of discourse structure in newspaper texts). Do not insert segment boundaries at commas that conjoin complex noun or verb phrases (for example, the italicized complex NP in "XY corporation manages *stocks, bonds, and mutual funds*" and the italicized complex VP in "XY corporation *buys, manages, and sells* mutual funds").

5. Insert segment boundaries at every quotation mark if they are not already present.

6. Insert segment boundaries at the contentful coordinating conjunctions listed in table 2.1 if they are not already present. For *and,* do not insert a segment boundary if it is used to conjoin verbs, adjectives, or nouns in a conjoined noun phrase.

B. Generate groupings of related discourse segments.

1. Group contiguous discourse segments that are enclosed by pairs of quotation marks.

2. Group contiguous discourse segments that are attributed to the same source.

3. Group contiguous discourse segments that belong to the same sentence (marked by periods, commas, semicolons, or colons).

4. Group contiguous discourse segments that are topically centered around the same entities or events.

C. Determine coherence relations between discourse segments and groups of discourse segments. For each previously unconnected (group of) discourse segment(s), test it for connections to any of the already-connected (groups of) discourse segments in the representation. Use the following steps for each decision.

1. Use pairs of quotation marks as a signal for attribution.

2. For pairs of (groups of) discourse segments that are already connected by one of the contentful coordinating conjunctions from table 2.1, choose the coherence relation that corresponds to the coordinating conjunction.

3. For pairs of (groups of) discourse segments that are not connected by any of the contentful coordinating conjunctions from table 2.1, do the following:

   a. Mentally connect the (groups of) discourse segments using one of the coordinating conjunctions from table 2.1.

   b. If the resulting passage sounds acceptable, choose the coherence relation that corresponds to the coordinating conjunction.

   c. If the passage does not sound acceptable, repeat step 3a until an acceptable coordinating conjunction is found.

   d. If the passage does not sound acceptable with any of the coordinating conjunctions from table 2.1, assume that the (groups of) discourse segments under consideration are not related.

4. Iterative procedure for steps C3a and C3b

   a. Start with any of the unambiguous coordinating conjunctions from table 2.1 (*because, although, if . . . then, . . . said, for example*).

   b. If none of the unambiguous coordinating conjunctions results in an acceptable passage, try the more ambiguous coordinating conjunctions (*and, but, while, also,* etc.).

As a result of practical issues that arose during the annotation project, we also took into account the following additional considerations for steps C2 and C3:

- *Example versus elaboration*   An *example* relation sets up an additional entity or event (the example), whereas an *elaboration* relation provides more detail about an already introduced entity or event (the one on which it elaborates).
- *Cause-effect*   Lascarides and Asher's (1993) Causal Law (see section 2.2.2) states that in a causal relation, the cause has to precede the effect. However, we noted in section 2.2.2 that this definition of the Causal Law might be too narrow. We therefore assume a modified version of the Causal Law, according to which the cause has to precede the effect at least partially. This allows for a causal relation in (40) in the case that John yawned during the film (i.e., the film event is the cause event even though it does not completely precede the yawning event).

(40)   The film was boring. John yawned.

- *Cause-effect versus temporal sequence*   Both cause-effect and temporal sequence entail a temporal ordering of events. However, only cause-effect relations have a causal relation between what is stated by the (groups of) discourse segments under consideration. Thus, if there is a causal relation between the (groups of) segments, assume cause-effect rather than temporal sequence (recall the Penguin Principle in Lascarides and Asher 1993).

2.3.5   Example of the Coding Procedure

To illustrate our approach for determining discourse structures, we use the following extract of a text from the *Wall Street Journal*:

(41)   *Example text for illustrating the coding procedure*
Three new issues began trading on the New York Stock Exchange today, and one began trading on the Nasdaq/National Market System last week. On the Big Board, Crawford & Co., Atlanta, (CFD) began trading today. Crawford evaluates health care plans, manages medical and disability aspects of worker's compensation injuries and is involved in claims adjustments for insurance companies. (Harman and Liberman 1993, text wsj-0607)

The following sections will illustrate how the coding procedure outlined in section 2.3.4 can be applied to (41).

2.3.5.1   Segmenting the Text   The first step in annotating (41) for discourse structure is to divide the text into discourse segments (steps A1 through A6 in the coding procedure).

Step A1   Insert segment boundaries at every period that marks a sentence boundary.

(42)   *Example text after applying step A1:*
  a.   S1: Three new issues began trading on the New York Stock Exchange today, and one began trading on the Nasdaq/National Market System last week.

    b. S2: On the Big Board, Crawford & Co., Atlanta, (CFD) began trading today.

    c. S3: Crawford evaluates health care plans, manages medical and disability aspects of worker's compensation injuries and is involved in claims adjustments for insurance companies.

Step A2   Insert segment boundaries at every semicolon that marks a sentence or clause boundary. There are no semicolons in the example text, so this step is skipped.

Step A3   Insert segment boundaries at every colon that marks a sentence or clause boundary. There are no colons in the example text, so this step is skipped.

Step A4   Insert segment boundaries at every comma that marks a sentence, clause, or modifying PP boundary. Notice that the comma in discourse segment 5 in (43) conjoins elliptic clauses (*Crawford evaluates health care plans, [Crawford] manages medical and disability aspects of worker's compensation injuries and [Crawford] is involved in claims adjustment . . .*).

(43)   *Example text after applying step A4:*

    a. S1: Three new issues began trading on the New York Stock Exchange today,

    b. S2: and one began trading on the Nasdaq/National Market System last week.

    c. S3: On the Big Board,

    d. S4: Crawford & Co., Atlanta, (CFD) began trading today.

    e. S5: Crawford evaluates health care plans,

    f. S6: manages medical and disability aspects of worker's compensation injuries and is involved in claims adjustments for insurance companies.

Step A5   Insert segment boundaries at every quotation mark. There are no quotations in the example text, so this step can be skipped.

Step A6   Insert segment boundaries at contentful coordinating conjunctions. There is one contentful coordinating conjunction, *and,* in discourse segment 6 in (43); it conjoins two clauses. Discourse segments 5, and 6 do not contain conjoined verbs because each verb (*evaluates, manages,* and *is involved in*) has its own object (*health care plans, medical and disability aspects of worker's compensation injuries,* and *claims adjustment for insurance companies,* respectively). When verbs are conjoined, all the verbs have the same object. For instance, in the example *XY Corporation manages and sells mutual funds*, the verbs *manages* and *sells* both have the same object (*mutual funds*). Instead, the discourse structure is as in (44), where segments 6 and 7 are elliptical constructions with *Crawford* being the elided subject for both.

(44)   *Example text after applying step A6:*

    a. S1: Three new issues began trading on the New York Stock Exchange today,

    b. S2: and one began trading on the Nasdaq/National Market System last week.

   c. S3: On the Big Board,

   d. S4: Crawford & Co., Atlanta, (CFD) began trading today.

   e. S5: Crawford evaluates health care plans,

   f. S6: manages medical and disability aspects of worker's compensation injuries

   g. S7: and is involved in claims adjustments for insurance companies.

2.3.6 Groupings of Discourse Segments

In the second step of annotating a text with a discourse structure, related contiguous discourse segments are grouped together (steps B1 through B4 in the coding procedure). Here is how this procedure is applied to (44):

Step B1   Group contiguous discourse segments that are enclosed by pairs of quotation marks. There are no quotation marks in the example text, so this step can be skipped.

Step B2   Group contiguous discourse segments that are attributed to the same source. Because there are no sources in the example text, this step can be skipped.

Step B3   Group contiguous discourse segments that belong to the same sentence. Discourse segments 1 and 2 are in the same sentence, so they form a group. Furthermore, discourse segments 3 and 4 form a single sentence, and 5, 6, and 7 form one as well. Thus, there are two more groups: one containing segments 3 and 4, and one with segments 5, 6, and 7.

Step B4   Group contiguous discourse segments that are topically centered around the same entities or events. Discourse segments 3 through 7 are about a company, Crawford. Therefore, these discourse segments are grouped together.

2.3.6.1 Coherence Relations between Discourse Segments and Groups of Discourse Segments   After grouping related contiguous discourse segments, we have the partial discourse structure for (44) shown in figure 2.9. To help distinguish group relations from other coherence relations and to avoid cluttering the figures with arc labels, group relation arcs are drawn in grey in the following figures.

The third step of annotating a text with a discourse structure consists of determining coherence relations between (groups of) discourse segments (steps C1 through C4 in the coding procedure). Here is how this procedure is applied to (44), repeated here as (45):

(45) *Example text*

   a. S1: Three new issues began trading on the New York Stock Exchange today,

   b. S2: and one began trading on the Nasdaq/National Market System last week.

   c. S3: On the Big Board,

   d. S4: Crawford & Co., Atlanta, (CFD) began trading today.

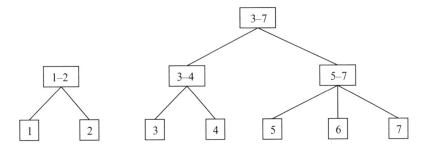

Figure 2.9
Partial discourse structure for (44) after discourse segment groupings

    e. S5: Crawford evaluates health care plans,
    f. S6: manages medical and disability aspects of worker's compensation injuries
    g. S7: and is involved in claims adjustments for insurance companies.

Step C1   Use pairs of quotation marks as a signal for attribution. This step is skipped because there are no quotation marks in the example text.

Step C2   Choose coherence relations for pairs of (groups of) discourse segments that are connected with a contentful coordinating conjunction. Discourse segments 1 and 2, and 6 and 7, respectively, are connected with *and*. Because of this, and because of their parallel sentence structures, these discourse segments are in similarity relations (discourse segments 1 and 2 are both about new issues that began trading on an exchange; discourse segments 6 and 7 both describe activities of the company Crawford). This results in the partial discourse structure shown in figure 2.10. Later on in the coding procedure, we will establish similarity relations between all three discourse segments, 5, 6, and 7 (see figure 2.13 below).

Steps C3-C4   Determine coherence relations for the (groups of) discourse segments that are not conjoined with contentful coordinating conjunctions. Since discourse segments 1 and 2 have already been connected, building a discourse structure for (45) will continue with integrating discourse segment 3 into the discourse structure built so far.

▪ *Discourse segment 3*   *Big Board* refers to *New York Stock Exchange* in discourse segment 1. Often when there is an anaphoric relation between two discourse segments, these discourse segments are also related by a coherence relation. However, in section 2.3.4, step C, we pointed out that if two (groups of) discourse segments are related by a coherence relation, mentally joining the two (groups of) discourse segments with a coordinating conjunction should result in an acceptable passage. This is not the case here because the resultant passage after concatenating discourse segments 1 and 3 is incomplete:

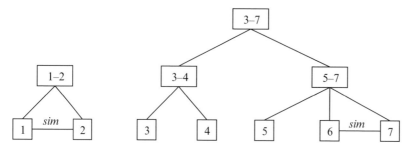

Figure 2.10
Partial discourse structure for (45) after applying step C2

(46)   *Resultant passage after concatenating discourse segments 1 and 3*
Three new issues began trading on the New York Stock Exchange today. On the big board

Therefore, we do not assign a coherence relation to discourse segments 1 and 3. However, later in the annotation procedure, we will assign an elaboration relation to the discourse segment group 3–4 and discourse segment 1 (see figure 2.12). There are no other coherence relations between discourse segment 3 and the discourse structure built so far.

• *Discourse segment 4*   Discourse segment 3 is a PP that modifies discourse segment 4 (it provides additional detail about where the trading described in segment 4 takes place). Therefore, an elaboration relation holds between discourse segments 3 and 4. There are no other coherence relations between discourse segment 4 and the discourse structure built so far. The result is the partial discourse structure shown in Figure 2.11.

• *Discourse segment group 3–4*   This group of discourse segments provides additional detail about discourse segment 1 (it provides details about a company mentioned in discourse segment 1 that began being traded on the New York Stock Exchange), so there is an elaboration relation between 3–4 and 1. There are no other coherence relations between 3–4 and the discourse structure built so far. The result is the partial discourse structure shown in figure 2.12.

• *Discourse segment 5*   Discourse segments 5 and 6 have parallel structure and both describe things that the company Crawford does. Therefore, there is a similarity relation between these two discourse segments. There is furthermore a similarity relation between discourse segments 5 and 7. This results in the partial discourse structure shown in figure 2.13.

• Discourse segment group 5–7: Instead of identifying individual coherence relations between discourse segments 5, 6, and 7 and the already-built structure, we assign these coherence relations to connect the group of discourse segments 5–7 and the rest of the structure. For the example text considered here, all relations that hold for the individual

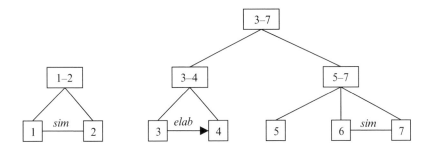

Figure 2.11
Partial discourse structure for (45) after integrating discourse segment 4

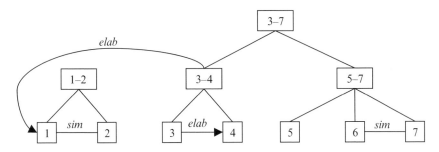

Figure 2.12
Partial discourse structure for (45) after integrating the group of discourse segments 3–4

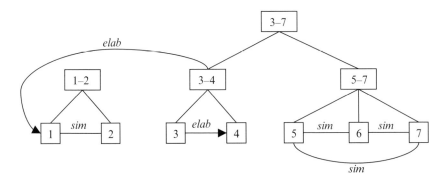

Figure 2.13
Partial discourse structure for (45) after integrating discourse segment 5

discourse segments in the group 5–7 also hold for that group as a whole. There is an elaboration relation between segment group 5–7 and discourse segment 4: 5–7 provides additional detail (business activities) about the company Crawford that is mentioned in discourse segment 4. The result is the partial discourse structure shown in figure 2.14.

• Discourse segment group 3–7: This group of discourse segments provides detail about one of the companies that began being traded on the New York Stock Exchange. Therefore, there is an elaboration relation between 3–7 and discourse segment 1 (which mentions the New York Stock Exchange). The result is the discourse structure shown in figure 2.15.

2.3.7 Annotators and Annotation Tools

The annotators for the database were MIT undergraduate students who worked in our research lab. The first author of this book provided training for the annotators, who received a manual that described the background of the project, discourse segmentation, coherence relations and how to recognize them, and the use of the annotation tools that we developed in our lab (Wolf et al. 2003). Training consisted of explaining the background of the project and the annotation method and of annotating example texts (these texts are not included in our database). Training took eight to ten hours in total, distributed over five days of a week. After the training, the annotators worked independently.

In doing the annotations, annotators used a simple Java-based tool that displayed the text to be annotated, the annotation commands, and a very simple display of the coherence graph annotated thus far. The tool used different colors for different kinds of coherence relations: green for similarity and contrast; blue for example, generalization, and elaboration; red for cause-effect, violated expectation, and condition; cyan for temporal

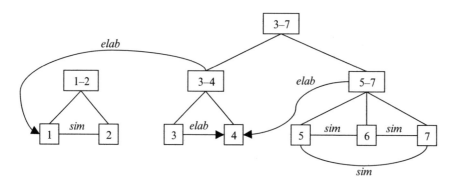

Figure 2.14
Partial discourse structure for (45) after integrating the group of discourse segments 5–7

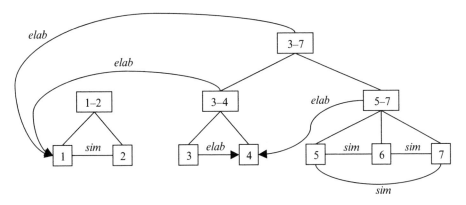

Figure 2.15
Discourse structure for (45) after integrating the group of discourse segments 3–7

sequence; orange for attribution; gray for same-segment. Groupings of discourse segments were indicated with open boxes in the coherence graph display. Figure 2.16 shows a screenshot of the annotation tool.

2.3.8 Statistics on the Annotated Database

To evaluate hypotheses about appropriate data structures for representing coherence structures, we collected a database of 135 texts from the *Wall Street Journal* (1987–1989) and the *AP Newswire* (1989) (both from Harman and Liberman 1993). First, the texts were segmented into their discourse units. A pilot study on 10 texts showed that agreement on this step, the number of common segments divided by the sum of the number of common segments and the number of differing segments, was never below 90 percent. Therefore, all 135 texts were segmented by two annotators together, resulting in segmentations that both annotators could agree on. Table 2.3 presents some descriptive statistics for these 135 texts.

Steps 2 (discourse segment grouping) and 3 (coherence relation annotation) of the coding procedure were performed independently by two annotators (the same two annotators as for step 1). In order to determine interannotator agreement for step 2, we calculated kappa statistics (Carletta 1996). We used the following procedure to construct a confusion matrix. First, all groups marked by either annotator were extracted. For the whole database, annotator 1 had marked 2616 groups, whereas annotator 2 had marked 3021 groups. The groups marked by the annotators consisted of 536 different discourse segment group types (for example, the first two discourse segments of a text, the first three discourse segments of a text, etc.). Therefore, the confusion matrix had 536 rows and columns. For all annotations of the 135 texts, agreement was 0.8449, per chance agreement was 0.0161,

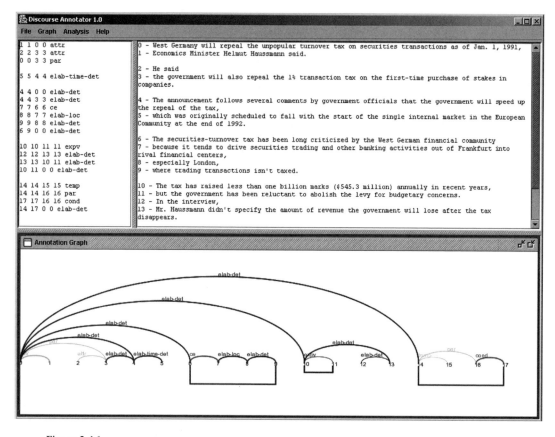

Figure 2.16
Screenshot of the annotation tool. Upper right window pane: text to be annotated, with numbered discourse segments; upper left window pane: annotation code entered by the annotators; lower window pane: simple display of the coherence graph annotated thus far

Table 2.3
Database statistics for 135 texts from *AP Newswire* (1989) (105 texts) and *Wall Street Journal* (1989) (30 texts)

	number of words	number of discourse segments
mean	545	61
minimum	161	6
maximum	1409	143
median	529	60

and kappa was 0.8424. Annotator agreement did not differ as a function of text length, arc length, or kind of coherence relation (all χ^2s < 1).

We also calculated kappa statistics to determine interannotator agreement for step 3 of the coding procedure.[7] For all annotations, the agreement was 0.8761, per chance agreement was 0.2466, and kappa was 0.8355. Annotator agreement did not differ as a function of text length ($\chi^2 = 1.27$; $p < 0.75$), arc length ($\chi^2 < 1$), or kind of coherence relation ($\chi^2 < 1$). Table 2.4 shows the confusion matrix for the database of 135 annotated texts that was used to compute the kappa statistics. The table shows, for example, that much of the interannotator disagreement seems to be driven by disagreement over how to annotate elaboration relations: in the whole database, annotator 1 marked 260 elaboration relations where annotator 2 marked no relation; annotator 2 marked 467 elaboration relations where annotator 1 marked no relation.

The only discourse annotation project comparable to ours that we are currently aware of is Carlson, Marcu, and Okurowski (2002). Because their procedure differed from ours (they used trees and split up the annotation process into different substeps), their annotator agreement figures are not directly comparable to ours. Furthermore, they do not report annotator agreement figures for their database as a whole, but for different subsets of four to seven documents that were each annotated by different pairs of annotators. For discourse segmentation, Carlson, Marcu, and Okurowski (2002) report kappa values ranging from 0.951 to 1.00; for annotation of discourse tree spans, their kappa values ranged from 0.778 to 0.929; for annotation of coherence relation nuclearity (whether a node in a discourse tree is a nucleus or a satellite), their kappa values ranged from 0.695 to 0.882; for assigning types of coherence relations, their kappa values ranged from 0.624 to 0.823.

2.4   Data Structures for Representing Coherence Relations

In order to represent the coherence relations between discourse segments in a text, most accounts of discourse coherence assume tree structures (Britton 1994; Carlson, Marcu, and Okurowski 2002; Corston-Oliver 1998; Grosz and Sidner 1986; Longacre 1983; Mann and Thompson 1988; Marcu 2000; Polanyi and Scha 1984; Polanyi 1996; Polanyi et al. 2004; van Dijk and Kintsch 1983; Walker 1998); some accounts do not allow crossed dependencies but allow nodes with multiple parents (Lascarides and Asher 1991).[8] Other accounts assume less constrained graphs that allow crossed dependencies as well as nodes with multiple parents (e.g., Bergler 1992; Birnbaum 1982; Danlos 2004; Hobbs 1985; McKeown 1985; Reichman 1985; Zukerman and McConachy 1995; for dialogue structure, see Penstein Rose et al. 1995).

Table 2.4

Confusion matrix of annotations for the database of 135 annotated texts (*contr = contrast; expv = violated expectation; ce = cause-effect; none = no coherence relation; gen = generalization; cond = condition; examp = example; ts = temporal sequence; attr = attribution; elab = elaboration; sim = similarity*)

	Annotator₂													
Annotator₁	contr	expv	ce	none	gen	cond	examp	temp	attr	elab	same	sim	sum	percent
contr	383	11	0	34	0	0	0	2	0	0	0	0	430	4.47
expv	4	113	0	7	0	0	0	0	0	0	0	0	124	1.29
ce	0	0	446	14	0	0	0	0	0	5	0	0	465	4.83
none	66	24	42	0	0	2	27	16	6	467	1	64	715	7.43
gen	0	0	0	1	21	0	0	0	0	1	0	0	23	0.24
cond	0	0	0	2	0	127	0	1	0	1	0	0	131	1.36
examp	0	0	1	18	0	0	219	0	0	3	0	0	241	2.51
temp	1	1	2	7	0	0	0	214	0	1	0	0	226	2.35
attr	0	0	0	5	0	0	0	0	1387	0	0	0	1392	14.47
elab	0	0	17	260	0	3	0	3	0	3913	1	0	4197	43.63
same	0	0	2	5	0	0	0	1	0	0	530	1	539	5.60
sim	7	0	3	43	0	0	0	6	0	0	3	1074	1136	11.81
sum	461	149	513	396	21	132	246	243	1393	4391	535	1139		
percent	4.79	1.55	5.30	4.12	0.20	1.37	2.56	2.53	14.50	45.60	5.56	11.80		

Some proponents of tree structures assume that trees are easier to formalize and to derive than less constrained graphs (Marcu 2000; Webber et al. 2003; but see Vogel, Hahn, and Branigan 1996). We demonstrate that in fact many coherence structures in naturally occurring texts cannot be adequately represented by trees. Therefore, we argue for less constrained graphs as an appropriate data structure for representing coherence, where nodes represent discourse segments and labeled directed arcs represent the coherence relations that hold between them.

Some proponents of more general graphs argue that trees cannot account for a full discourse structure that represents informational, intentional, and attentional discourse relations. For example, Moore and Pollack (1992) point out that Rhetorical Structure Theory (Mann and Thompson 1988) has both informational and intentional coherence relations but forces annotators to decide on only one coherence relation between any two discourse segments. Moore and Pollack (1992) argue that there is often an informational as well as an intentional coherence relation between two discourse segments: this presents a problem for RST, since only one of the relations can be annotated. Thus, Moore and Pollack (1992) propose allowing more than one coherence relation between two discourse segments (i.e., one intentional and one informational), which violates the tree constraint against nodes with multiple parents.

Reichman (1985) argues that tree-based story grammars are not sufficient to account for discourse structure. Instead, she argues that in order to account for intentional structure of discourse, more general data structures are needed. We argue that the same is true for the informational structure of discourse. Moore and Pollack (1992), Moser and Moore (1996), and Reichman (1985) argue that trees are insufficient for representing together informational, intentional, and attentional discourse structure. Although the focus of our work is on informational coherence relations, not on intentional relations, we do not wish to imply that we think that attentional or intentional structure should not be part of a full account of discourse structure. Rather, we agree with the above accounts that trees are inadequate for representing informational, intentional, and attentional discourse structure together, and we argue that trees are not descriptively adequate to describe even informational discourse structure by itself.

As pointed out in section 2.2.1, Webber, Knott, Stone et al. (1999), Webber et al. (2003), and Knott (1996) hypothesize that discourse structure is represented by two different levels: a structural level, which allows nodes with multiple parents but no crossed dependencies, and a nonstructural level, which allows crossed dependencies. As also noted in section 2.2.1, Knott (1996) makes empirically testable claims about how structural and nonstructural levels of representation might be distinguished. We will test these claims in sections 2.5.1.2 and 2.5.2.2.

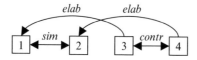

Figure 2.17
Coherence graph for (47); *Sim = similarity; contr = contrast; elab = elaboration*

2.4.1 Crossed dependencies

Consider the text passage in (47), whose coherence graph is shown in figure 2.17. The arrowheads of the arcs represent directionality for asymmetrical relations (elaboration) and bidirectionality for symmetrical relations (similarity, contrast).

(47) *Example text (modified from SAT practice materials [College Board 2004])*
  a. S1: Schools tried to teach students history of science.
  b. S2: At the same time, they tried to teach them how to think logically and inductively.
  c. S3: Some success has been reached in the first of these aims.
  d. S4: However, none at all has been reached in the second.

The coherence structure for (47) can be derived as follows:

• *Similarity* relation between discourse segments 1 and 2: both segments describe teaching different things to students
• *Contrast* relation between discourse segments 3 and 4: both segments describe varying degrees of success (some vs. none)
• *Elaboration* relation between discourse segments 3 and 1: segment 3 provides more details (the degree of success) about the teaching described in segment 1
• *Elaboration* relation between discourse segments 4 and 2: segment 4 provides more details (the degree of success) about the teaching described in segment 2

The similarity relation between discourse segments 1 and 2 could be a contrast relation instead. If it is a similarity relation, the emphasis is on the fact that students are taught things at the same time; if it is a contrast relation, the emphasis is on the fact that students were taught different things (history of science vs. how to think logically and inductively). However, this does not change the point we are trying to make here, namely, that the coherence structure for (47) has a crossed dependency between {4, 2} and {3, 1}.

The discourse structure for (47) might also be represented as shown in figure 2.18. However, such a representation would not distinguish (47) from (48). In (48), the amount of success in discourse segment 3 has basically been switched: in (47), some success has been reached in teaching students history of science, while in (48), no success has been reached

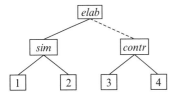

Figure 2.18
Tree-based representation of the coherence structure of (47)

at all. Similarly, in discourse segment 4, no success at all has been reached at teaching students how to think logically in (47); in (48), however, some success has been reached there. This difference is not captured by the tree structure in figure 2.18, which indicates only that there was some success in one goal and none in the other, but not which goal has met with some success and which one has not.

(48) a. S1: Schools tried to teach students history of science.
     b. S2: At the same time they tried to teach them how to think logically and inductively.
     c. S3: No success at all has been reached in the first of these aims.
     d. S4: However, some success has been reached in the second.

In order to represent a structure like the one for (47) in a tree without violating validity assumptions about tree structures (Diestel 2000), one might consider augmenting a tree either with feature propagation (Shieber 1986) or with a coindexation mechanism (Chomsky 1973). But there is a problem for both feature propagation and coindexation mechanisms: the tree structure itself and the features and coindexations represent the same kind of information (coherence relations), and it is unclear how one could decide which part of a text coherence structure should be represented by the tree structure and which part should be represented by the augmentation. Other areas of linguistics have faced this issue as well. Researchers investigating data structures for representing intrasentential structure, for instance, generally fall into two groups. One group tries to formulate principles that allow representing some aspects of structure in the tree itself and other aspects in some augmentation formalism (e.g., Chomsky 1973; Marcus et al. 1994). Another group argues that it is more parsimonious to assume a unified dependency-based representation that drops the tree constraints disallowing crossed dependencies (e.g., Brants et al. 2002; Skut et al. 1997; König and Lezius 2000). Our approach falls into the latter group. As we will point out, there does not seem to be a well-defined set of constraints on crossed dependencies in discourse structures. Without such constraints, it does not seem viable to represent discourse structures as augmented tree structures.

An important question is how many different kinds of crossed dependencies occur in naturally occurring discourse. If there are only a very limited number of different structures with crossed dependencies, one could make special provisions to account for these structures and otherwise assume tree structures. Example (47), for instance, has a listlike structure. It is possible that listlike examples are exceptional in natural texts. However, there are many other naturally occurring nonlistlike structures that contain crossed dependencies. As an example of a nonlistlike structure with a crossed dependency (between {4, 2} and {3, 1–2}), consider (49):

(49)   a.   S1: Susan wanted to buy some tomatoes
        b.   S2: and she also tried to find some basil
        c.   S3: because her recipe asked for these ingredients.
        d.   S4: The basil would probably be quite expensive at this time of the year.

The coherence structure for (49), shown in figure 2.19, can be derived as follows:

• *Similarity* relation between discourse segments 1 and 2: both describe shopping for grocery items.
• *Cause-effect* relation between segments 3 and 1–2: 3 describes the cause for the shopping described by 1 and 2.
• *Elaboration* relation between segments 4 and 2: 4 provides details about the basil in 2.

Example (50) has a similar structure:

(50)   *Example text from the* AP Newswire *(1989) corpus (Harmon and Liberman 1993, ap890109-0012)*
        a.   S1: The flight Sunday took off from Heathrow Airport at 7:52pm
        b.   S2: and its engine caught fire 10 minutes later,
        c.   S3: the Department of Transport said.
        d.   S4: The pilot told the control tower he had the engine fire under control.

The coherence structure for (50) can be derived as follows:

• *Temporal sequence* relation between discourse segments 1 and 2: 1 describes the takeoff that happens before the engine fire described by 2 occurs.
• *Attribution* relation between segments 3 and 1–2: 3 mentions the source of what is said in 1-2.
• *Elaboration* relation between segments 4 and 2: 4 provides more detail about the engine fire in 2.

The resulting coherence structure, shown in figure 2.20, contains a crossed dependency between {4, 2} and {3, 1–2}.

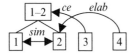

Figure 2.19
Coherence graph for (49); *Sim = similarity; ce = cause-effect; elab = elaboration*

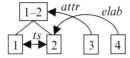

Figure 2.20
Coherence graph for (50); *Ts = temporal sequence; attr = attribution; elab = elaboration*

Consider example (51).

(51) *Example text from the* Wall Street Journal *(1989) corpus (Harmon and Liberman 1993, wsj_0655)*

    a. S1: [Mr. Baker's assistant for inter-American affairs,]$_{1a}$ [Bernard Aronson,]$_{1b}$

    b. S2: while maintaining

    c. S3: that the Sandinistas had also broken the cease-fire,

    d. S4: acknowledged:

    e. S5: "It's never very clear who starts what."

Annotations are presented with the discourse segmentation based on the guidelines in Carlson, Marcu, and Okurowski (2002) and based on our own guidelines from section 2.3.1. The only difference between these two approaches to segmentation in (51) is that Carlson, Marcu, and Okurowski (2002) assume discourse segment 1 to be a single segment. By contrast, our segmentation guidelines divide discourse segment 1 into two segments (because the comma does not separate a complex NP or VP), as indicated by the subscripted brackets below:[9]

(52) [Mr. Baker's assistant for inter-American affairs,]1a [Bernard Aronson,]1b

We then derive the coherence structure for (51) as follows:

• *Elaboration* relation between 1a and 1b: if discourse segment 1 is segmented into 1a and 1b (following our guidelines), 1b provides additional detail (a name) about what is stated in 1a (Mr. Baker's assistant)

• *Same-segment* relation between segments 1 (or 1a) and 4: the subject NP in 1 (*Mr. Baker's assistant . . .*) is separated from its predicate in 4 (*acknowledged*) by intervening discourse segments 2 and 3 (and 1b in our discourse segmentation)

- *Attribution* relation between segments 2 and 3: segment 2 provides the source for what is stated in 3 (the source in 2 is the elided *Mr. Baker*)
- *Elaboration* relation between the group of discourse segments 2–3 and discourse segment 1 (or segment group 1a–1b in our discourse segmentation): segments 2 and 3 provide additional detail (a remark about a political process) about what is stated in 1 (Mr. Baker's assistant)
- *Attribution* relation between segments 4 (and by virtue of the *same-segment* relation also 1 or 1a) and 5: segment 4 provides the source (Mr. Baker's assistant) for what is stated in 5.
- *Violated expectation* relation between the group of discourse segments 2–3 and the group of discourse segments 4–5: although Mr. Baker's assistant confirmed cease-fire violations by one side (discourse segments 2 and 3), he acknowledged that it is in fact difficult to clearly blame only one side for the violations (discourse segments 4 and 5).

The resulting coherence structure, shown in figure 2.21 (Carlson, Marcu, and Okurowski's 2002 segmentation) and figure 2.22 (our segmentation), contains a crossed dependency: the same-segment relation between discourse segment 1/1a and discourse segment 4 crosses the violated expectation relation between the segment group 2–3 and the group 4–5.

Figure 2.23 represents a tree-based RST annotation for (51) from Carlson, Marcu, and Okurowski (2002); dashed lines represent the start of asymmetric coherence relations, and continuous lines indicate the end of asymmetric coherence relations; symmetric coherence relations have two continuous lines (the *ss* node in figure 2.23 is a symmetric co-

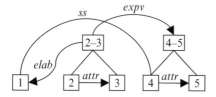

Figure 2.21
Coherence graph for (51); *Expv = violated expectation, ss = same-segment*

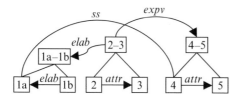

Figure 2.22
Coherence graph for (51) with discourse segment 1 split up into two segments

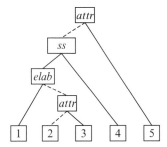

Figure 2.23
Tree-based RST annotation for (51) from Carlson, Marcu, and Okurowski (2002); *attr = attribution; elab = elaboration, ss = same-segment*. Dashed lines represent the start of asymmetric coherence relations; continuous lines represent the end of asymmetric coherence relations; symmetric coherence relations have two continuous lines (see section 2.3.3).

herence relation). We do not have a description of how these researchers derived a tree-based RST structure for (51). Therefore, we show instead a comparison of the RST structure and our chain graph-based structure in table 2.5. The RST structure does not represent the violated expectation relation between 2–3 and 4–5; that relation could not be annotated without violating the tree constraint disallowing crossed dependencies. Furthermore, in the RST structure, the same-segment relation dominates the elaboration relation between the group of 2–3 and segment 1. This does not seem to represent the targeted discourse meaning of (51). Instead, it seems to be a consequence of the fact that trees cannot represent nodes with multiple parents: according to the targeted discourse meaning, discourse segment 1 should be dominated by the same-segment relation as well as by an elaboration relation that holds between discourse segment 1 and the group of discourse segments 2–3 (see section 2.4.2 for a detailed discussion of nodes with multiple parents in discourse structures).

2.4.2 Nodes with Multiple Parents

In addition to including crossed dependencies, many coherence structures for natural texts include nodes with multiple parents. Such nodes cannot be represented in tree structures. Consider example (53).

(53) *Example text from the* AP Newswire *(1989) corpus (Harman and Liberman 1993, ap890103-0014)*
   a. S1: "Sure I'll be polite,"
   b. S2: promised one BMW driver
   c. S3: who gave his name only as Rudolf.
   d. S4: "As long as the trucks and the timid stay out of the left lane."

Table 2.5
Comparison of tree-based RST structure from Carlson, Marcu, and Okurowski (2002) and of our chain graph-based structure for (51)

Tree-based RST structure	Our chain graph–based structure
(1a and 1b are one discourse segment)	Elaboration between 1a and 1b
Same-segment between 1–3 and 4	Same-segment 1 (or 1a) and 4
Attribution between 1 and 2	Attribution between 1 and 2
Elaboration between 2–3 and 1	Elaboration between 2–3 1a–1b
Attribution between 1–4 and 5	Attribution between 4 and 5
(no relation)	Violated expectation between 2–3 and 4–5

The coherence structure for (53) can be derived as follows:

• *Attribution* relations between segments 2 and 1 and between 2 and 4: 2 states the source of what is stated in 1 and in 4.

• *Elaboration* relation between segments 2 and 1: segment 2 provides additional detail (the name) about the BMW driver in 1.

• *Condition* relation between segments 3 and 1: segment 3 states the BMW driver's condition for being polite, given in 1.[10] This condition relation is also indicated by the phrase *as long as*.

In the resultant coherence structure for (53), node 1 has two parents—one attribution and one condition ingoing arc (see figure 2.24).

   As another example of a discourse structure that contains nodes with multiple parents, consider the structure of (54) also from the *Wall Street Journal* (1989) corpus. The segmentation reflects Carlson, Marcu, and Okurowski's analysis.

(54)   *Example text (Harman and Liberman 1993, wsj_0655)*
   a.   S1: "The administration should now state
   b.   S2: that
   c.   S3: if the February election is voided by the Sandinistas
   d.   S4: they should call for military aid,"
   e.   S5: said former Assistant Secretary of State Elliott Abrams.
   f.   S6: "In these circumstances, I think they'd win."

[*They* in 4 and 6 = *Contra supporters;* this is clear from the whole text wsj_0655]

The only difference between our structure and Carlson, Marcu, and Okurowski's (2002) is that discourse segments 1 and 2 constitute one segment in our analysis (represented by the node 1 + 2 in figure 2.25). Carlson, Marcu, and Okurowski (2002) always represent

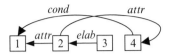

Figure 2.24
Coherence graph for (53). *Cond = condition*

the subordinating conjunction *that* as a separate discourse segment, as in (54), segment 2. It is unclear why these researchers have adopted this procedure instead of making *that* part of discourse segments 1 or 3.

The discourse structure for (54) can be derived as follows:

- According to our discourse segmentation guidelines (section 2.3.1), 1 and 2 should be a single discourse segment; therefore, merge 1 and 2 into a single segment, 1 + 2 (see figure 2.25 below).
- *Attribution* relation between 1/1 + 2 and 3–4: 1/1 + 2 provide the source (the administration) for what is stated in 3-4.
- *Condition* relation between segments 3 and 4: segment 3 provides the condition for what is stated in 4 (the condition relation is also signaled by the cue phrase *if* in 3).
- *Attribution* relation between segments 5 and 1–4: segment 5 provides the source for what is stated in 1–4.
- *Attribution* relation between segments 5 and 6: segment 5 provides the source for what is stated in 6.
- *Evaluation-s* relation between segments 6 and 3–4:[11] segment group 3–4 states what is evaluated by 6—the Contra supporters should call for military aid, and if the February election is voided (discourse segment group 3–4), the Contra supporters might win (discourse segment 6). Notice that in our coherence scheme, the evaluation-s relation would be an elaboration relation (segment 6 provides additional detail about 3–4: Elliott Abrams's opinion on the Contras' chances to win).

In the resultant coherence structure for (54), shown in figure 2.25, node 3–4 has multiple parents or ingoing arcs—one attribution ingoing arc and one evaluation-s ingoing arc. Figure 2.26 shows the tree-based annotation from Carlson, Marcu, and Okurowski (2002).

We present a comparison of the RST annotation and our chain graph-based annotation in table 2.6. Notice in particular that the attribution relation between segments 5 and 6 cannot be represented in the RST tree structure because doing so would require nodes with multiple parents. Notice furthermore that the RST tree contains an evaluation-s relation between segments 6 and 1–5. However, this evaluation-s relation seems to hold rather

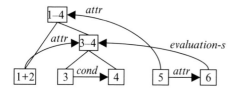

Figure 2.25
Coherence graph for (54) with discourse segments 1 and 2 merged into a single discourse segment

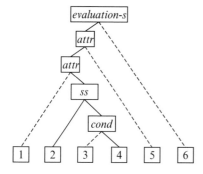

Figure 2.26
Tree-based RST annotation for (54) from Carlson, Marcu, and Okurowski (2002). Dashed lines represent the start of asymmetric coherence relations; continuous lines represent the end of asymmetric coherence relations; symmetric coherence relations have two continuous lines (see section 2.3.3).

Table 2.6
Comparison of tree-based RST structure from Carlson, Marcu, and Okurowski (2002) and of our chain graph-based structure for (54)

Tree-based RST structure	Our chain graph–based structure
Same between 2 and 3–4	Same-segment between 1 and 2, or merging of 1 and 2 to 1 + 2
Attribution between 1 and 2–4	Attribution between 1 or 1 + 2 and 3–4
Condition between 3 and 4	Condition between 3 and 4
Attribution between 5 and 1–4	Attribution between 5 and 1–4
(no relation)	Attribution between 5 and 6
Evaluation-s between 6 and 1–5	Evaluation-s between 6 and 3–4

between segments 6 and 3–4: what is being evaluated is a chance for the Contras to win a military conflict under certain circumstances. But annotating a coherence relation between 6 and 3–4 can not be accommodated in a tree structure.

2.5 Statistics

We performed a number of statistical analyses on our annotated database to test our hypotheses. Each set of statistics was calculated for both annotators separately. However, since the statistics for both annotators were never different (as confirmed by significant R^2s > 0.9 and by χ^2s < 1), we report the statistics for only one annotator in the following sections.

An important question regarding the phenomena discussed in section 2.4 is how frequently they occur. The more frequent they are, the more urgent the need for a data structure that can adequately represent them. The following sections report statistical results on crossed dependencies (section 2.5.1) and on nodes with multiple parents (section 2.5.2).

2.5.1 Crossed Dependencies

2.5.1.1 Frequency of Crossed Dependencies To track the frequency of crossed dependencies for the coherence structure graph of each text, we counted the minimum number of arcs that would have to be deleted in order to make the coherence structure graph free of crossed dependencies. The example graph in figure 2.27 illustrates this process. This graph contains the following crossed dependencies: {0, 2} crosses with {1, 3}, {2, 4} with {1, 3}, and {4, 6} with {5, 7}. By deleting {1, 3}, we can eliminate the crossing of {0, 2} and {1, 3} and the crossing of {2, 4} with {1, 3}. By deleting either {4, 6} or {5, 7} the remaining crossed dependency (between {4, 6} and {5, 7}) can be eliminated. Therefore, two edges would have to be deleted from the graph in figure 2.27 to make it free of crossed dependencies.

Table 2.7 shows the results of the crossed dependency deletions. On average for the 135 annotated texts, 12.5 percent of arcs in a coherence graph have to be deleted in order to make the graph free of crossed dependencies. Seven texts out of 135 had no crossed dependencies, and the mean number of arcs for the coherence graphs of these texts was 36.9 (minimum: 8; maximum: 69; median: 35). The mean number of arcs for the other 128

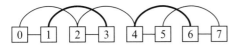

Figure 2.27
Graph with crossed dependencies

Table 2.7
Percentages of arcs to be deleted in order to eliminate crossed dependencies

	Mean	Minimum	Maximum	Median
Percent	12.5	0	44.4	10.9

coherence graphs (those with crossed dependencies) was 125.7 (minimum: 20; maximum: 293; median: 115.5). Thus, the graphs with no crossed dependencies have significantly fewer arcs than those with crossed dependencies ($\chi^2(1) = 15330.35$ (Yates's correction for continuity applied); $p < 10^{-6}$). This is a likely explanation for why these seven texts had no crossed dependencies.

More generally, linear regressions show a correlation between the number of arcs in a coherence graph and the number of crossed dependencies. The more arcs a graph has, the higher the number of crossed dependencies ($R^2 = 0.39$; $p < 10^{-4}$; see figure 2.28). The same linear correlation holds between text length and number of crossed dependencies—the longer a text, the more crossed dependencies it has in its coherence structure graph (for text length in discourse segments: $R^2 = .29$, $p < 10^{-4}$; for text length in words: $R^2 = .24$, $p < 10^{-4}$).

2.5.1.2 Types of Coherence Relations Involved in Crossed Dependencies In addition to the question of how frequent crossed dependencies are, another question is whether there are certain types of coherence relations that participate more or less frequently in crossed dependencies than other types of coherence relations. For an arc to participate in a crossed dependency, that arc must be in the set of arcs that would have to be deleted from a coherence graph in order to make that graph free of crossed dependencies (recall the procedure outlined in the beginning of section 2.5.1.1). The question, then, is whether the frequency distribution over types of coherence relations is different for arcs of this type compared to the overall frequency distribution over types of coherence relations in the whole database.

Figure 2.29 shows that the overall distribution over types of coherence relations participating in crossed dependencies is not different from the distribution over types of coherence relations overall. This is confirmed by a linear regression, which shows a significant correlation between the two distributions of percentages ($R^2 = 0.84$; $p < .0001$). The overall distribution includes only arcs with length greater than one, since arcs of length one could not participate in crossed dependencies. (For a description of how we calculated arc length, please see section 2.5.1.3).

However, there are some differences for individual coherence relations. Some types of coherence relations occur considerably less frequently in crossed dependencies than overall in the database. Table 2.8 shows the data from figure 2.29 ranked by the ratio of the

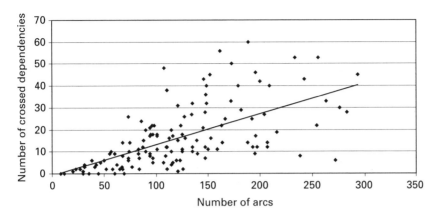

Figure 2.28
Correlation between number of arcs and number of crossed dependencies

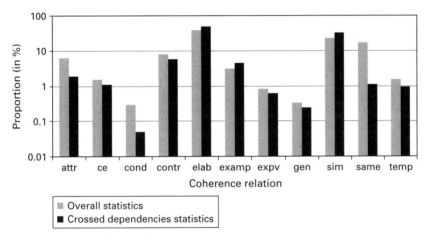

Figure 2.29
Distributions over types of coherence relations. For each condition (overall statistics and crossed dependencies statistics), the sum over all coherence relations is 100; each bar in each condition represents a fraction of the total of 100 in that condition. The y-axis uses a $\log_{10}$ scale.

Table 2.8
Proportions of coherence relations

Coherence relation	Proportion of coherence relations participating in crossed dependencies (%)	Proportion of overall coherence relations (%)	Factor (= overall/crossed dependencies)
Same-segment	1.13	17.21	15.23
Condition	0.05	0.28	5.59
Attribution	1.93	6.31	3.27
Temporal sequence	0.94	1.56	1.66
Generalization	0.24	0.34	1.40
Contrast	5.84	7.93	1.36
Cause-effect	1.13	1.53	1.35
Violated expectation	0.61	0.82	1.40
Elaboration	50.52	37.97	0.71
Example	4.43	3.15	1.34
Similarity	33.18	22.91	0.69

proportion of overall coherence relations to the proportion of coherence relations participating in crossed dependencies. The proportion of same-segment relations, for instance, is 15.23 times greater, and the percentage of condition relations is 5.59 times greater overall in the database than in crossed dependencies; these two relations are rarely involved in crossed dependencies. We do not yet understand the reason for these differences and plan to address this question in future research.

Another way of testing whether certain coherence relations contribute more than others to crossed dependencies is to remove coherence relations of a certain type from the database and then count the remaining number of crossed dependencies. For example, the number of crossed dependencies is likely to be reduced once all elaboration relations are removed from the database because elaboration relations are very frequent, and they are very frequently involved in crossed dependencies. Table 2.9 shows that by removing all elaboration relations from the database, the percentage of coherence relations involved in crossed dependencies is reduced from 12.5 percent to 4.96 percent of the remaining coherence relations. To further reduce the proportion of remaining crossed dependencies, it is necessary to remove similarity relations in addition to elaboration relations. Table 2.9 shows that when all elaboration and similarity relations are removed, the percentage of coherence relations involved in crossed dependencies is reduced to 0.84 percent. This pattern of results is not predicted by any literature that we are aware of, although it seems to provide partial support for Knott's (1996) hypothesis that elaboration relations, but not sim-

Table 2.9

The effect of removing different types of coherence relations on the percentage of coherence relations involved in crossed dependencies

Coherence relation removed	Remaining percentage of coherence relations involved in crossed dependencies			
	Mean	Min	Max	Median
Same-segment	13.08	0	44.44	11.39
Condition	12.63	0	45.28	10.89
Attribution	13.44	0	44.86	11.36
Temporal sequence	12.53	0	44.44	10.87
Generalization	12.53	0	44.44	10.84
Contrast	11.88	0	46.15	9.86
Cause-effect	12.67	0	49.47	11.03
Violated expectation	12.51	0	44.44	10.87
Elaboration	4.96	0	47.47	1.23
Example	12.08	0	44.44	9.89
Similarity	7.32	0	24.56	7.04
Elaboration and similarity	0.84	0	10.68	0.00

ilarity relations, are less constrained than other types of coherence relations (see the discussion of Knott 1996 in section 2.4).

However, there is a possible alternative hypothesis to Knott (1996). In particular, elaboration relations are very frequent (37.97 percent of all coherence relations, see table 2.8). It is possible that removing elaboration relations from the database reduces the number of crossed dependencies only because a large number of coherence relations are removed. In other words, the reduced number of crossed dependencies may result from having less dense coherence graphs (i.e., the less dense the coherence graphs, the lower the chance for crossed dependencies). We tested this hypothesis by correlating the proportion of coherence relations removed with the proportion of crossed dependencies that remain after removing a certain type of coherence relation.[12] Figure 2.30 shows that the higher the proportion of removed coherence relations, the lower the proportion of coherence relations involved in crossed dependencies. This correlation is confirmed by a linear regression (all data points: $R^2 = 0.7697$; $p < .0005$; after removing the elaboration data point: $R^2 = 0.4504$; $p < .05$; after removing the similarity data point: $R^2 = 0.7381$; $p < .002$; after removing both the elaboration and similarity data points: $R^2 = 0.0941$; $p < .43$). In any case, what this correlation shows is that while removing certain types of coherence relations reduces the number of crossed dependencies, the result is a very impoverished representation of coherence structure. After removing all elaboration and similarity relations, only 39.12 percent of all

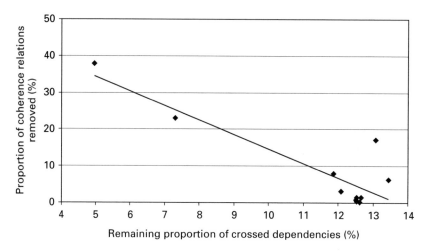

Figure 2.30
Correlation between removed proportion of overall coherence relations and remaining proportion of crossed dependencies. Note that the data point for elaboration + similarity is not included. Both axes represent percent values. $R^2 = 0.7699$; $p < .0005$.

coherence relations would still be represented (see table 2.8); 52.13 percent of all coherence relations would still be represented if the distribution over coherence relations included those relations with absolute arc length 1.

2.5.1.3 Arc Length of Coherence Relations Involved in Crossed Dependencies Another question of importance is how great the distance typically is between discourse segments that participate in crossed dependencies. One possible measure of distance is in terms of the number of intervening discourse segments. Thus, according to this metric, the distance between the first discourse segment in a text and the fourth is three segments.

A possible hypothesis is that crossed dependencies primarily involve long-distance arcs and that more local crossed dependencies are disfavored. For example, in Webber et al. (2003), structural relations (which, according to Webber et al. (2003), do not allow crossed dependencies) generally seem to be short-distance relations. By contrast, nonstructural relations (which, according to Webber et al. (2003), allow crossed dependencies) seem to also involve long-distance relations. It could be that short-distance relations tend to be subject to stronger constraints and that long-distance relations tend to be based on anaphoric relations, which might be subject to fewer constraints.[13] However, figure 2.31 shows that the distribution over arc lengths is practically identical for the overall database and for coherence relations participating in crossed dependencies (linear regression: $R^2 = 0.937, p < 10^{-4}$),

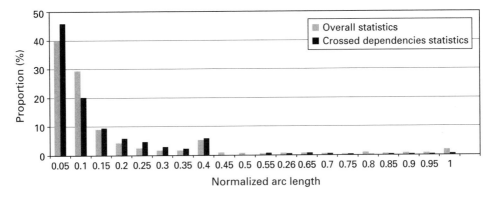

Figure 2.31
Comparison of normalized arc length distributions. For each condition (overall statistics and crossed dependencies statistics), the sum over all coherence relations is 100; each bar in each condition represents a fraction of the total of 100 in that condition.

suggesting a strong locality bias for coherence relations overall as well as for those participating in crossed dependencies.[14] The arc lengths are normalized in order to abstract from texts of different length. Normalized arc length is calculated by dividing the absolute length of an arc by the maximum length that that arc could have, given its position in a text. For example, if there is a coherence relation between discourse segment 1 and discourse segment 3 in a text, the raw distance would be 3. If these discourse segments are part of a text that has five discourse segments total (i.e., 1 to 5), the normalized distance would be 3/4 = 0.75 (because 4 would be the maximum possible length of an arc that originates in discourse segment 1 or 4, given that the text has five discourse segments in total).

In addition to computing statistics on normalized arc lengths, we also computed statistics on raw arc lengths. We did this because normalized arc lengths assign different values to local attachments, depending on text length (a local attachment occurs when there is a coherence relation between two adjacent discourse segments, resulting in a raw distance of 1). For example, if there are four discourse segments in total in a text, the length of a local attachment is 1/4 = 0.25. But if a text has twenty discourse segments in total, the length of a local attachment is 1/20 = 0.05.

Figure 2.32 shows that the results for raw arc lengths confirm the results for normalized arc lengths. Arcs of length 1 are not included because such arcs could not participate in crossed dependencies. As for normalized arc lengths, the distribution over raw arc lengths for the overall database is highly correlated with the distribution over raw arc lengths for coherence relations participating in crossed dependencies (linear regression: $R^2 = 0.7844$, $p < 10^{-4}$).

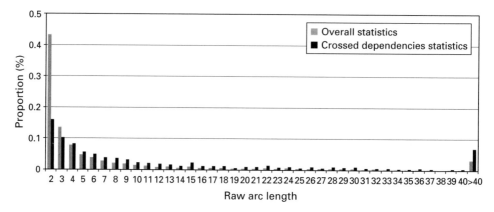

Figure 2.32
Comparison of raw arc length distributions. For each condition (overall statistics and crossed dependencies statistics), the sum over all coherence relations is 100; each bar in each condition represents a fraction of the total of 100 in that condition.

2.5.1.4 Summary on Crossed Dependencies Statistics Taken together, statistical results suggest that crossed dependencies are too frequent to be ignored by accounts of coherence relations. Furthermore, the results suggest that any type of coherence relation can participate in a crossed dependency. However, there are cases where knowing the type of coherence relation that an arc represents can be informative as to how likely that arc is to participate in a crossed dependency. The statistical results reported here also suggest that crossed dependencies occur primarily locally, as evidenced by the distribution over lengths of arcs participating in crossed dependencies.

2.5.2 Nodes with Multiple Parents

2.5.2.1 Frequency of Nodes with Multiple Parents We determined the frequency of nodes with multiple parents by counting the number of nodes with an in-degree (i.e., number of parents) greater than 1. The result of our count indicated that 41.22 percent of all nodes in the database have an in-degree greater than 1. In addition, table 2.10 shows that the mean in-degree of all nodes in the investigated database is 1.6. Furthermore, a linear regression showed a significant correlation between the number of arcs in a coherence graph and the number of nodes with multiple parents (see figure 2.33; $R^2 = 0.7258$, $p < 10^{-4}$; for text length in discourse segments: $R^2 = .6999$, $p < 10^{-4}$; for text length in words: $R^2 = .6022$, $p < 10^{-4}$). The proportion of nodes with in-degree greater than 1 and the mean in-degree of the nodes in our database suggest that even if a mechanism could be derived for represent-

Table 2.10
In-degrees of nodes in the overall database

	Mean	Minimum	Maximum	Median
In-degree	1.60	1	12	1

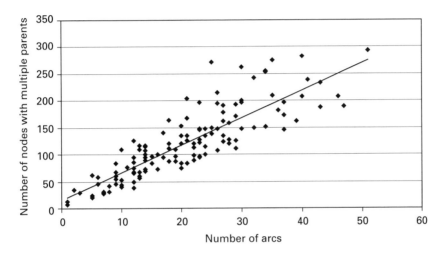

Figure 2.33
Correlation between number of arcs and number of nodes with multiple parents

ing crossed dependencies in (augmented) tree graphs, nodes with multiple parents present another significant problem for using trees to represent coherence structures.

2.5.2.2 Types of Coherence Relations Ingoing to Nodes with Multiple Parents As with crossed dependencies, an important question for multiple-parent nodes is whether there are certain types of coherence relations that occur more or less frequently ingoing to nodes with multiple parents than other types of coherence relations. In other words, is the frequency distribution over types of coherence relations different for arcs ingoing to nodes with multiple parents when compared to the overall frequency distribution over types of coherence relations in the whole database? Figure 2.34 shows that the overall distribution over types of coherence relations ingoing to nodes with multiple parents is not different from the distribution over types of coherence relations overall.[15] This is confirmed by a linear regression, which shows a significant correlation between the two distributions of percentages ($R^2 = 0.967$ $p < 10^{-4}$).

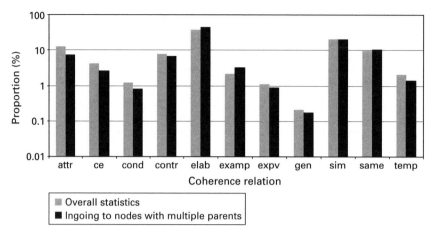

Figure 2.34
Distributions over types of coherence relations. For each condition (overall statistics and ingoing to nodes with multiple parents), the sum over all coherence relations is 100; each bar in each condition represents a fraction of the total of 100 in that condition. The y-axis uses a $\log_{10}$ scale.

Unlike for crossed dependencies (see table 2.8), there appear to be no noticeable differences for individual coherence relations. Table 2.11 shows the data from figure 2.34 ranked by the ratio of proportion of overall coherence relations to the proportion of coherence relations ingoing to nodes with multiple parents.

As for crossed dependencies, we also tested to see whether removing certain kinds of coherence relations reduces the mean in-degree (number of parents), the proportion of nodes with in-degree greater than 1 (more than one parent), or both. Table 2.12 shows that removing all elaboration relations from the database reduces the mean in-degree of nodes from 1.60 to 1.238 and the proportion of nodes with in-degree greater than 1 from 41.22 percent to 20.29 percent. Removing all elaboration as well as all similarity relations reduces these numbers further to 1.142 and 11.24 percent, respectively. As table 2.12 also shows, removing other types of coherence relations does not lead to as great a reduction of the mean in-degree and proportion of nodes with in-degree greater than 1.

However, as with crossed dependencies (see section 2.5.1.2), we also tested to see whether the reduction in nodes with multiple parents could be due simply to removing more coherence relations (i.e., the less dense a graph, the smaller the chance that there are nodes with multiple parents). We correlated the proportion of coherence relations removed with the mean in-degree of the nodes after removing different types of coherence relations. In the correlations in this chapter, the proportions of removed coherence relations include

Table 2.11
Proportion of coherence relations

Coherence relation	Proportion of coherence relations ingoing to nodes with multiple parents (%)	Proportion of overall coherence relations (%)	Factor (= overall/ingoing to nodes with multiple parents)
Attribution	7.38	12.68	1.72
Cause-effect	2.63	4.19	1.59
Temporal sequence	1.38	2.11	1.53
Condition	0.83	1.21	1.46
Violated expectation	0.90	1.13	1.26
Generalization	0.17	0.21	1.22
Contrast	6.72	7.62	1.13
Same-segment	10.72	9.74	0.91
Similarity	20.22	20.79	1.03
Elaboration	45.83	38.13	0.83
Example	3.20	2.19	0.68

Table 2.12
The effect of removing different types of coherence relations on the mean in-degree of nodes and on the proportion of nodes with in-degree > 1.

Coherence relation removed	In-degree of nodes				Proportion of nodes with in-degree > 1 (%)
	Mean	Min	Max	Median	
Same-segment	1.519	1	12	1	35.85
Condition	1.599	1	12	1	41.01
Attribution	1.604	1	12	1	41.18
Temporal sequence	1.599	1	12	1	41.12
Generalization	1.6	1	12	1	41.16
Contrast	1.569	1	12	1	39.45
Cause-effect	1.599	1	12	1	41.14
Violated expectation	1.598	1	12	1	40.96
Elaboration	1.238	1	11	1	20.29
Example	1.574	1	11	1	40.37
Similarity	1.544	1	12	1	36.25
Elaboration and similarity	1.142	1	11	1	11.24

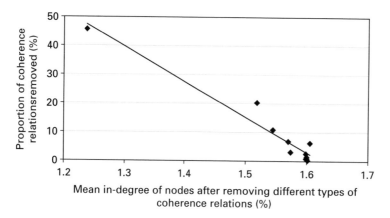

Figure 2.35
Correlation between proportion of removed coherence relations and mean in-degree of remaining nodes. $R^2 = 0.9455$; $p < 10^{-4}$.

coherence relations of absolute arc length 1, because removing these coherence relations also has an effect on the mean in-degree of nodes and the proportion of nodes with in-degree greater than 1. Thus, the proportions of coherence relations removed in figures 2.35 and 2.36 are from the third column of table 2.11. Figure 2.35 shows that the higher the proportion of removed coherence relations, the lower the mean in-degree of the nodes in the database. This correlation is confirmed by a linear regression ($R^2 = 0.9455$; $p < 10^{-4}$; after removing the elaboration data point: $R^2 = 0.8310$; $p < .0005$; after removing the similarity data point: $R^2 = 0.9462$; $p < 10^{-4}$; after removing both the elaboration and the similarity data points: $R^2 = 0.8254$; $p < .0008$). We also correlated the proportion of coherence relations removed with the proportion of nodes with in-degree greater than 1 after removing different types of coherence relations. Figure 2.36 shows that the higher the proportion of removed coherence relations, the lower the proportion of nodes with in-degree greater than 1. This correlation is also confirmed by a linear regression ($R^2 = 0.9574$, $p < 10^{-4}$; after removing the elaboration data point: $R^2 = 0.8146$, $p < .0005$; after removing the similarity data point: $R^2 = 0.9602$; $p < 10^{-4}$; after removing both the elaboration and the similarity data points: $R^2 = 0.9002$; $p < .0002$).

As was the case for crossed dependencies, while removing certain types of coherence relations reduces the mean in-degree of nodes and the proportion of nodes with in-degree greater than 1, the result is a very impoverished coherence structure (see section 2.5.1.2). For example, after removing both elaboration and similarity relations, only 52.13 percent of all coherence relations would be represented.

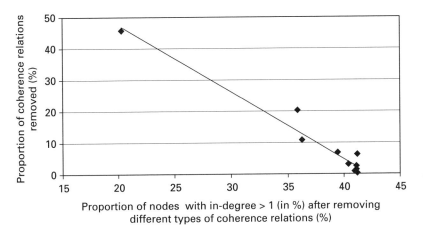

Figure 2.36
Correlation between proportion of removed coherence relations and proportion of nodes with in-degree > 1. $R^2 = 0.9574$; $p < 10^{-4}$.

2.5.2.3 Arc Lengths of Coherence Relations Ingoing to Nodes with Multiple Parents As we did for crossed dependencies, we also compared arc lengths for nodes with multiple parents. We compared the length of arcs that are ingoing to nodes with multiple parents to the overall distribution of arc length. Again, we compared normalized arc lengths (see section 2.5.1.3 for the normalization procedure). By contrast to the comparison for crossed dependencies, we included arcs of (absolute) length 1 because such arcs can be ingoing to nodes with either single or multiple parents. Figure 2.37 shows that the distribution over arc lengths is practically identical for the overall database and for arcs ingoing to nodes with multiple parents (linear regression: $R^2 = 0.993$, $p < 10^{-4}$), suggesting a strong locality bias for coherence relations overall as well as for those ingoing to nodes with multiple parents.

As for crossed dependencies, we also computed statistics on raw arc lengths. The results for raw arc lengths are basically the same as the results for normalized arc lengths. Figure 2.38 shows that the distribution over raw arc lengths is practically identical for the overall database and for arcs ingoing to nodes with multiple parents (linear regression: $R^2 = 0.9760$, $p < 10^{-4}$).

2.5.2.4 Summary of Statistical Results on Nodes with Multiple Parents In sum, statistical results on nodes with multiple parents suggest that they are a frequent phenomenon and that they are not limited to certain kinds of coherence relations. However, as was the case with crossed dependencies, removing certain kinds of coherence relations (elaboration

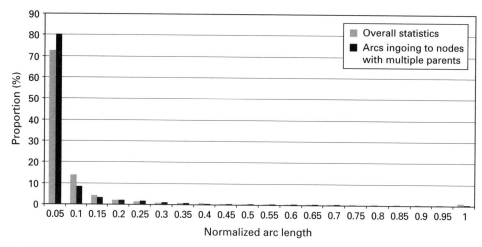

Figure 2.37
Comparison of normalized arc length distributions. For each condition (overall statistics and arcs ingoing to nodes with multiple parents), the sum over all coherence relations is 100; each bar in each condition represents a fraction of the total of 100 in that condition.

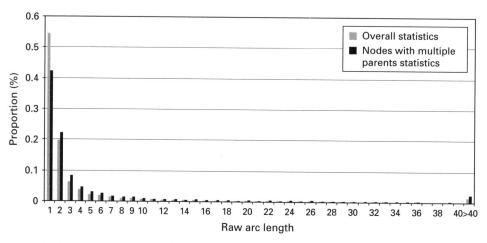

Figure 2.38
Comparison of raw arc length distributions. For each condition (overall statistics and arcs ingoing to nodes with multiple parents), the sum over all coherence relations is 100; each bar in each condition represents a fraction of the total of 100 in that condition.

and similarity) can reduce the mean in-degree of nodes and the proportion of nodes with in-degree greater than 1. But, as was also the case with crossed dependencies, our data at present do not indicate whether this reduction in nodes with multiple parents is due to a property of the coherence relations removed (elaboration and similarity), or whether it is just that removing coherence relations simply reduces the chance for nodes to have multiple parents. In addition to the results on frequency of nodes with multiple parents and types of coherence relations ingoing to nodes with multiple parents, the statistical results reported here suggest that ingoing arcs to nodes with multiple parents are primarily local.

2.6   Conclusion

The goals of this chapter have been to present a set of coherence relations that are easy to code and to test the adequacy of trees as a data structure for representing discourse coherence structures. We developed a coding scheme with high interannotator reliability and used that scheme to annotate 135 texts with coherence relations. An investigation of these annotations has shown that discourse structures of naturally occurring texts contain various kinds of crossed dependencies as well as nodes with multiple parents. Neither phenomenon can be represented using trees. This implies that existing databases of coherence structures that use trees are not descriptively adequate.

Our statistical results suggest that crossed dependencies and nodes with multiple parents are not restricted phenomena that could be disregarded or accommodated with a few exception rules. Furthermore, we found that removing certain kinds of coherence relations (elaboration and similarity) can reduce the number of crossed dependencies and nodes with multiple parents. However, it is not clear that this is due to some property of these coherence relations. Instead, our results are also consistent with a more parsimonious alternative hypothesis: removing coherence relations might simply reduce the chance for relations to be involved in crossed dependencies or for nodes to have multiple parents.

Because trees are neither a descriptively adequate data structure for representing coherence structures nor easier to derive, we hypothesize that it is simpler to start with less constrained graphs as a data structure for representing coherence structures. In particular, we argue for a representation such as chain graphs. Such less constrained graphs would have the advantage of being able to adequately represent coherence structures in a single data structure (see Brants et al. 2002; König and Lezius 2000; Skut et al. 1997). Furthermore, they are no harder to derive than (augmented) tree structures. The greater descriptive adequacy might in fact make them easier to derive. However, this is still an open issue and will have to be addressed in future research.

3.1 Introduction

An important component of language comprehension in most natural language contexts involves connecting clauses and phrases to establish a coherent discourse. One critical way in which coherence can be established between clauses is by the use of referring expressions, such as pronouns (Garnham 2001; Haliday and Hassan 1976; Johnson-Laird 1983; Kintsch and van Dijk 1978; Sanford and Garrod 1989). Thus an important part of discourse comprehension involves discovering how antecedents for pronouns are resolved.

A number of different approaches to pronoun resolution have been proposed. Some have argued that pronouns prefer to have antecedents (referents) in certain grammatical or semantic positions (e.g., Brennan, Friedman, and Pollard 1987; Chambers and Smyth 1998; Grosz, Joshi, and Weinstein 1995; Smyth 1994). Others have proposed that pronouns are assigned to antecedents based on causal inference (e.g., Winograd 1972). Furthermore, there are accounts which argue that pronoun resolution strategies depend on the coherence relation between the clause containing the pronoun and the clause containing the antecedent (Hobbs 1979; Kehler 2002). We will describe these accounts in more detail in section 3.2 and test some of their predictions in an online comprehension experiment (section 3.3) and an off-line production study (section 3.4).

3.2 Accounts of Pronoun Processing

One well-known account of discourse processing with implications on pronominal resolution is Centering Theory, which, for two-sentence discourses such as the ones investigated in this chapter, predicts that pronouns prefer to have antecedents in subject position (Brennan, Friedman, and Pollard 1987; Grosz, Joshi, and Weinstein 1995; see also Wundt 1911). This prediction is based on attentional, not informational, discourse structure (see section 2.2 for an explanation of this distinction). Consider example (55):

(55)   Fiona complimented Susan, and she congratulated James.

Most people have a preference for interpreting the pronoun *she* as referring to Fiona rather than to Susan.[16] We can also see the effects of pronominal resolution complexity in reading times on corresponding unambiguous sentence stimuli. In (56), *Susan* has been replaced by *Craig,* with the result that the pronoun *she* in (56a) unambiguously refers to Fiona, whereas the pronoun *he* in (56b) unambiguously refers to Craig. People will generally read (56a)—the sentence in which the pronoun refers to the preceding sentence's subject—faster than (56b)—the sentence in which the pronoun refers to the preceding sentence's object.

(56)   a.   Fiona complimented Craig, and she congratulated James.
       b.   Fiona complimented Craig, and he congratulated James.

In further support of Centering Theory, Gordon, Grosz, and Gilliom (1993) found that there is a preference for using pronouns to refer to entities in subject position but not to entities in object position. Conversely, they found that a pronoun is easy to process when it refers to an entity in the subject position of the preceding sentence, but harder to process when it refers to an entity that is not in the subject position of the preceding sentence. Consider the sentences in (57):

(57)   a.   Fiona complimented Craig, and she congratulated James.
       b.   Fiona complimented Craig, and Fiona congratulated James.
       c.   Fiona complimented Craig, and he congratulated James.
       d.   Fiona complimented Craig, and Craig congratulated James.

Gordon, Grosz, and Gilliom (1993) found that (57a) was easier to process (i.e., it was read faster) than (57b). The only difference between these two items is that (57a) uses a pronoun, whereas (57b) uses a repeated name. This pattern of results, where the item containing the pronoun was read faster than the item containing the repeated name, has been labeled the *repeated name penalty* by Gordon, Grosz, and Gilliom (1993). For (57c) and (57d), these researchers found the reverse pattern, that is, (57d), which contains a repeated name, was read faster than (57c), which contains a pronoun.

However, a problem for Centering Theory is provided by the contrast in (58):

(58)   a.   Fiona complimented Craig, and James congratulated her.
       b.   Fiona complimented Craig, and James congratulated him.

Centering Theory predicts that (58a) should be read faster than (58b), but Chambers and Smyth (1998) found in a self-paced reading experiment that sentences like (58b) were read faster than sentences like (58a). This pattern of results motivates the Parallel Preference account (Chambers and Smyth 1998; Smyth 1994; see Lappin and Leass 1994 for a combination of Centering Theory and Parallel Preference). Under the Parallel Preference account

(Smyth 1994), pronouns are argued to prefer antecedents in a parallel position when the sentences containing the pronoun and the antecedent have the following properties: (1) both sentences have the same global constituent structure, and (2) the thematic roles of the verbs in both sentences concur. When these conditions are met, subject pronouns should prefer subject antecedents, and object pronouns should prefer object antecedents. This is the case in (57) and (58) above. In (57), people prefer the preceding clause's subject as the referent for the subject pronoun, whereas in (58), people prefer the preceding clause's object as the referent for the object pronoun.

Although a Parallel Preference account can explain the preferences in (57) and (58), it does not explain the preferences in (59), from Winograd (1972):

(59) a. The city council denied the demonstrators the permit because they advocated violence.

      b. The city council denied the demonstrators the permit because they feared violence.

In sentence (59a) the pronoun *they* refers to the demonstrators, whereas in sentence (59b) it refers to the city council. Neither sentence seems particularly difficult to process. Notice, however, that both Centering Theory and Parallel Preference predict a preference for *they* to refer to the subject, *the city council;* in Centering Theory, the subject antecedent is in the center of attention in (59), and in Parallel Preference, there is a preference for an antecedent in a parallel position. Examples like (59) motivate causal inference-based accounts of pronoun processing (Hobbs 1979; Hobbs et al. 1993; Kehler 2002). According to such accounts, *they* refers to the demonstrators in sentence (59a) because advocating violence is assumed to be a good reason for being denied a permit. In sentence (59b) *they* refers to the city council because fearing violence by demonstrators is a good reason for denying a permit to these demonstrators.

Experimental evidence relevant to causal inference-based accounts of pronominal resolution is provided by Ehrlich (1980), who used an off-line questionnaire to investigate people's preferred pronoun resolution. Ehrlich found that pronoun resolution is driven only by causal inferences (Caramazza et al. 1977; Stewart, Pickering, and Sanford 2000) when the clauses containing the pronoun and the antecedent are in a causal relation. When there is no such causal relation, Ehrlich found that people prefer antecedents in topic or subject position (as in Centering Theory, Grosz, Joshi, and Weinstein 1995). Topic position refers to material preceding the verb. Thus, in active sentences, the agent of the verb is in topic (and subject) position (e.g., *the city council* in *the city council denied the demonstrators the permit*), whereas in passive sentences, the theme of the verb is in topic position (e.g., *the demonstrators* in *the demonstrators were denied a permit by the city council*).

Although cause-based strategies can explain the effects in (59), they do not explain the patterns in (57) and (58) because there is no causal connection between the two clauses in either of these sentences. Furthermore, resorting to a topic-based strategy like Centering Theory, as suggested by Ehrlich (1980), makes the right prediction for (57) but not for (58), where the pronoun with an object antecedent is easier to process. Following Hobbs (1979), Kehler (2002) provides a hypothesis that aims to explain all of these patterns of pronoun resolution. Instead of arguing for pronoun-specific processing mechanisms, Kehler, like Hobbs (1979), proposes that pronoun resolution is a byproduct of establishing coherence. Kehler extends Hobbs's (1979) key insight that the establishment of coherence guides pronoun resolution and vice versa, noting that discourse coherence and pronoun resolution also mutually constrain each other. Thus, Kehler hypothesizes that how a pronoun is resolved may depend on the coherence relation between the clauses.

Two classes of coherence relations that are particularly relevant to the examples that have been discussed in the pronoun resolution literature are cause-effect, similarity, and contrast. A cause-effect relation holds between two clauses if a plausible causal relation can be inferred to hold between the events described by the two clauses. This is the case in (59a). Because the demonstrators advocated violence, the city council denied them a permit to demonstrate. Kehler (2002) argues that the pronoun is interpreted such that a plausible cause-effect relation between the two clauses can be established. Pairing *they* with *the demonstrators* provides a more plausible interpretation for (59a) than pairing *they* with *the city council*. A similar analysis applies to the pronoun resolution of *they* in (59b).

The similarity and contrast discourse relations are relevant to explaining the pattern of preferences in (57) and (58). A similarity relation holds between two clauses if the entities and events they described are similar; a contrast relation holds if the entities and events described are contrastive (recall section 2.3.3). Consider the following examples from Kehler (2002):

(60) *Similarity*
    a. Gephardt organized rallies for Gore,
    b. and Daschle distributed pamphlets for him.

(61) *Contrast*
    a. Gephardt supported Gore,
    b. but Armey opposed him.

Kehler hypothesizes that the first step in establishing a similarity or a contrast relation between clauses is to find parallel corresponding entities and events. Then, these entities and events are linked by similarity or contrast relations. For example, in sentence (60a), *orga-*

nized rallies is parallel and similar to *distributed pamphlets* in sentence (60b) (both are predicates describing actions of supporting a political candidate), and *Dick Gephardt* in sentence (60a) is parallel and similar to *Tom Daschle* in sentence (60b) (both are American politicians who supported Al Gore). Then, Kehler (2002) argues, the pronoun *him* in sentence (60a) is paired with its parallel preceding element, *Gore,* in sentence (60b). In sentence (61a), *supported* is parallel and in contrast to *opposed* in sentence (61b). *Gephardt* in sentence (61a) is parallel and in contrast to *Armey* in sentence (61b) (both are politicians, but one of them supported Gore and the other one opposed him). Then, as in example (60), the pronoun *him* in sentence (61a) is paired with its parallel preceding element, *Gore,* in sentence (61b). Thus, in both examples (60) and (61), the pronoun is bound to its antecedent during the establishment of similarity and contrast coherence relations, respectively, when parallel entities are matched.

The pronoun in (60) could also be resolved using general inference mechanisms: someone organized rallies for Gore, suggesting that Gore is a political candidate (and not Gephardt). Daschle distributed pamphlets for someone; usually pamphlets are distributed by someone who is not a political candidate (i.e., Daschle) for someone who is a political candidate. Since Gore is the most plausible political candidate of the three, and since *him* should refer to a political candidate (because pamphlets are usually distributed for political candidates), it is most likely that *him* refers to Gore. However, such general inferences are not sufficient for resolving the pronoun in (61): it is not clear why the fact that Gephardt supported Gore should make it more plausible for Armey to oppose Gore than to oppose Gephardt (particularly since opposing Gephardt could also be interpreted as indirectly opposing Gore—Gephardt may be opposed because of his support for Gore).

The similarity relation is the most plausible coherence relation between each of the clauses in the sentences in (57) and (58). In particular, the use of the similar verbs *complimented* and *congratulated* in the absence of any other cues induces a similarity relation between each pair of clauses. Kehler's (2002) theory then predicts that a Parallel Preference strategy would be in effect under the similarity relation, which has been observed experimentally in such sentences (Chambers and Smyth 1998). A prediction of Kehler's theory is that pronoun resolution preferences can be altered depending on the coherence relation between clauses. The experiments presented below test this prediction directly.

3.3 Experiment 1

Experiment 1 describes an online self-paced reading experiment to test the different predictions of the pronoun processing accounts discussed above.

3.3.1 Method

3.3.1.1 Participants Forty participants from the MIT community were paid for their participation. All were native speakers of English and were naive as to the purpose of the study.

3.3.1.2 Materials Twenty sets of sentences were constructed, each with four conditions in a 2 × 2 design: coherence relation (similarity, cause-effect) × parallel reference (parallel, nonparallel). An example item is presented in (62):

(62) a. *Similarity, parallel reference*
Fiona complimented Craig, and similarly James congratulated him after the match, but nobody took any notice.
  b. *Similarity, nonparallel reference*
Fiona complimented Craig, and similarly James congratulated her after the match, but nobody took any notice.
  c. *Cause-effect, parallel reference*
Fiona defeated Craig, and so James congratulated him after the match, but nobody took any notice.
  d. *Cause-effect, nonparallel reference*
Fiona defeated Craig, and so James congratulated her after the match, but nobody took any notice.

Each sentence consisted of three clauses. The second clause was the target clause, which consisted of the same words across the coherence manipulation. We manipulated the coherence relation between similarity and cause-effect by making two changes to the items: (1) by using different connectives between the clauses (*and similarly* vs. *and so*), and (2) by using a different verb in the first clause. For similarity, the verbs in the two clauses were semantically similar according to the WordNet lexical database (Fellbaum 2001), for example, *compliment* and *congratulate* in (62). For the cause-effect conditions, the verb of the first clause was chosen so that there was a plausible causal relation between the two clauses which in turn entailed that the object pronoun referred to the subject of the first clause, for example, *defeat* and *congratulate* in (62). The first-clause verb in the cause-effect conditions always differed from the first-clause verb in the similarity conditions. The remainder of the sentences consisted of a prepositional phrase and a third clause. This portion of the items was the same across the four conditions. Overall, the only differences between the similarity and cause-effect conditions were the verbs of the first clause and the connectives relating the two clauses.

Note that this experiment did not explore the relative contribution of different coherence cues to changing pronoun interpretation preferences. This did not diminish the intent of the design, which was simply to show that changing the coherence relation by using one or more cues may alter pronoun interpretation preferences.

The target sentences were combined with seventy-six fillers of various types in four lists balancing all factors in a Latin Square design. Appendix A provides a complete list of the stimuli, which were pseudorandomized separately for each participant so that at least one filler item intervened between two targets.

3.3.1.3 Procedure   The task involved self-paced, word-by-word reading with a moving window display (Just, Carpenter, and Woolley 1982) using Linux computers running software developed in our lab. Each trial began with a series of dashes marking the length and position of the words in the sentences, printed approximately a third of the way down the screen. Participants pressed the spacebar to reveal each word of the sentence. As each new word appeared, the preceding word disappeared. The amount of time the participant spent reading each word was recorded as the time between key presses. After the final word of each item, a question appeared which asked about information contained in the sentence (e.g., *Did James congratulate Fiona?*). Participants pressed one of two keys to respond *yes* or *no*. After an incorrect answer, the word *INCORRECT* flashed briefly on the screen. No feedback was given for correct responses. Participants were asked to read sentences at a natural rate and to be sure that they understood what they read. They were told to answer the questions as quickly and accurately as they could and to take wrong answers as an indication to read more carefully. Before the main experiment, a short list of practice items and questions was presented to familiarize the participant with the task. A session averaged twenty-five minutes.

3.3.2   Predictions
The predictions were made in terms of reading times on the pronoun plus the next word, because in self-paced reading, effects often spill over to the next word (Sanford and Garrod 1989). Faster reading times are assumed to reflect easier processing of the pronoun. Centering Theory predicts that pronouns referring to antecedents in subject position should always be read faster. Thus, the pronouns in sentences (62b) and (62d) should be read faster than those in sentences (62a) and (62c). Parallel Preference makes the opposite prediction for sentences (62a) and (62b). Because the pronouns in the experimental items are in object position, Parallel Preference predicts that pronouns referring to antecedents in (parallel) object position should be read faster. Thus, the pronouns in sentence (62a) should be read

faster than those in sentence (62b). Parallel Preference does not apply to sentences (62c) and (62d) because these sentences do not meet Smyth's (1994) criteria for parallelism.

Causal inference-based accounts do not apply to sentences (62a) and (62b), because the events described by the clauses are not causally related. Ehrlich's (1980) proposal, in which a topic-based strategy applies when there is no causal relation, predicts that the pronoun in (62b) should be read faster than the pronoun in (62a). Causal-inference accounts predict that the pronoun in sentence (62d) should be read faster than in (62c) because a causal inference to resolve the pronoun is much easier to establish in (62d); in (62c), it is hard to see why James should congratulate Craig, because Craig lost the match.

Kehler's (2002) coherence-based theory predicts that the cues in sentences (62a) and (62b) will indicate a similarity relation between the clauses, so that a Parallel Preference strategy will be in effect. Thus, the pronoun in sentence (62a) should be read faster than the one in sentence (62b). Kehler's account furthermore predicts that the cues in sentences (62c) and (62d) will indicate a cause-effect relation between the clauses, with the consequence that the pronoun in sentence (62d) should be read faster than the pronoun in sentence (62c) because of the more plausible causal inference for sentence (62d). Thus Kehler's (2002) account predicts an interaction between coherence relations and pronominal reference.

3.3.3   Results

Table 3.1 shows the question-answering performance for the experiment. A 2×2 ANOVA, coherence relation (similarity, cause-effect) by reference (parallel, nonparallel), revealed an interaction that was significant in the participants analysis ($F1(1,39) = 8.150$, MSE = 1210, $p < .01$) and marginally significant in the items analysis ($F2(1,19) = 3.385$, MSE = 605, $p = .08$). Pairwise comparisons by subject showed that under the similarity relation, question-answering performance was better under parallel than under nonparallel reference ($F1(1,39) = 5.354$, MSE = 845, $p < .05$). There was no significant difference under cause-effect ($F1(1,39) = 2.395$, MSE = 405, $p = .13$).

We analyzed reading times only for items for which the comprehension question was answered correctly. Reading times beyond three SD from the mean for a given condition and

Table 3.1
Question-answering performance in percent correct.

Pronoun reference	Coherence relation	
	Similarity	Cause-effect
Parallel	86	80.5
Nonparallel	79.5	85

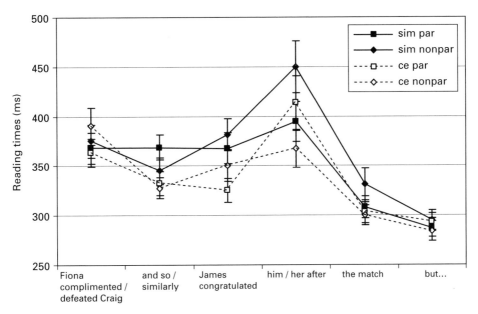

Figure 3.1

Plot of mean word-by-word reading times; *sim par = similarity, parallel; sim nonpar = similarity, non-parallel; ce par = cause-effect, parallel; ce nonpar = cause-effect, nonparallel*

position were excluded from the analysis. This affected 2.79 percent of the data. Mean word-by-word reading times in the by-subject analysis are shown in figure 3.1.

A 2 × 2 ANOVA, coherence relation by reference, was computed for a region including the pronoun and the following word. It showed a significant interaction of coherence relation and reference ($F1(1,39) = 14.669$, MSE $= 103997$, $p < .001$; $F2(1,19) = 13.398$, MSE $= 67545$, $p < .005$). There was also a main effect of coherence relation—cause-effect items were read faster than similarity items ($F1(1,39) = 4.431$, MSE $= 40563$, $p < .05$; $F2(1,19) = 3.898$, MSE $= 22222$, $p = .06$). For the region containing the pronoun and the region preceding that region, there was a significant three-way interaction of coherence relation, reference, and region ($F1(1,39) = 12.111$, MSE $= 64630$, $p < .005$; $F2(1,19) = 20.126$, MSE $= 44344$, $p < .0005$). There were no other significant effects.

Pairwise comparisons showed that under similarity, parallel was read faster than non-parallel ($F1(1,19) = 7.849$, MSE $= 60866$, $p < .01$; $F2(1,19) = 5.785$, MSE $= 40196$, $p < .05$). Under cause-effect, nonparallel was read faster than parallel ($F1(1,39) = 4.822$, MSE $= 43829$, $p < .05$; $F2(1,19) = 5.785$, MSE $= 27907$, $p < .05$).

3.3.4 Discussion

The results of Experiment 1 showed that under a similarity discourse relation, pronouns with an antecedent in parallel object position were read faster than pronouns with an antecedent in subject position. This is predicted by the Parallel Preference account as well as by Kehler's (2002) account. By contrast, Centering Theory and Ehrlich's (1980) account would have predicted a subject antecedent preference. Causal inference-based accounts make no prediction for pronoun preferences in the absence of causal relations between the clauses containing pronoun and antecedent.

Under the cause-effect discourse relations in our items, pronouns referring to a subject antecedent were read faster. This is predicted by causal inference-based accounts as well as Kehler's (2002) account, but not by the Parallel Preference account. Centering Theory does predict this preference, but not as a part of a causal inference process.

To summarize, the only account that makes the correct predictions for all conditions is Kehler's (2002). It predicts different preferences in pronoun resolution depending on the coherence relation between the clauses containing the pronoun and the antecedent.

3.4 Experiment 2

Experiment 2 was a corpus study that tested the predictions of the pronoun processing accounts described above. Whereas Experiment 1 tested online language comprehension preferences, Experiment 2 tested off-line language production preferences.

3.4.1 Method

3.4.1.1 Materials We extracted materials from the *Wall Street Journal* and the Brown corpora (Marcus et al. 1994). The materials we used were clauses containing pronouns and clauses containing antecedents of these pronouns. The next section describes how we collected the materials.

3.4.1.2 Procedure We used the following procedure to collect materials and determine frequencies of interest:

1. Extract all sentences containing nonreflexive pronouns from both the *Wall Street Journal* and the Brown corpora.
2. From the materials collected in step 1
   a. To collect cause-effect materials: extract examples containing *because* with the pronoun in the second clause (i.e., in the clause following the word *because*).

   b. To collect similarity and contrast materials
      i. Extract examples containing *and* as a sentential conjunction with a pronoun in the second clause (i.e., in the clause following the word *and*).
      ii. From these materials, extract those where the clauses conjoined by *and* are in a similarity or contrast relation. This relation was determined by a human annotator.
3. Determine pronoun antecedents.
4. Extract grammatical roles for pronouns and antecedents.
5. Keep only those materials that had the structure *S V O and/because S V O* and where the pronouns and the antecedents were in either subject or direct object position.

Using this procedure, we extracted 410 pairs of pronouns and antecedents from the *Wall Street Journal* corpus (205 cause-effect; 205 similarity/contrast), and 470 pairs of pronouns and antecedents from the Brown corpus (235 cause-effect; 235 similarity/contrast).

Below are two examples from the *Wall Street Journal*, one for each type of coherence relation. The pronouns and their antecedents are in boldface. In (63), an object pronoun refers to an antecedent in object position. In (64), a subject pronoun refers to an object antecedent.

(63) *Similarity*
      The Exchequer Nigel Lawson's resignation slapped **the market,** and Wall Street's rapid selloff knocked **it** down.

(64) *Cause-effect*
      They shredded **the document** simply because **it** contained financial information.

3.4.2 Predictions

The predictions were made in terms of frequencies of subject and object position pronouns and subject and object position antecedents. Higher frequencies of a type are assumed to reflect a preference for producing that type. Thus, while Experiment 1 tested preferences in language comprehension, Experiment 2 tested preferences in language production.

   Centering Theory predicts that there should always be more pronoun antecedents in subject position than pronoun antecedents in object position. It does not make predictions about the frequency of pronouns in subject versus object positions. Parallel Preference predicts that there should be more subject pronouns with subject antecedents than object antecedents. Furthermore, it predicts that there should be more object pronouns with object antecedents than subject antecedents.

   Causal inference-based accounts could not be tested in Experiment 2. They would predict higher frequencies of types that reflect more plausible causal inferences. However, the dependent variable in Experiment 2 was distributional patterns of grammatical roles and functions of pronouns and their antecedents, and we could not formalize testable hypotheses about causal inferences that make predictions in terms of distributional patterns.

Kehler's (2002) coherence-based theory predicts that under similarity or contrast, there should be more subject pronouns with subject antecedents than object antecedents. Furthermore, it predicts that under similarity or contrast, there should be more object pronouns with object antecedents than subject antecedents. Thus, Kehler's (2002) prediction for similarity or contrast are the same as the predictions made by Parallel Preference. By contrast, we could not formalize a testable hypothesis for Kehler's (2002) theory for cause-effect, for the same reason that we could not test causal inference-based accounts: the question of plausibility in causal inferences is orthogonal to the question of grammatical function.

3.4.3 Results

The results of the counts are shown in figures 3.2 through 3.5. In order to test differences in the distributions for significance, we conducted a series of chi-square tests. The results are given below.

- *Wall Street Journal* corpus
  - *Cause-effect*
    - More pronouns in subject than in object position ($\chi^2(1) = 96.14$, $p = 0.0000001$)
    - More antecedents in subject than in object position ($\chi^2(1) = 5.22$, $p = 0.02$)
    - No significant interaction ($\chi^2(1) < 1$)

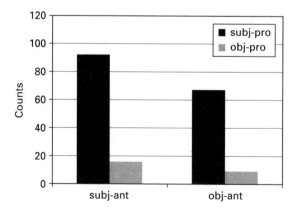

Figure 3.2
Cause-effect data from the *Wall Street Journal* corpus; *subj = subject, obj = object, pro = pronoun, ant = antecedent*

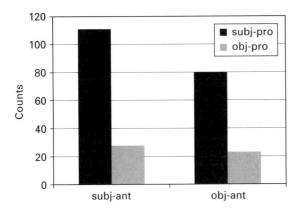

Figure 3.3
Cause-effect data from the *Brown* corpus; *subj = subject, obj = object, pro = pronoun, ant = antecedent*

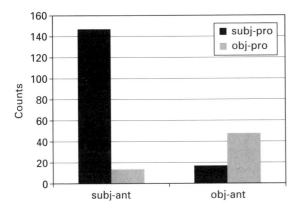

Figure 3.4
Similarity data from the *Wall Street Journal* corpus; *subj = subject, obj = object, pro = pronoun, ant = antecedent*

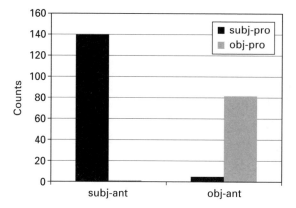

Figure 3.5
Similarity data from the *Brown* corpus; *subj = subject, obj = object, pron = pronoun, ant = antecedent*

- *Similarity*
  - More pronouns in subject than in object position ($\chi^2(1) = 45.14$, $p = 0.0000001$)
  - More antecedents in subject than in object position ($\chi^2(1) = 38.27$, $p = 0.0000001$)
  - Significant interaction ($\chi^2(1) = 99.31$, $p = 0.0000001$)
- Brown corpus
  - *Cause-effect*
    - More pronouns in subject than in object position ($\chi^2(1) = 79.84$, $p = 0.0000001$)
    - More antecedents in subject than in object position ($\chi^2(1) = 5.06$, $p = 0.02$)
    - No significant interaction ($\chi^2(1) < 1$)
  - *Similarity*
    - More pronouns in subject than in object position ($\chi^2(1) = 16.32$, $p = 0.000053$)
    - More antecedents in subject than in object position ($\chi^2(1) = 12.32$, $p = 0.000448$)
    - Significant interaction ($\chi^2(1) = 199.33$, $p = 0.0000001$)

3.4.4 Discussion

The results of Experiment 2 showed that under a similarity discourse relation, there are more subject pronouns with subject than object antecedents, and more object pronouns with object than subject antecedents. This is predicted by the Parallel Preference account as well as by Kehler's (2002) account. By contrast, Centering Theory and Ehrlich's (1980) account would have predicted there to be more subject antecedents than object antecedents, independent of pronoun position. In the absence of a causal relation between the clause containing the pronoun and the clause containing the antecedent, causal inference-based accounts do not apply (see section 3.4.2).

We did not find a preference for parallel pronoun and antecedent positions under cause-effect. Instead, we found that there was a preference for subject and object pronouns to have subject antecedents. This is not predicted by the Parallel Preference account. Causal inference-based accounts do not make grammatical function frequency predictions, nor does Kehler's (2002) account, under a cause-effect relation. The only account that predicts more subject antecedents is Centering Theory. However, while Centering Theory makes the correct prediction for cause-effect, it does not predict the observed interaction in frequency distributions between cause-effect and similarity.

Across the conditions (cause-effect and similarity), we found more pronouns and antecedents in subject position than pronouns and antecedents in object position. Centering Theory predicts this. A possible explanation for this result might be that pronouns tend to refer to given rather than to new information; often, given information is found in subject rather than in object position (see Grosz, Joshi, and Weinstein 1995; Wundt 1911).

In sum, Kehler's (2002) account is the only one that predicts the observed interaction between cause-effect and similarity. We also observed an overall preference for pronouns and antecedents in subject position across cause-effect and similarity, which is predicted by Centering Theory.

3.5 Conclusions

The results from the experiments reported here support the idea that the preferences observed in pronoun processing depend on the coherence relation between the clause containing the pronoun and the clause containing the antecedent (Kehler 2002). However, this is not to say that other factors, such as focusing attention on specific discourse elements (Grosz, Joshi, and Weinstein 1995; Wundt 1911), play no role in pronoun processing; the overall preference for subject antecedents and pronouns observed in Experiment 2 supports this hypothesis. In fact, Kehler (2002) also points out that in narratives, shifting attention to different discourse entities is an important factor in pronoun processing preferences. He argues that under such circumstances the observed preferences may be more as predicted by accounts such as Centering Theory. Note, however, that of the accounts considered here, Kehler's (2002) is the only one that predicts all observed preferences to be not a result of the operations of pronoun-specific mechanisms, but a byproduct of more general cognitive mechanisms and their interaction—establishing coherence and focusing attention.

The goal of this chapter has not been to describe a full account of pronoun processing. It is possible that there are other, non-coherence-based factors that influence preferences in pronoun processing. However, the results from the experiments reported here have implications for psychologically plausible taxonomies of coherence relations. For language production as well as comprehension, our experiments suggest that people use different approaches to pronoun resolution, depending on whether there is a cause-effect or a similarity coherence relation between the clause containing the pronoun and the clause containing the antecedent. For taxonomies of coherence relations that are based on different cognitive inference mechanisms underlying different coherence relations, these results suggest that such taxonomies should at least distinguish between cause-effect and similarity coherence relations.

Appendix A: Items for Experiment 1 in Chapter 3

1. Charles commended/saved Harriet and similarly/so Richard praised her/him in the newspaper but everything was just a big show.
2. David reprimanded/betrayed Sarah and similarly/so Helen chastised her/him after the holidays but all the criticism showed very little effect.
3. Michael disciplined/attacked Shirley and similarly/so Leonard punished her/him two days ago but in the end they reached an agreement.
4. Peter questioned/assaulted Julie and similarly/so Carol interrogated her/him for an hour but a few moments later the police arrived at the scene.
5. Stuart honored/liberated Martha and similarly/so Joseph admired her/him a great deal but unfortunately the feeling was not mutual.
6. Nathan disliked/abandoned Alyssa and similarly/so Nicole hated her/him for a while and in the end they all avoided each other.
7. Ryan safeguarded/feared Emma and similarly/so Adam protected her/him in the evening but all their caution would probably not have been necessary.
8. Kevin rebuked/kicked Claire and similarly/so Grace scolded her/him in the house but nobody else cared about all these quarrels.
9. Erik embraced/rescued Lisa and similarly/so Liam hugged her/him with great enthusiasm and everybody was a little bit relieved.
10. Brian scolded/harassed Cathy and similarly/so Scott lectured her/him after the meeting and everybody ended up hating each other.
11. Fiona complimented/defeated Craig and similarly/so James congratulated him/her after the match but nobody took any notice.
12. Christina lectured/pestered Christopher and similarly/so Stephanie reprimanded him/her for one hour although nobody thought it would have any effect.
13. Jonathan despised/denounced Madeline and similarly/so Patricia scorned her using harsh language but after a while everybody was reconciled again.

14. Rebecca interrogated/punched Anthony and similarly/so Suzanne cross-examined him/her for a while but nothing interesting was said.

15. Melissa suspected/deceived William and similarly/so Natalie distrusted him/her in the end and the whole working atmosphere was spoiled.

16. Tina thanked/supported Robert and similarly/so Fred acknowledged him/her at the conference but nobody seemed to be sincere.

17. Sophia admired/outdid Joshua and similarly/so Gloria respected him/her in the beginning but very soon things changed.

18. Melanie hired/impressed Bradley and similarly/so Malcolm recruited him/her after the interview but not all of the co-workers were satisfied with the situation.

19. Heather hit/insulted Aaron and similarly/so Caitlin punched him/her in the nose and the result was a big fight.

20. Hannah appointed/outperformed Michael and similarly/so George nominated him/her for the job although some people were not happy with the decision.

4.1 Introduction

Automatic generation of text summaries is a natural language engineering application that has received considerable interest, more recently in particular due to the ever-increasing volume of text information available through the Internet. For humans, generating a summary generally involves three tasks (Brandow, Mitze, and Rau 1995; Mitra, Singhal, and Buckley 1997): (1) understanding a text, (2) ranking text pieces (sentences, paragraphs, phrases, etc.) for importance, and (3) generating a new text (the summary). Like most approaches to summarization, we are concerned with the second task (e.g., Carlson et al. 2001; Goldstein et al. 1999; Gong and Liu 2001; Jing et al. 1998; Luhn 1958; Mitra, Singhal, and Buckley 1997; Sparck-Jones and Sakai 2001; Zechner 1996). Furthermore, we are concerned with obtaining generic rather than query-relevant importance rankings: in generic importance rankings, text pieces are ranked for importance with respect to the overall content of the text; by contrast, in query-relevant importance rankings, text pieces are ranked for importance with respect to the content of a certain query (see Goldstein et al. 1999 and Radev, Hovy, and McKeown 2002 for that distinction).

Sentence rankings might be influenced by coherence structures. That is, it is possible that the saliency of a discourse segment (e.g., a sentence) is based on its position in the informational structure of a discourse. But there are also other approaches to sentence ranking that are not based on coherence structures. For example, some accounts hypothesize that sentence importance is based on document layout features or on the importance of words in a sentence. Section 4.2 will describe the different approaches to sentence ranking in more detail.

In section 4.4, we will evaluate the approaches to automated sentence ranking against human sentence rankings. To obtain human sentence rankings, we asked people to read fifteen texts from the *Wall Street Journal* on a wide variety of topics (e.g., economics, foreign and domestic affairs, political commentaries). For each of the sentences in the text, they provided a ranking of how important that sentence was with respect to the content of the text, on an integer scale from 1 (not important) to 7 (very important). The approaches we evaluated included a simple layout-based approach that serves as a baseline, two word-based algorithms, and three coherence-based approaches. We furthermore evaluated the *Microsoft Word* summarizer/sentence ranker.

In our experiments, we did not use any machine learning techniques to boost performance of the algorithms we tested. Therefore, performance of the algorithms tested here will almost certainly be below the level of performance that could be reached if we had augmented the algorithms with such techniques (e.g., Carlson et al. 2001). However, we think that a comparison between "bare-bones" algorithms is viable because it allows us to see how performance differs due to distinct basic approaches to sentence ranking, and not due to potentially different effects of different machine learning algorithms on distinct basic approaches to sentence ranking.

4.2   Approaches to Sentence Ranking

4.2.1   Coherence-Based Approaches

Coherence-based approaches to sentence ranking are based on the informational structure of texts. By informational structure, we mean the set of informational relations that hold between sentences in a text. This set can be represented in a graph, where the nodes represent sentences and labeled directed arcs represent informational relations that hold between the sentences (recall Hobbs 1985; also sections 2.3 and 2.4). Often, informational structures of texts have been represented as trees (e.g., Carlson et al. 2001; Corston-Oliver 1998; Mann and Thompson 1988; Ono, Sumita, and Miike 1994). We will present one coherence-based approach that assumes trees as a data structure for representing discourse structure, and one approach that assumes less constrained graphs. As we will show, the approach based on less constrained graphs performs better than the tree-based approach when compared to human sentence rankings.

4.2.2   Layout-Based Approaches

In layout-based approaches, sentence importance is determined based on the layout of a text. The idea behind such approaches is that if information is important, it is often placed at a prominent position within a text and not, for example, in a footnote. Layout-based methods have often been used in domains where layout information is easily accessible, for example, in the form of HTML markup tags (see Raghavan and Garcia-Molina 2001). Furthermore, people are often instructed to write so that important information comes first (see Eden and Mitchell 1986).

We tested a simple layout-based approach using paragraph structure as its basis. Sentences at the beginning of a paragraph are usually more important than sentences further down, due in part to the way people are instructed to write. Conceivably, the simplest way to instantiate this idea is to identify the first sentences of each paragraph as important, and the other sentences as not important. We included this approach merely as a simple baseline.

4.2.3 Word-Based Approaches

Word-based approaches to summarization are based on the idea that discourse segments are important if they contain "important" words. These approaches have different definitions of what an important word is. For example, Luhn (1958), in a classic approach to summarization, argues that sentences are more important if they contain many significant words. Significant words are those that do not occur in a predefined stoplist of words with high overall corpus frequency.[17] Once significant words are marked in a text, clusters of significant words are formed. A cluster has to start and end with a significant word, and fewer than n insignificant words must separate any two significant words (we chose $n = 3$, following Luhn 1958). Next, the weight of each cluster is calculated by dividing the square of the number of significant words in the cluster by the total number of words in the cluster. Sentences can contain multiple clusters. The weight of a sentence is then the maximum of the weights of all clusters in that sentence. The higher the weight of a sentence, the higher its ranking. Figure 4.1 shows the formula for calculating the importance of a sentence according to Luhn (1958): i_s is the importance of a sentence; n is the number of clusters in a sentence; n_c is the current cluster in a sentence; w_{sig} is the number of significant words in a cluster; w_{insig} is the number of insignificant words in a cluster.

A more recent, frequently used word-based method for text piece ranking is *tf.idf* (Manning and Schuetze 2000; Salton and Buckley 1988; Sparck-Jones and Sakai 2001; Zechner 1996). The *tf.idf* measure relates the frequency of words in a text piece, in the text, and in a collection of texts, respectively. The intuition behind *tf.idf* is to give more weight to sentences that contain terms with high frequency in a document but low frequency in a reference corpus. Figure 4.2 shows a formula for calculating *tf.idf*, where ds_{ij} is the *tf.idf* weight of sentence i in document j, n_{si} is the number of words in sentence i, k is the kth word

$$i_s = \sum_{n_c=1}^{n} \frac{w_{sig}^2}{w_{sig} + w_{insig}}$$

Figure 4.1
Formula for calculating the importance of a sentence according to Luhn (1958)

$$ds_{ij} = \sum_{k=1}^{n_{si}} tf_{jk} \cdot \log\left[\frac{n_d}{df_k}\right]$$

Figure 4.2
Formula for calculating *tf.idf* (Salton and Buckley 1988)

in sentence *i*, tf_{jk} is the frequency of word *k* in document *j*, n_d is the number of documents in the reference corpus, and df_k is the number of documents in the reference corpus in which word *k* appears.

We compared both Luhn's (1958) measure and *tf.idf* scores to human rankings of sentence importance. We will show that both methods performed remarkably well, although some coherence-based methods performed better.

4.3   Coherence-Based Sentence Ranking Revisited

This section will discuss in more detail the data structures we used to represent discourse structure, as well as the algorithms based on discourse structures used to calculate sentence importance.

4.3.1   Representing Coherence Structures

4.3.1.1   Discourse Segments   As pointed out in section 2.3.1, discourse segments can be defined as nonoverlapping spans of prosodic units (Hirschberg and Nakatani 1996), intentional units (Grosz and Sidner 1986), phrasal units (Lascarides and Asher 1993), or sentences (Hobbs 1985). We adopted a mostly clause unit-based definition of discourse segments for the coherence-based approach that assumes chain graphs (see section 2.3.1). For the coherence-based approach that assumes trees, we used Marcu's (2000) more fine-grained definition of discourse segments because we used the discourse trees from Carlson, Marcu, and Okurowski's (2002) database of coherence-annotated texts.

4.3.1.2   Kinds of Coherence Relations   For the coherence structure-based summarization approaches discussed in this chapter, we assume the set of coherence relations that was introduced in section 2.3.3. As a reminder, examples of each coherence relation are given below.

(65)   *Cause-effect*
       [There was bad weather at the airport]$_a$ [and so our flight got delayed.]$_b$

(66)   *Violated expectation*
       [The weather was nice]$_a$ [but our flight got delayed.]$_b$

(67) *Condition*
      [If the new software works,]ₐ [everyone will be happy.]_b

(68) *Similarity*
      [There is a train on platform A.]ₐ [There is another train on platform B.]_b

(69) *Contrast*
      [John supported Bush]ₐ [but Susan opposed him.]_b

(70) *Elaboration*
      [A probe to Mars was launched this week.]ₐ [The European-built *Mars Express* is scheduled to reach Mars by late December.]_b

(71) *Attribution*
      [John said that]ₐ [the weather would be nice tomorrow.]_b

(72) *Temporal sequence*
      [Before he went to bed,]ₐ [John took a shower.]_b

As pointed out in section 2.3.3, cause-effect, violated expectation, condition, elaboration, temporal sequence, and attribution are asymmetrical or directed relations, whereas similarity and contrast are symmetrical or undirected relations (Mann and Thompson 1988; Marcu 2000). As also pointed out in section 2.3.3, in the chain graph-based approach, the directions of asymmetrical or directed relations are as follows:

- cause → effect for *cause-effect*
- cause → absent effect for *violated expectation*
- condition → consequence for *condition*
- elaborating → elaborated for *elaboration*
- source → attributed for *attribution*
- sooner → later for *temporal sequence*

In the tree-based approach, the asymmetrical or directed relations link a more important discourse segment, or a nucleus, and a less important discourse segment, or a satellite (Mann and Thompson 1988). The nucleus is the equivalent of the arc destination, and the satellite the equivalent of the arc origin, in the chain graph-based approach. The symmetrical or undirected relations link two discourse elements of equal importance, or two nuclei. Below, we will explain how the difference between satellites and nuclei is considered in tree-based sentence rankings.

4.3.1.3 Data Structures for Representing Discourse Coherence   As mentioned above, we used two alternative representations for discourse structure, trees and chain graphs. As an illustration of both data structures, let us begin with (73):

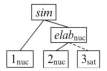

Figure 4.3
Coherence tree for (73)

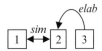

Figure 4.4
Coherence chain graph for (73)

(73) a. S1: Susan wanted to buy some tomatoes.
      b. S2: She also tried to find some basil.
      c. S3: The basil would probably be quite expensive at this time of the year.

Figure 4.3 shows one possible tree representation of the coherence structure of (73).[18] *Sim* represents a similarity relation, and *elab* an elaboration relation. Furthermore, nodes with a *nuc* subscript are nuclei, and nodes with a *sat* subscript are satellites; nucleus relations are also indicated by solid lines and satellite relations by dashed lines. Figure 4.4 shows a chain graph representation of the coherence structure of (73). Here, the heads of the arrows represent the directionality of a relation.

4.3.2 Coherence-Based Sentence-Ranking
This section explains the algorithms for the tree- and the chain graph-based sentence-ranking approaches.

4.3.2.1 Tree-Based Approaches We used Marcu's (2000) algorithm to determine sentence rankings based on tree discourse structures. In this algorithm, sentence saliency is determined based on the level of a discourse segment in the coherence tree. Figure 4.5 shows Marcu's (2000) algorithm, where $r(s, D, d)$ is the rank of a sentence s in a discourse tree D with depth d. Every node in discourse tree D has a promotion set *promotion(D),* which is the union of all nucleus children of that node. Associated with every node in discourse tree D is also a set of parenthetical nodes *parentheticals(D)* (for example, in *Mars—half the size of Earth—is red, half the size of Earth* would be a parenthetical node in a discourse tree).

Both *promotion(D)* and *parentheticals(D)* can be empty sets. Furthermore, each node has a left subtree, *lc(D),* and a right subtree, *rc(D).* Both *lc(D)* and *rc(D)* can also be empty.

We illustrate how Marcu's (2000) algorithm works in an example shown in figures 4.6 through 4.11. The gray numbers on the right side of each figure represent inverse tree levels, which are used for determining discourse segment ranks. As in the examples in sections 2.4.1 and 2.4.2, solid lines represent nucleus relations and dashed lines represent satellite relations (see Mann and Thompson 1988). Terminal nodes can only be promoted through nucleus relations. The promotions are illustrated by the arrows in the figures. The rank for each segment or terminal node is determined by the highest level in the tree to which the node can be promoted. The segment ranks are shown in boldface below the terminal nodes. We demonstrate below how the discourse segment ranks for the tree in figure 4.6 were derived.

• *Discourse segment 0 (see figure 4.7):* Discourse segment 0 is in a nucleus relation with a nonterminal node at inverse tree level 2, so discourse segment 0 gets promoted to inverse tree level 2. The nonterminal node at inverse tree level 2 is in a nucleus relation with another nonterminal node at inverse tree level 3, so discourse segment 0 gets promoted to inverse tree level 3. The nonterminal node at inverse tree level 3 is in a nucleus relation with a nonterminal node (the root node) at inverse tree level 4, so discourse segment 0 gets promoted to inverse tree level 4. Thus discourse segment 0 gets rank 4 by Marcu's (2000) algorithm.

$$r\,(s,D,d) = \begin{cases} 0 & \text{if } D \text{ is NIL,} \\ d & \text{if } s \in promotion\,(D), \\ d-1 & \text{if } s \in parentheticals\,(D), \\ \max\,(r\,(s,lc\,(D),d-1), \\ \qquad r\,(s,rc\,(D),d-1)) & otherwise \end{cases}$$

Figure 4.5
Formula for calculating coherence tree-based sentence rank (Marcu 2000)

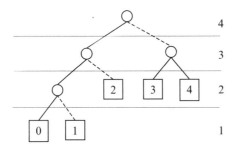

Figure 4.6
Example tree for illustrating Marcu's (2000) algorithm

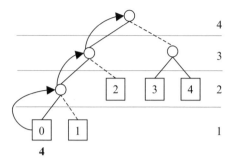

Figure 4.7
Determining the ranking for segment 0

• *Discourse segment 1:* Discourse segment 1 is in a satellite relation. Therefore discourse segment 1 does not get promoted and gets rank 1 by Marcu's (2000) algorithm (see figure 4.8).
• *Discourse segment 2:* Discourse segment 2 is in a satellite relation. Therefore discourse segment 2 does not get promoted and gets rank 2 by Marcu's (2000) algorithm (see figure 4.9).
• *Discourse segment 3 (see figure 4.10):* Discourse segment 3 is in a nucleus relation with a nonterminal node at inverse tree level 3, so discourse segment 3 gets promoted to inverse tree level 3. Because the nonterminal node at inverse tree level 3 is in a satellite relation with the nonterminal node at the next-higher inverse tree level, discourse segment 3 does not get promoted further. Thus, discourse segment 3 gets rank 3 by Marcu's (2000) algorithm.
• *Discourse segment 4 (see figure 4.11):* Discourse segment 4 is in a nucleus relation with a nonterminal node at inverse tree level 3, so discourse segment 4 gets promoted to inverse tree level 3. Because the nonterminal node at inverse tree level 3 is in a satellite relation with the nonterminal node at the next-higher inverse tree level, discourse segment 4 does not get promoted further. Thus, discourse segment 4 gets rank 3 by Marcu's (2000) algorithm.

The discourse segments in Carlson, Marcu, and Okurowski's (2002) database are often subsentential. Therefore, we had to calculate sentence rankings from the rankings of the discourse segments that form the sentence under consideration. We did this by calculating the average ranking, the minimal ranking, and the maximal ranking of all discourse segments in a sentence. Our results showed that choosing the minimal ranking performed best, followed by the average ranking, followed by the maximal ranking (see section 4.4.4).

4.3.2.2 Chain Graph-Based Approaches We used three different methods to determine sentence rankings for the coherence chain graphs.[19] All three methods implement the intuition that sentences are more important if other sentences relate to them (Sparck-Jones 1993).

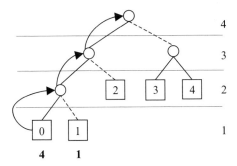

Figure 4.8
Determining the ranking for segment 1

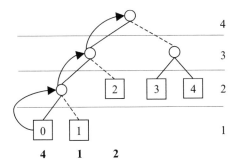

Figure 4.9
Determining the ranking for segment 2

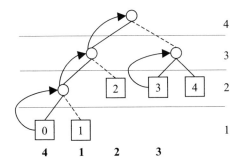

Figure 4.10
Determining the ranking for segment 3

The first method consists of simply determining the in-degree of each node in the graph.[20] A node represents a sentence, and the in-degree of a node represents the number of sentences that relate to that sentence. The higher the in-degree of a node, the higher the ranking of the sentence that the node represents (i.e., the more other sentences relate to a sentence, the more important that sentence becomes). To implement this method, we treated coherence graphs as unlabeled, directed graphs. Arcs representing symmetrical or undirected coherence relations (i.e., similarity, contrast, same-segment) were replaced by two directed arcs (one arc in each direction).

The second method is based on the idea that a discourse segment is more important if other important discourse segments relate to it. To implement this idea, we used Page et al.'s (1998) PageRank algorithm, which is used, for example, in the Google™ search engine. Instead of just determining the in-degree of a node, PageRank takes into account the importance of sentences that relate to a sentence. Figure 4.12 shows how PageRank is calculated. PR_n is the PageRank of the current sentence, PR_{n-1} is the PageRank of the sentence that relates to sentence n, o_{n-1} is the out-degree of sentence $n-1$, and α is a damping parameter that is set to a value between 0 and 1. We report results for α set to 0.85 because this is a value often used in applications of PageRank (e.g., Ding et al. 2002; Page et al. 1998). We also calculated PageRanks for α set to values between 0.05 and 0.95, in increments of 0.05; changing α did not affect performance. For calculating PageRank, we

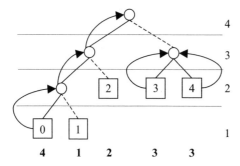

Figure 4.11
Determining the ranking for segment 4

$$PR_n = 1 - \alpha + \alpha \frac{PR_{n-1}}{O_{n-1}}$$

Figure 4.12
Formula for calculating PageRank (Page et al. 1998)

1.   **for** each discourse segment vertex ds in $V(G_{discourse\text{-}structure})$ **do**

2. $rank_{ds} \leftarrow 0$

3.   initialize container L_0 to contain vertex ds

4. $i \leftarrow 0$

5.   **while** L_i is not empty **do**

6.   create container L_{i+1} to initially be empty

7.   **for** each vertex v in L_i **do**

8.   **if** edge e is unexplored **then**

9.   let w be the other endpoint of e

10.   **if** vertex w is unexplored **then**

11.   label e as a discovery edge

12.   insert w into L_{i+1}

13.   **else**

14.   label e as a cross edge

15. $rank_{ds} \leftarrow rank_{ds} + \alpha^{i+1} \cdot \|L_{i+1}\|$

16. $i \leftarrow +1$

Figure 4.13

Pseudocode for cRank, based on pseudocode for a breadth-first search algorithm in Goodrich and Tamassia (2001)

treated coherence graphs as unlabeled directed graphs and replaced undirected arcs (those arcs that represent symmetrical or undirected coherence relations, i.e., similarity, contrast, same-segment) by two directed arcs (one arc in each direction).

The third method, cRank (for *coherence-rank*), is based on the idea that a discourse segment ds_0 is more important the more other discourse segments relate to it. Furthermore, in cRank, the more directly these other discourse segments relate to ds_0, the more they boost its importance. In order to determine how directly discourse segments relate to ds_0, cRank conducts a breadth-first search through the coherence graph, starting at ds_0 (this ranking procedure is done for every node in the coherence graph). Pseudocode for cRank is shown in figure 4.13 (based on breadth-first search pseudocode from Goodrich and Tamassia 2001):

- i: counter for the rounds of the breadth-first search algorithm
- L_i: container for graph vertices at round i of the breadth-first search algorithm
- ds: discourse segment vertex
- $rank_{ds}$: rank of discourse segment vertex ds

- $V(G_{discourse\text{-}structure})$: set of discourse segment vertices in the graph representing the discourse structure, $G_{discourse\text{-}structure}$
- e: edge in the coherence graph
- v, w: vertices adjacent to an edge e
- α: parameter set to $]0..1]$
- $\|L_{i+1}\|$: number of elements in container L_{i+1}
- discovery edge: an edge that leads to a previously unvisited vertex
- cross edge: an edge that leads to a previously visited vertex

For implementing cRank, we treated coherence graphs as unlabeled, undirected graphs. Note furthermore that we set the parameter α to 1, thus effectively reducing line 15 of the algorithm to a parameter-free form:

15. $rank_{ds} \rightarrow rank_{ds} + (i + 1) \cdot \|L_{i+1}\|$

The effect of setting α to a value between 0 and 1 would be that the nodes further up in a breadth-first traversal tree would add more to $rank_{ds}$ than nodes that are further down. This could be done to optimize the performance of cRank. However, that was not the goal here.

We illustrate cRank with $\alpha = 1$ for the graph shown in figure 4.14. Trees representing breadth-first graph traversals for each node in the graph are shown in figures 4.15 through 4.20. The gray numbers in the figures represent the inverse tree levels. Note that it does not make a difference whether the inverse tree level for the starting node of each breadth-first graph traversal is included in the calculations of cRank because it would affect the rank of all nodes equally.

Using the breadth-first graph traversals shown in figures 4.15 through 4.20, the rank for each node in the graph in figure 4.14 can be determined as follows (with parameter $\alpha = 1$):

Node 0:

$$
\begin{aligned}
& 3 \cdot 3 \quad \text{(nodes 1, 2, and 3)} \\
+\ & 1 \cdot 2 \quad \text{(node 4)} \\
+\ & 1 \cdot 1 \quad \text{(node 5)} \\
=\ & 12;
\end{aligned}
$$

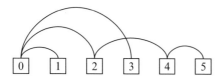

Figure 4.14
Example graph for illustrating cRank

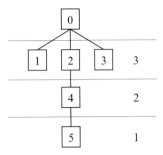

Figure 4.15
Breadth-first graph traversal starting at node 0

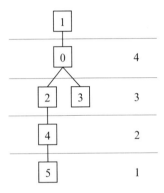

Figure 4.16
Breadth-first graph traversal starting at node 1

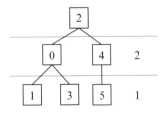

Figure 4.17
Breadth-first graph traversal starting at node 2

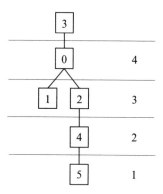

Figure 4.18
Breadth-first graph traversal starting at node 3

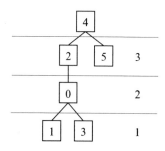

Figure 4.19
Breadth-first graph traversal starting at node 4

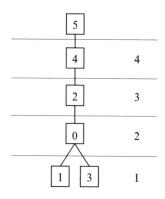

Figure 4.20
Breadth-first graph traversal starting at node 5

Node 1:

$$1 \cdot 4 \quad \text{(node 0)}$$
$$+ \quad 2 \cdot 3 \quad \text{(nodes 2 and 3)}$$
$$+ \quad 1 \cdot 2 \quad \text{(node 4)}$$
$$+ \quad 1 \cdot 1 \quad \text{(node 5)}$$
$$= \quad 13;$$

Node 2:

$$2 \cdot 2 \quad \text{(nodes 0 and 4)}$$
$$+ \quad 3 \cdot 1 \quad \text{(nodes 1, 3, and 5)}$$
$$= \quad 7;$$

Node 3:

$$1 \cdot 4 \quad \text{(node 0)}$$
$$+ \quad 2 \cdot 3 \quad \text{(nodes 1 and 2)}$$
$$+ \quad 1 \cdot 2 \quad \text{(node 4)}$$
$$+ \quad 1 \cdot 1 \quad \text{(node 5)}$$
$$= \quad 13;$$

Node 4:

$$2 \cdot 3 \quad \text{(nodes 2 and 5)}$$
$$+ \quad 1 \cdot 2 \quad \text{(node 0)}$$
$$+ \quad 2 \cdot 1 \quad \text{(nodes 1 and 3)}$$
$$= \quad 10;$$

Node 5:

$$1 \cdot 4 \quad \text{(node 4)}$$
$$+ \quad 1 \cdot 3 \quad \text{(node 2)}$$
$$+ \quad 1 \cdot 2 \quad \text{(node 0)}$$
$$+ \quad 2 \cdot 1 \quad \text{(nodes 1 and 3)}$$
$$= \quad 11;$$

Thus, by cRank, node 0 has rank 12, node 1 has rank 13, node 2 has rank 7, node 3 has rank 13, node 4 has rank 10, and node 5 has rank 11, as shown in figure 4.21. As can be seen in figures 4.15 through 4.20, as well as in the above cRank calculations for each node, the cRank value of a discourse segment is determined by two factors: the depth of the breadth-first traversal tree and the branching factor of the traversal tree (either the branching factor at a certain tree level, or some kind of average across the branching factors at all tree levels in a breadth-first search traversal tree). Parameters could be used to determine which of these two factors is more important for calculating cRank.

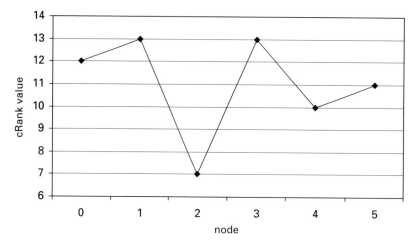

Figure 4.21
cRank values for the nodes in the graph shown in figure 4.14

Note that all chain graph-based algorithms treated coherence graphs as unlabeled graphs. One possible refinement of chain graph-based methods for sentence ranking would be to assign different weights to arcs representing different coherence relations. For example, weights could be assigned such that arcs representing causal coherence relations (cause-effect, violated expectation, condition) contribute more weight than arcs representing elaboration coherence relations. Thus, sentences that are part of causal coherence structures in a text would be ranked as more important (see also Kintsch's (1998) results, suggesting better memory for information that is embedded in causal structures). We plan to address this issue in future research.

4.4 Experiments

In order to test algorithm performance, we compared algorithm sentence rankings to human sentence rankings. This section describes the experiments we conducted. In Experiment 1, the texts were presented with paragraph breaks; in Experiment 2, the texts were presented without paragraph breaks. This was done to control for the effect of paragraph information on human sentence rankings.

4.4.1 Materials for the Coherence-Based Approaches

In testing the tree-based approach, we took coherence trees for 15 texts from a database of 385 texts from the *Wall Street Journal* that were annotated for coherence (Carlson, Marcu, and Okurowski 2002). The database was independently annotated by six annotators. Interannotator agreement was determined for six pairs of two annotators each, resulting in kappa values (Carletta 1996) ranging from 0.62 to 0.82 for the whole database (Carlson, Marcu, and Okurowski 2003). No kappa values were available for just the 15 texts we used.

For the chain graph-based approach, we used coherence graphs for 15 texts from a database of 135 texts from the *Wall Street Journal* and the *AP Newswire,* annotated for coherence. Each text was independently annotated by two annotators. For the 15 texts we used, kappa was 0.78, for the whole database, kappa was 0.84.

4.4.2   Experiment 1: With Paragraph Information

Fifteen participants from the MIT community were paid for their participation. All were native speakers of English and were naive as to the purpose of the study (i.e., none of the subjects were familiar with theories of coherence in natural language, for example).

Participants were asked to read fifteen texts from the *Wall Street Journal* and, for each sentence in each text, to provide a ranking of how important that sentence is with respect to the content of the text, on an integer scale from 1 to 7 (1 = not important; 7 = very important).

The texts were selected so that there was a coherence tree annotation available in Carlson, Marcu, and Okurowski's (2002) database. Text lengths for the fifteen texts we selected ranged from 130 to 901 words (five to forty-seven sentences); average text length was 442 words (twenty sentences), median was 368 words (sixteen sentences). Additionally, texts were selected so that they were about as diverse topics as possible.

The experiment was conducted in front of personal computers. Texts were presented in a web browser as one webpage per text; for some texts, participants had to scroll to see the whole text. Each sentence was presented on a new line. Paragraph breaks were indicated by empty lines; this was pointed out to the participants during the instructions for the experiment.

4.4.3   Experiment 2: Without Paragraph Information

The method used here was the same as in Experiment 1, except that texts in Experiment 2 did not include paragraph information. Each sentence was presented on a new line. None of the fifteen participants for Experiment 2 had participated in Experiment 1.

4.4.4   Results of the Experiments

Human sentence rankings did not differ significantly between Experiment 1 and Experiment 2 for any of the fifteen texts (all Fs < 1). This suggests that paragraph information does not have a large effect on human sentence rankings, at least not for the fifteen texts that we examined. Figure 4.22 shows the results from both experiments for one text.

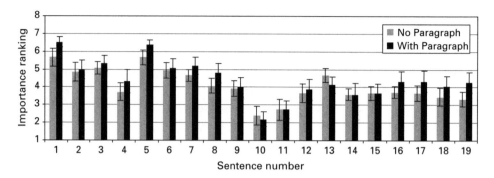

Figure 4.22
Human ranking results for one text (*wsj_1306*). The error bars represent standard errors of the mean.

We compared human sentence rankings to different algorithmic approaches. The layout-based rankings do not provide scaled importance rankings but only binary ones: *important* versus *not important*. Therefore, to compare human rankings to the layout-based baseline approach, we calculated point biserial correlations (see Bortz 1999). We obtained significant correlations between layout-based rankings and human rankings for only one of the fifteen texts.

All other algorithms provided scaled importance rankings. Many evaluations of scalable sentence ranking algorithms are based on precision/recall/*F*-scores (e.g., Carlson et al. 2001; Ono, Sumita, and Miike 1994). However, Jing et al. (1998) argue that such measures are inadequate because they distinguish only between hits and misses or false alarms, and do not account for a degree of agreement. For example, imagine a situation where the human ranking for a given sentence is 7 (very important) on an integer scale ranging from 1 to 7, algorithm A gives the same sentence a ranking of 7 on the same scale, algorithm B gives a ranking of 6, and algorithm C gives a ranking of 2. Intuitively, algorithm B performs better than Algorithm C, although it does not reach perfect performance. Precision/recall/*F*-scores do not account for this difference; they would rate algorithm A as "hit" (successful) but algorithm B as well as algorithm C as "miss" (unsuccessful). To collect performance measures that are more adequate to the evaluation of scaled importance rankings, we computed Spearman's rank correlation coefficients. The rank correlation coefficients were corrected for tied ranks because in our rankings it was possible for more than one sentence to have the same importance rank, that is, to have tied ranks (Horn 1942; Bortz 1999).

In addition to evaluating word-based and coherence-based algorithms, we evaluated one commercially available summarizer, the *Microsoft Word* (*MS Word*) summarizer, against human sentence rankings. Our reason for including an evaluation of the *MSWord* summarizer was to have a more useful baseline for scalable sentence rankings than the layout-based approach provides.

We used Carlson, Marcu, and Okurowski's (2002) discourse trees as input to Marcu's (2000) algorithm. That means that Marcu's algorithm operated on subsentential discourse segments. By contrast, the human rankings, and all the rankings obtained from the other algorithms, were for entire sentences. We therefore had to convert the rankings obtained from Marcu's (2000) algorithm from rankings of subsentential segments into rankings of sentences. We did this in three different ways:

- *MarcuAvg* sentence rankings were calculated as the average of the rankings of all discourse segments in that sentence
- *MarcuMin* sentence rankings were the minimum of the rankings of all discourse segments in that sentence
- *MarcuMax* sentence rankings were the maximum of the rankings of all discourse segments in that sentence

Figure 4.23 shows average rank correlations (ρ_{avg}) of each algorithm and human sentence ranking for the fifteen texts. It shows that the *MSWord* summarizer performed numerically worse than most other algorithms, except MarcuMax. Figure 4.23 also shows that cRank performed numerically better than all other algorithms and significantly better than most other algorithms:

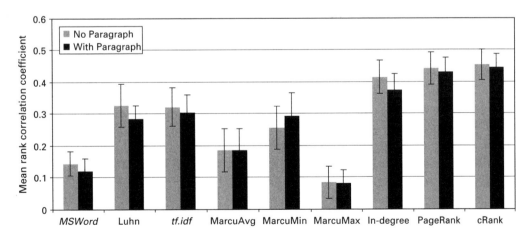

Figure 4.23
Average rank correlations (ρ_{avg}) of algorithm and human sentence rankings. The error bars represent standard errors of the mean.

- *MSWord*
  - NoParagraph: $F(1,28) = 24.779$, $p = 0.001$
  - WithParagraph: $F(1,28) = 31.832$, $p = 0.001$
- Luhn
  - WithParagraph: $F(1,28) = 7.326$, $p = 0.011$
- MarcuAvg
  - NoParagraph: $F(1,28) = 10.382$, $p = 0.003$
  - WithParagraph: $F(1,28) = 10.821$, $p = 0.004$
- MarcuMin
  - NoParagraph: $F(1,28) = 5.527$, $p = 0.026$
- MarcuMax
  - NoParagraph: $F(1,28) = 27.722$, $p = 0.0001$
  - WithParagraph: $F(1,28) = 37.778$, $p = 0.0001$

cRank performed marginally better than *tf.idf,* WithParagraph ($F(1,28) = 4.162$, $p = 0.051$).

cRank did not perform significantly better than the following algorithms:

- Luhn
  - NoParagraph: $F(1,28) = 2.298$, $p = 0.141$
- *tf.idf*
  - NoParagraph: $F(1,28) = 2.858$, $p = 0.102$
- MarcuMin
  - WithParagraph: $F(1,28) = 3.287$, $p = 0.081$
- In-degree, NoParagraph and WithParagraph: all $Fs < 1$
- PageRank, NoParagraph and WithParagraph: all $Fs < 1$

As mentioned above, human sentence rankings did not differ significantly between Experiment 1 and Experiment 2 for any of the fifteen texts (all $Fs < 1$). Therefore, to lend more power to our statistical tests, we collapsed the data for each text for the WithParagraph and the NoParagraph conditions and treated them as one experiment. Figure 4.24 shows that when the data from Experiments 1 and 2 are collapsed, cRank performed significantly better than all other algorithms except In-degree and PageRank, as shown by two-tailed *t*-tests:

- *MSWord:* $F(1,58) = 57.881$, $p = 0.0001$
- Luhn: $F(1,58) = 8.108$, $p = 0.006$
- *tf.idf:* $F(1,58) = 7.104$, $p = 0.010$
- MarcuAvg: $F(1,58) = 21.928$, $p = 0.0001$

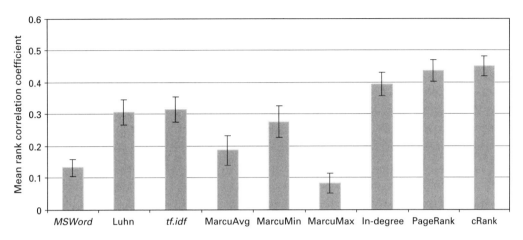

Figure 4.24
Average rank correlations (ρ_{avg}) of algorithm and human sentence rankings with collapsed data. The error bars represent standard errors of the mean.

- MarcuMin: $F(1,58) = 8.946$, $p = 0.004$
- MarcuMax: $F(1,58) = 66.076$, $p = 0.0001$
- In-degree: $F(1,58) = 1.350$, $p = 0.250$
- PageRank: $F(1,58) < 1$

4.5 Discussion

4.5.1 *MSWord* and Word-Based Algorithms

The results of our experiments showed that *MSWord* showed the second-worst performance of all algorithms tested; only MarcuMax was numerically worse, although the difference was not significant. Unfortunately, we cannot determine why *MSWord* did not perform better because it is a proprietary product. Part of the problem might be, however, that the *MSWord* summarizer might have been optimized for sentence selection rather than sentence ranking.[21] Sentence selection and sentence ranking are two different tasks. For instance, if there are multiple sentences with similar content, a sentence selection algorithm might (but a sentence ranking algorithm would not) try to select one of these sentences over the others, bypass all the other high-ranked sentences with similar content, and move to a different topic.

It is difficult to evaluate why the word-based methods (Luhn and *tf.idf*) did not perform better. However, word-based methods provide a very high baseline.

4.5.2 Coherence-Based Algorithms That Operate on Trees

Our results showed that coherence-based algorithms that operate on trees (MarcuMin, MarcuMax, MarcuAvg) performed worse than coherence-based algorithms that operate on chain graphs (In-degree, PageRank, cRank). The difference between tree-based and chain graph-based algorithms was significant ($F(1,70) = 7.057$; $p = .01$) (see figure 4.25).

One possible reason for this could be that trees introduce biases that hurt performance on sentence ranking. In particular, one problem could be that trees cannot represent nodes with multiple parents. Consider the coherence structure shown in figure 4.26. In that structure, R_1, R_2, and R_3 represent three different kinds of coherence relations. Based on any of the algorithms tested in this chapter that operate on chain graphs (In-degree, PageRank, cRank), node 1 would obtain the highest rank, whereas nodes 2, 3, and 4 would all obtain the same rank, which is lower than the rank of node 1.

However, the nodes would be ranked differently if a tree-based representation is used for the structure in figure 4.26. The problem with a structure such as the one shown in figure 4.26 is that it contains nodes with multiple parents. Figure 4.27 shows a tree representing that structure, where the grey numbers on the right indicate inverse tree level, solid lines in the tree indicate nucleus relations, and dashed lines indicate satellite relations.[22] By Marcu's (2000) algorithm, node 1 would obtain the highest rank (rank 4, see section 4.3.2.1, figure 4.5, for the algorithm). However, in contrast to chain graph-based ranking algorithms, Marcu's algorithm would assign each of the other nodes different ranks: node 2 would get rank 1, node 3 would get rank 2, and node 4 would get rank 3 (because they are in satellite relations, these nodes do not get promoted). Note that these ranks are a byproduct of the tree data structure.

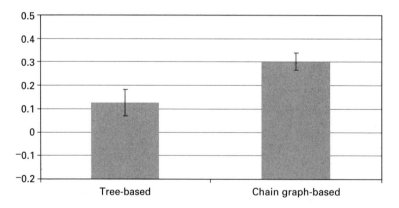

Figure 4.25
Performance of tree-based and chain graph-based algorithms compared. The error bars represent standard errors of the mean.

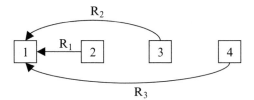

Figure 4.26
Example of a coherence structure containing a node with multiple parents (node 1)

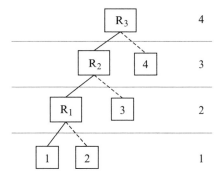

Figure 4.27
Tree-based representation for the coherence structure shown in figure 4.26. The gray numbers on the right indicate inverse tree levels. Solid lines indicate nucleus relations and dashed lines indicate satellite relations.

Our experimental text segment-ranking results provide some support for this idea, although we did not obtain enough data from our experiments to allow a quantitative analysis; we plan to perform such an analysis in future research. An example is the discourse structure for text wsj_1148 from the *Wall Street Journal* corpus (Harman and Liberman 1993), segmented into sentences (as we used them for the human sentence-ranking experiments):

(74) a. S1: Mobil Corp. is preparing to slash the size of its work force in the U.S., possibly as soon as next month, say individuals familiar with the company's strategy.

   b. S2: The size of the cuts isn't known, but they'll be centered in the exploration and production division, which is responsible for locating oil reserves, drilling wells and pumping crude oil and natural gas.

   c. S3: Employees haven't yet been notified.

   d. S4: Sources said that meetings to discuss the staff reductions have been scheduled for Friday at Mobil offices in New Orleans and Denver.

e. S5: This would be a second round of cuts by Mobil, which along with other oil producers and refiners reduced its work force by 15% to 20% during the mid-1980s as part of an industrywide shakeout.

f. S6: Mobil's latest move could signal the beginning of further reductions by other oil companies in their domestic oil-producing operations.

g. S7: In yesterday's third-quarter earnings report, the company alluded to a $40 million provision for restructuring costs involving U.S. exploration and production operations.

h. S8: The report says that "the restructuring will take place over a two-year period and will principally involve the transfer and termination of employees in our U.S. operations."

i. S9: A company spokesman, reached at his home last night, would only say that there will be a public announcement of the reduction program by the end of the week.

j. S10: Most oil companies, including Mobil, have been reporting lower third-quarter earnings, largely as a result of lower earnings from chemicals as well as refining and marketing businesses.

k. S11: Individuals familiar with Mobil's strategy say that Mobil is reducing its U.S. work force because of declining U.S. output.

l. S12: Yesterday, Mobil said domestic exploration and production operations had a $16 million loss in the third quarter, while comparable foreign operations earned $234 million.

m. S13: Industrywide, oil production in this country fell by 500,000 barrels a day to 7.7 million barrels in the first eight months of this year.

n. S14: Daily output is expected to decline by at least another 500,000 barrels next year.

o. S15: Some Mobil executives were dismayed that a reference to the cutbacks was included in the earnings report before workers were notified.

p. S16: One Mobil executive said that the $40 million charge related to the action indicates "a substantial" number of people will be involved.

q. S17: Some will likely be offered severance packages while others will be transferred to overseas operations.

The discourse structure for this text, when represented in a tree, is very similar to the one shown in figure 4.27, and it is schematically represented in figure 4.28. Figure 4.28 shows that node 17, which represents the last text segment in the text, gets rank 11 by Marcu's (2000) algorithm. This is the second-highest rank; only node 1 is ranked higher, because it

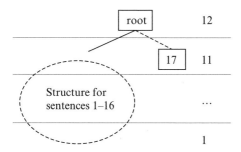

Figure 4.28
Partial representation of the tree discourse structure for text *wsj_1148* (Carlson, Marcu, and Okurowski 2002)

is promoted to rank 12 through nucleus relations.[23] However, in our human rankings (both with and without paragraph information), node 17 is ranked lowest of all nodes.

It is possible that human rankings of the last sentence of a text might be artificially low. This might be due in part to certain ways people are taught to read and write texts. However, in the discourse structure for the same text, node 13 is ranked third by Marcu's (2000) algorithm, but only twelfth by human judges (both with and without paragraph information). Again, the high ranking of that node by Marcu's algorithm is due to the tree representation's not allowing nodes with multiple parents, which enforces representations as shown in figures 4.27 and 4.28, and results in an artificially high ranking for node 13.

4.5.3 Coherence-Based Algorithms That Operate on Chain Graphs

Our results show that coherence-based algorithms that operate on chain graphs (In-degree, PageRank, cRank) performed best. However, we have identified a systematic problem for these algorithms. Consider the following example:

(75) a. S1: Susan plans to do the following things tomorrow morning:
      b. S2: She needs to go grocery shopping.
      c. S3: She also has to pick up clothes from the drycleaner.
      d. S4: And she has to get some wine for dinner.

A possible coherence structure for (75) is shown in figure 4.29.[24] By any of the chain graph-based ranking algorithms discussed in this chapter, segment 1 would get the highest ranking because of all the ingoing arcs leading to it. However, human raters would probably not rank segment 1 very high because it does not contain a lot of useful information.

An example of this phenomenon from our experimental results is from text wsj_2354. The first sentence of that text is given in (76):

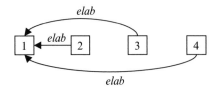

Figure 4.29
Coherence structure for (75)

(76) *First sentence of wsj_2354, Harman and Liberman (1993)*
      Call it the "we're too broke to fight" defense.

This sentence is followed by a range of statements that elaborate on it, resulting in a structure that is similar to the one shown in figure 4.29. Thus, by all chain graph-based ranking algorithms, that sentence is ranked first out of 16. However, the human rankings (with and without paragraph) placed it at only fifth out of 16.

A possible way of dealing with this problem could be to combine coherence chain graph-based ranking algorithms with measures of text segment informational content. Then, a text segment that is ranked high by a coherence chain graph-based algorithm would lose some of its rank if it has very low informational content. Possible ways of determining informational content could be measures of word entropy or measures like *tf.idf*.

4.6 Conclusion

The goal of this chapter was to evaluate the results of three different kinds of sentence-ranking algorithms and one commercially available summarizer. To evaluate the algorithms, we compared their sentence rankings to human sentence rankings of fifteen texts of varying length from the *Wall Street Journal*.

Our results indicated that a simple layout-based algorithm that was intended as a baseline performed very poorly, and that word-based and some coherence-based algorithms showed the best performance. The only commercially available summarizer that we tested, the *MSWord* summarizer, showed worse performance than most other algorithms. Furthermore, we found that a coherence-based algorithm that uses cRank and takes coherence chain graphs as input performed significantly better than most versions of a coherence-based algorithm that operates on coherence tree graphs. When data from Experiments 1 and 2 were collapsed, the cRank algorithm performed significantly better than all other algorithms, except the other coherence-based algorithms that operate on coherence chain graphs.

We found that coherence-based algorithms operating on chain graphs performed better than those performing on trees. Some preliminary results from our experiments suggest that this might in part be due to the fact that trees cannot represent nodes with multiple parents, leading possibly to artificially inflated sentence rankings. We plan to address this question in a more quantitative study in future research.

Note that the weaknesses of tree-based algorithms discussed in section 4.5.2 seem to be different from the weaknesses of chain graph-based algorithms discussed in section 4.5.3. The issue with tree-based algorithms seems to be that they might operate on a descriptively inadequate representation of coherence structures. On the other hand, the results for chain graph-based algorithms discussed in section 4.5.3 seem to suggest that there are additional, non-coherence-based factors contributing to sentence importance. If our preliminary results reported in section 4.5.3 can be supported in a larger, quantitative study, it would suggest that sentence informational content is another factor relevant to determining sentence importance, besides the relative position of a sentence in a coherence structure.

5 | General Conclusion

We have addressed three main issues within the general topic area of coherence in natural language. The first issue was the development of an easily codable, descriptively adequate data structure for representing coherence. The second issue we discussed was the role of coherence in psycholinguistic processes; more specifically, we discussed coherence as a factor in pronoun processing. Finally, the third issue addressed in this book was the relation between coherence structures and the relative saliency of discourse segments. The following sections will address each issue in turn and point out potential questions for future research.

5.1 Data Structures for Representing Discourse Coherence

In order to address the question of descriptively adequate data structures for representing coherence, we first compared a number of current approaches to representing discourse coherence. In doing that, we focused on comparing different taxonomies of coherence relations, constraints on inferences for determining coherence relations, and assumptions about data structures for representing discourse coherence.

Based on that discussion, we developed a coding scheme for coherence, where coherence refers to informational relations between segments of text. The coding scheme used a small taxonomy of coherence relations so that it would be compatible with as many different accounts of coherence as possible and be easier to code. Furthermore, we tried to make as few a priori theoretical assumptions as possible about representational data structures. In particular, we did not enforce a tree structure for coherence graphs.

The coding scheme was used to annotate for coherence structure a set of 135 naturally occurring texts. We used these coherence structures to test hypotheses about descriptively adequate data structures for representing discourse coherence. In particular, we tested for tree structure constraint violations in these manually annotated coherence structures. Our results indicated that there are many crossed dependencies and nodes with multiple parents in coherence structures of naturally occurring texts. Furthermore, there do not seem to be any obvious constraints on where those violations can occur. Therefore, it does not seem feasible to disregard these violations and accept a certain error rate, or to develop an augmented tree representation in order to represent these tree structure violations. By contrast, we have argued that more powerful data structures are needed to represent discourse coherence. In particular, we have argued for labeled chain graphs, where an ordered array of nodes represents text segments, and labeled directed or undirected arcs represent the coherence relations that hold between the text segments. However, we are not arguing that there are no constraints on discourse structure but rather that tree constraints are not the right kinds of constraints. Furthermore, dispensing with tree structures does not necessarily mean that discourse structures can be completely arbitrary. Future research should investigate questions such as whether there are structural constraints on coherence graphs (e.g., as proposed by Danlos 2004), or whether there are systematic structural differences between the coherence graphs of texts that belong to different genres (e.g., as proposed by Bergler 1992).

In section 2.3.3, we briefly illustrated the possibility of a more fine-grained discourse segmentation than used here. While such a detailed annotation of coherence relations was beyond the scope of the current project, future research should address this issue. A more fine-grained discourse segmentation could also facilitate integrating discourse-level with sentence-level structural descriptions.

Another issue to be addressed in future research is the complexity of inferring coherence structures. It is possible, for example, that certain coherence relations are harder to infer than others. Furthermore, features of a partially built discourse structure might influence the complexity of integrating additional arcs or nodes into that structure. Another factor influencing complexity might be the kinds of inferences necessary to infer a coherence relation; for instance, some inferences involved in a causal coherence relation might be harder to make than others.

Future research should also address the question of what the relation is between the processes underlying the establishment of discourse coherence and other linguistic or more general inference processes (see Hobbs 1985; Hobbs et al. 1993; Kehler 2002; Kintsch 1998; Winograd 1972). One hypothesis could be that inference processes underlying the establishment of discourse coherence form a specific cognitive module that is separate from other linguistic or more general cognitive processes (although this would not necessarily mean that coherence-related inference processes could not communicate with other cognitive processes; see Fodor 1983). On the other hand, it could be that coherence-related inference processes are part of more general cognitive inference processes that are used in other domains as well. This is hypothesized, for example, by Hobbs (1985), Hobbs et al. (1993), and Kehler (2002), who point out that their taxonomies of coherence relations are based on taxonomies of general inference processes that go back to Hume (1748) and Aristotle (Nestle 1977; see also section 2.3.3; Kintsch 1998; and Winograd 1972). There is also evidence that coherence relations can influence other cognitive processes (see section 1.1). For example, people are better at remembering information that is embedded in causal relations than elaborative relations (Kintsch 1998; Kintsch and van Dijk 1978). Furthermore, there is evidence that different pronoun processing strategies are used under different coherence relations (recall section 3). But there is no direct evidence yet about what exactly the different cognitive processing mechanisms are which underlie different coherence relations.

There are, however, hypotheses about the kinds of information that might be useful for establishing different coherence relations. For example, Kehler (2002) has proposed that in order to establish a similarity or a contrast relation, linguistic structures could be important: predicate-argument structures could be used to find corresponding entities and/or events between which a similarity or a contrast relation holds. To determine such similarity or contrast relations, it is necessary to have knowledge about similarities and contrasts between entities and events in the world (see also resources such as WordNet [Fellbaum 2001] or FrameNet [Johnson et al. 2003]). On the other hand, in order to establish elaboration relations, knowledge about super- and subclass relations, as well as mereological (part-whole) relations could be useful because elaboration relations describe a coherence relation between a more general and a more specific statement.

Establishing causal relations, however, seems to rely on different kinds of information (Kehler 2002): in determining whether a causal relation holds between two discourse segments, it is not very informative to know whether the discourse segments under consideration have similar predicate-argument structures. Ontological relations (similarities, contrasts, super- or subclass membership, or mereological relations between entities or events) are also not likely to be very informative. Instead, for causal relations, it is necessary to have knowledge about what causal inferences are plausible.

It is unclear how exactly the different kinds of information described above are used in online processing. For example, it is possible that certain kinds of information are accessed first, or that information is accessed first if it is particularly salient, regardless of what kind of information it is. Alternatively, there might be no such ranked access of information. Furthermore, it is unclear whether cognitive mechanisms for discourse processing are based on serial- or on parallel-processing architectures. Note that these questions have been addressed by many studies of human sentence and pronoun processing (e.g., Frazer and Clifton 1996; Gibson 1998; Gibson and Pearlmutter 1998; Jurafksy 2003; Tanenhaus and Trueswell 1995 for sentence processing; Garnham 2001; Sanford and Garrod 1989; and Stewart, Pickering, and Sanford 2000 for pronoun processing). However, to our knowledge, there have so far been no such studies on a discourse level.

5.2 Discourse Coherence and Pronoun Processing

The second goal of this book has been to test the role of coherence in psycholinguistic processes. In particular, we examined whether coherence can influence preferences in pronoun processing. In addressing this question, we conducted online comprehension and off-line production studies.

We tested several different accounts of pronoun processing. Most of these were specific to pronoun processing and made predictions based on the structural positions of the pronoun and its referent. The alternative to these pronoun-specific accounts was a coherence-based account where preferences in pronoun comprehension and production are a byproduct of more general cognitive processes used in determining discourse coherence. Both the comprehension and the production study indicated that structural, pronoun-specific approaches are not able to account for the full range of observed experimental results. Instead, the results from both studies supported the coherence-based account.

We have not described a full account of pronoun processing, and it is possible that other, non-coherence-based factors also affect pronoun processing. However, our results suggested that coherence is not just an arbitrary theoretical construct but that it can be validated through its influence on other cognitive processes. Furthermore, we showed that under cause-effect coherence relations, there are different pronoun processing preferences than under similarity coherence relations. This suggests that psychologically valid taxonomies of coherence relations should at least distinguish between these kinds of coherence relations.

Future work on pronoun processing should investigate pronoun processing preferences under other coherence relations than the ones we examined (similarity and cause-effect). Additionally, the time course of pronoun processing under different coherence relations should be explored: it is unclear, for example, whether the processing of coherence-relevant information (e.g., causal inferences or taxonomic relations) and linguistic information (e.g., predicate-argument structure or semantic roles) happens serially or in parallel. Similar questions have been addressed extensively for sentence-level processing (e.g., Frazer and Clifton 1996; Gibson 1998; Jurafksy 2003) and other aspects of pronoun processing that are not directly related to discourse coherence as defined in this book (Garnham 2001; Sanford and Garrod 1989; Stewart, Pickering, and Sanford 2000). Notice that investigating the time course of pronoun processing under different coherence relations would also require a better understanding of the time course of cognitive mechanisms underlying the establishment of coherence (see section 5.1).

Another open question concerning the relation between coherence and pronoun processing is what happens in longer discourses. We investigated preferences for two-clause sentences, but it is unclear, for example, how coherence and pronoun resolution are related if there is a greater distance between the clause containing the pronoun and the clause containing the referent. Another open question is what pronoun processing preferences are if coherence suggests one preference but other factors such as pronoun-referent distance suggest another preference.

5.3   Discourse Coherence and Discourse Segment Rankings

The third issue addressed in this book was the relation between coherence structures and the relative saliency of discourse segments. Using a set of naturally occurring texts, we compared human rankings with rankings derived from different approaches to discourse segment ranking. The approaches we tested included one layout-based, two word-based, and six coherence-based algorithms. We furthermore tested the commercially available *MSWord* summarizer.

The results from our study indicated that word-based algorithms provide a high baseline. A simple layout-based approach performed poorly. The *MSWord* summarizer also showed relatively weak performance, although this might result in part from the fact that the algorithm was probably optimized for the task of text summarization rather than discourse segment ranking per se (recall section 4.5.1). When compared to human discourse segment rankings, the best performance was shown by coherence-based algorithms that operate on chain graphs.

Our study furthermore showed that coherence-based algorithms operating on chain graphs perform better than coherence-based algorithms operating on tree graphs. So far, we do not have enough data to explore that difference in a more detailed quantitative study. But preliminary results from our experiment seem to indicate that the difference in performance might in part be due to the fact that chain graphs but not (unaugmented) trees can represent nodes with multiple parents.

While our results suggested that coherence-based algorithms operating on chain graphs performed best, we could also identify situations in which these algorithms do not make correct predictions about discourse segment importance. While these results are preliminary, they seem to indicate that in addition to a coherence-based measure of sentence importance, one should take into account measures of the informational content of discourse segments. Note, however, that this is probably an issue for tree-based approaches as well, in addition to their problems regarding nodes with multiple parents.

Future research on discourse segment ranking should investigate the performance difference between coherence-based algorithms operating on trees and algorithms operating on chain graphs. Our results indicated that the problem for tree-based algorithms might be that trees cannot represent nodes with multiple parents. However, our results concerning this issue are preliminary, and larger-scale, quantitative studies are needed.

Another question that should be addressed in the context of sentence-ranking algorithms is what factors contribute to sentence importance other than relative position of a sentence in a coherence structure. In section 4.5.3, we discussed one potential non-coherence-based factor, that is, the informational content of a sentence. Future research should investigate what good measures of informational content are, and how exactly they interact with coherence-based measures of sentence importance.

Yet another question that might be addressed in future research is how coherence-based ranking algorithms compare to algorithms operating on sentence similarity graphs. In sentence similarity graphs, links between sentences are based on lexical similarity rather than on coherence relations (e.g., Mihalcea 2004).

Other possible extensions of the work on sentence ranking reported here could be rankings on weighted coherence graphs. Such weighted graphs could implement the idea that under some circumstances, certain coherence relations are more important than others (e.g., causal coherence relations might be more important than elaborative coherence relations). Another possible extension would be to add weights for query-specific sentence rankings, rather than using generic sentence rankings as reported here.

Notes

1. In what follows, we will use the terms *coherence structure* and *discourse structure* interchangeably.

2. A connected graph is a graph where every node relates to some other node in the graph. A fully connected graph is a graph where every node relates to every other node in the graph.

3. Webber et al. (2003) do not include discourse segment 2 (11b) in their structure. Figure 2.5 shows an elaboration relation between discourse segments 1 and 2 as one way in which discourse segment 2 might be included in the structure for (11). This would mean that discourse segment 1 would have two parents: a succession and an elaboration relation. However, this does not change the point that Webber et al. (2003) make, namely, that discourse segment 3 has two parents.

4. Webber, Knott, Stone et al. (1999) do not specify the names for the relations in (12), so we use relation names R_1 through R_4, the focus here is not on what kinds of coherence relations there are in the discourse structure for (12) but on the topology of the coherence structure.

5. The Penguin Principle derives its name from the following: assume a knowledge base such that (1) birds can fly, (2) penguins are birds, (3) penguins cannot fly. In order to resolve the logical contradiction here between (1) and (3), one of these statements needs to be given priority over the other. Statement (3) is selected because it holds of a more specific class (penguins) than (1) (birds). By analogy, the Penguin Principle says that for discourse coherence, a more specific relation is preferred over a less specific relation if the conditions for both are met.

6. The 25 coherence relations are a superset of the 400.

7. Interannotator agreement for step 3 was influenced by interannotator agreement for step 2. For example, one annotator might mark a group of discourse segments 2 and 3, whereas the second annotator might not mark that group of discourse segments. If the first annotator then marks, for example, a cause-effect coherence relation between discourse segment 4 and the group of discourse segments 2-3, while the second annotator marks a

cause-effect coherence relation between discourse segment 4 and discourse segment 3, this would count as a disagreement. Thus, our measure of interannotator agreement for step 3 is conservative.

8. Although Lascarides and Asher (1991) do not explicitly disallow crossed dependencies, they argue that when building a discourse structure, the right frontier of an already-existing discourse structure is the only possible attachment point for a new discourse segment (see also Polanyi 1996; Polanyi and Scha 1984; Webber et al. 1999). This constraint on building discourse structures effectively disallows crossed dependencies.

9. Based on our segmentation guidelines, the complementizer *that* in discourse segment 3 would be part of discourse segment 2 instead of 3 (see (35) in section 2.3.3). However, this would not make a difference in terms of the resulting discourse structure.

10. A cultural reference may be useful here: it is only lawful to pass on the left on German highways. Thus, Rudolf is essentially saying that he will be polite as long as "the trucks and the timid" do not keep him from passing other cars.

11. The relation evaluation-s is part of the annotation scheme in Carlson, Marcu, and Okurowski (2002) but is not part of ours. In an evaluation-s relation, the situation presented in the satellite assesses the situation presented in the nucleus. An evaluation-s relation would be an elaboration relation in our annotation scheme.

12. Note that the proportions of removed coherence relations do not include coherence relations of absolute arc length 1, since removing those coherence relations cannot have any influence on the number of crossed dependencies. Thus, the proportions of coherence relations removed in figure 2.30 come from the third column of table 2.8.

13. Note that the hypothesis about a possible relation between arc length and frequency of crossed dependencies does not come from Webber et al. (2003).

14. The arc length distribution for the database overall does not include arcs of (absolute) length 1, since such arcs could not participate in crossed dependencies.

15. Note that, unlike in section 2.5.1.2, the distribution over coherence relations for all coherence relations includes arcs with length 1, since this time there was no reason to exclude them.

16. We follow the processing literature in focusing on the interpretation of unstressed pronouns. See Akmajian and Jackendoff (1970), among others, for a discussion of the interpretation of stressed pronouns.

17. A stoplist is a list of words that do not help distinguish one document from another (e.g., *the, a, of, under, above,* etc.). Instead of stoplists, *tf.idf* values have also been used to determine significant words (e.g., Buyukkokten, Garcia-Molina, and Paepcke 2001).

18. Another possible tree structure might be (elab (sim (1, 2), 3)). The structure chosen would probably mostly depend on how the similarity relation is defined: if it can hold only

between what is actually in a similarity relation (1 and 2 are, but 3 has no corresponding parallel entities or events anywhere), then (elab (sim (1, 2), 3)) should be chosen over (sim (1, elab (3, 2))).

19. None of these methods could be implemented for coherence trees since Marcu's (2000) tree-based algorithm assumes binary-branching trees. Thus, the in-degree for all nonterminal nodes is always 2.

20. The in-degree of a node is the number of arcs ingoing or pointing to that node. The out-degree would be the number of arcs outgoing or originating from that node, and the overall degree would be the number of ingoing plus the number of outgoing arcs (Diestel 2000).

21. We would like to thank Andy Kehler for this observation.

22. Note that the point of the example is that R_1, R_2, and R_3 are different kinds of relations. Therefore a structure like R_1 (0, R_2 (1, 2, 3)) does not represent the target discourse meaning.

23. Note that the original tree structure for text wsj_1148 in Carlson, Marcu, and Okurowski's (2002) database has forty-three nodes. However, for the purpose of this section, we collapsed their text segments into sentences to make them comparable to our human rankings. Collapsing the forty-three text segments results in seventeen sentences.

24. Note that there might be similarity relations between 1, 2, and 3 (all these text segments talk about similar things—things Susan has to do). However, these similarity relations have no bearing on the point made here, and are therefore left out to keep the graph structure simple.

References

Akmajian, A., and R. Jackendoff. 1970. Coreferentiality and stress. *Linguistic Inquiry* 1: 124–126.

Ariel, M. 1990. *Accessing NP antecedents*. London: Routledge.

Bateman, J., and K. Rondhuis. 1994. *Coherence relations: Analysis and specifications*. Technical report. Darmstadt, Germany: GMD-IPSI.

Bergler, S. 1991. The semantics of collocational patterns for reporting verbs. Paper presented at the 5th Conference of the European Chapter of the Association for Computational Linguistics, Berlin, Germany.

Bergler, S. 1992. Evidential analysis of reported speech. PhD diss., Brandeis University, Waltham, MA.

Birnbaum, L. 1982. Argument molecules: A functional representation of argument structures. Paper presented at the Third National Conference on Artificial Intelligence (AAAI-82), Pittsburgh, PA.

Bortz, J. 1999. *Statistik fuer Sozialwissenschaftler*. Berlin: Springer Verlag.

Brandow, R., K. Mitze, and L. F. Rau. 1995. Automatic condensation of electronic publications by sentence selection. *Information Processing and Management* 31 (5): 675–685.

Brants, S., S. Dipper, S. Hansen, W. Lezius, and G. Smith. 2002. The TIGER Treebank. Paper presented at the Workshop on Treebanks and Linguistic Theories, Sozopol, Bulgaria.

Brennan, S. E., M. W. Friedman, and C. J. Pollard. 1987. A centering approach to pronouns. Paper presented at the 25th Meeting of the Association for Computational Linguistics, Stanford, CA.

Britton, B. K. 1994. Understanding expository text. In *Handbook of psycholinguistics,* ed. M. A. Gernsbacher, 641–674. San Diego, CA: Academic Press.

Buyukkokten, O., H. Garcia-Molina, and A. Paepcke. 2001. Seeing the whole in parts: Text summarization for web browsing on handheld devices. Paper presented at the 10th International WWW Conference, Hong Kong.

Caramazza, A., E. Grober, C. Garvey, and J. Yates. 1977. Comprehension of anaphoric pronouns. *Journal of Verbal Learning and Verbal Behavior* 16: 601–609.

Carletta, J. 1996. Assessing agreement on classification tasks: The kappa statistic. *Computational Linguistics* 22 (2): 249–254.

Carlson, L., J. M. Conroy, D. Marcu, D. P. O'Leary, M. E. Okurowski, A. Taylor and W. Wong. 2001. An empirical study on the relation between abstracts, extracts, and the discourse structure of texts. Paper presented at the DUC-2001, New Orleans, LA.

Carlson, L., D. Marcu, and M. E. Okurowski. 2002. *RST Discourse Treebank*. Philadelphia: Linguistic Data Consortium.

Carlson, L., D. Marcu, and M. E. Okurowski. 2003. Building a discourse-tagged corpus in the framework of rhetorical structure theory. In *Current directions in discourse and dialogue,* ed. J. van Kuppevelt and R. Smith. New York: Kluwer.

Chambers, C. C., and R. Smyth. 1998. Structural parallelism and discourse coherence: A test of Centering Theory. *Journal of Memory and Language* 39: 593–608.

Chomsky, N. 1973. Conditions on transformations. In *A Festschrift for Morris Halle,* ed. S. Anderson and P. Kiparsky, 232–286. New York: Holt, Rinehart, and Winston.

Corston-Oliver, S. 1998. Computing representations of the structure of written discourse. Microsoft Research Technical Report MSR-TR-98-15. Redmond, WA: Microsoft.

Danlos, L. 2004. Discourse dependency structures as DAGs. Paper presented at the SigDIAL2004, Cambridge, MA.

Diestel, R. 2000. *Graph theory.* New York: Springer Verlag.

Ding, C., X. He, P. Husbands, H. Zha, and H. Simon. 2002. *PageRank, HITS, and a unified framework for link analysis.* Lawrence Berkeley National Laboratory Technical Report 49372. Berkeley, CA: LBNL.

Dowty, D. 1986. The effects of aspectual class on the temporal structure of discourse: Semantics or pragmatics? *Linguistics and Philosophy* 9: 37–61.

Eden, R., and R. Mitchell. 1986. Paragraphing for the reader. *College Composition and Communication* 37 (4): 416–430.

Ehrlich, K. 1980. Comprehension of pronouns. *Quarterly Journal of Experimental Psychology* 32: 247–255.

Fellbaum, C., ed. 2001. *WordNet—An electronic lexical database.* Cambridge, MA: MIT Press.

Fodor, J. A. 1983. *The modularity of mind.* Cambridge, MA: MIT Press.

Frazer, L., and C. Clifton. 1996. *Construal.* Cambridge, MA: MIT Press.

Garnham, A. 2001. *Mental models and the interpretation of anaphora.* Hove, UK: Psychology Press.

Gibson, E. 1998. Linguistic complexity: Locality of syntactic dependencies. *Cognition* 68: 1–76.

Gibson, E., and M. Breen. 2003. The difficulty of processing crossed dependencies in English. Unpublished manuscript, MIT, Cambridge, MA.

Gibson, E., and N. J. Pearlmutter. 1998. Constraints on sentence comprehension. *Trends in Cognitive Sciences* 2: 262–268.

Goldstein, J., M. Kantrowitz, V. O. Mittal, and J. O. Carbonell. 1999. Summarizing text documents: Sentence selection and evaluation metrics. Paper presented at the SIGIR-99, Melbourne, Australia.

Gong, Y., and X. Liu. 2001. Generic text summarization using relevance measure and latent semantic analysis. Paper presented at the Annual ACM Conference on Research and Development in Information Retrieval, New Orleans, LA.

Goodrich, M. T., and R. Tamassia. 2001. *Data structures and algorithms in Java.* New York: John Wiley.

Gordon, P. C., B. J. Grosz, and L. A. Gilliom. 1993. Pronouns, names, and the centering of attention in discourse. *Cognitive Science* 17: 311–347.

Grice, H. P. 1975. Logic and conversation. In *Speech Acts,* vol. 3, *Syntax and semantics,* ed. P. Cole and J. Morgan, 41–58. New York: Academic Press.

Grosz, B. J., A. K. Joshi, and S. Weinstein. 1995. Centering: A framework for modeling the local coherence of discourse. *Computational Linguistics* 21 (2): 203–225.

Grosz, B. J., and C. L. Sidner. 1986. Attention, intentions, and the structure of discourse. *Computational Linguistics* 12 (3): 175–204.

Haliday, M. A., and R. Hassan. 1976. *Cohesion in English.* London: Longman.

Harman, D., and M. Liberman. 1993. *TIPSTER complete.* Philadelphia: Linguistic Data Consortium.

Hearst, M. 1997. TextTiling: Segmenting text into multi-paragraph subtopic passages. *Computational Linguistics* 23 (1): 33–64.

Hirschberg, J., and C. H. Nakatani. 1996. A prosodic analysis of discourse segments in direction-giving monologues. Paper presented at the 34th annual meeting of the Association for Computational Linguistics, Santa Cruz, CA.

Hobbs, J. R. 1979. Coherence and coreference. *Cognitive Science* 3: 67–90.

Hobbs, J. R. 1985. *On the coherence and structure of discourse.* Center for the Study of Language and Information Technical Report 85-37. Stanford, CA: CSLI Publications.

Hobbs, J. R., M. E. Stickel, D. E. Appelt, and P. Martin. 1993. Interpretation as abduction. *Artificial Intelligence* 63: 69–142.

Horn, D. 1942. A correction for the effect of tied ranks on the value of the rank difference correlation coefficient. *Journal of Educational Psychology* 33: 686–690.

Hovy, E., and E. Maier. 1995. *Parsimonious or profligate: How many and which discourse relations?* Unpublished manuscript. Marina del Rey, CA: Information Sciences Institute of the University of Southern California.

Hume, D. 1748. *An enquiry concerning human understanding.* http://www.infidels.org/library/historical/david_hume/human_understanding.html.

Jing, H., K. R. McKeown, R. Barzilay, and M. Elhadad. 1998. Summarization evaluation methods: Experiments and analysis. Paper presented at the AAAI-98 Spring Symposium on Intelligent Text Summarization, Stanford, CA.

Johnson, C. R., M. R. L. Petruck, C. F. Baker, M. Ellsworth, J. Ruppenhofer, and C. J. Fillmore. 2003. *FrameNet: Theory and practice.* http://www.icsi.berkeley.edu/~framenet/book/book.html

Johnson-Laird, P. 1983. *Mental models.* Cambridge, MA: Harvard Univ. Press.

Joshi, A. K., and S. Kuhn. 1979. Centered logic: The role of entity centered sentence representation in natural language inferencing. Paper presented at the 6th International Joint Conference on Artificial Intelligence, Tokyo.

Joshi, A. K., and Y. Schabes. 1997. Tree-adjoining grammars. In *Handbook of formal languages,* ed. G. Rozenberg and A. Salomaa, 69–123. New York: Springer Verlag.

Jurafksy, D. 2003. Probabilistic modeling in psycholinguistics: Linguistic comprehension and production. In *Probabilistic linguistics,* ed. R. Bod, J. Hay, and S. Jannedy, 39–96. Cambridge, MA: MIT Press.

Just, M. A., P. A. Carpenter, and J. D. Woolley. 1982. Paradigms and processing in reading comprehension. *Journal of Experimental Psychology: General* 111: 228–238.

Kehler, A. 2002. *Coherence, reference, and the theory of grammar.* Stanford, CA: CSLI Publications.

Kintsch, W. 1998. *Comprehension: A paradigm for cognition.* Cambridge: Cambridge Univ. Press.

Kintsch, W., and T. A. van Dijk. 1978. Toward a model of text comprehension and production. *Psychological Review* 85: 363–394.

Knott, A. 1996. A data-driven methodology for motivating a set of coherence relations. PhD diss., University of Edinburgh.

König, E., and W. Lezius. 2000. A description language for syntactically annotated corpora. Paper presented at the Computational Linguistics Conference (COLING), Saarbrücken, Germany.

Lappin, S., and H. Leass. 1994. An algorithm for pronominal anaphora resolution. *Computational Linguistics* 20 (4): 535–561.

Lascarides, A., and N. Asher. 1991. Discourse relations and defeasible knowledge. Paper presented at the 9th annual meeting of the Association for Computational Linguistics, Berkeley, CA.

Lascarides, A., and N. Asher. 1993. Temporal interpretation, discourse relations and common sense entailment. *Linguistics and Philosophy* 16 (5), 437–493.

Longacre, R. E. 1983. *The grammar of discourse*. New York: Plenum Press.

Luhn, H. P. 1958. The automatic creation of literature abstracts. *IBM Journal of Research and Development* 2 (2): 159–165.

Mann, W. C., and S. A. Thompson. 1988. Rhetorical structure theory: Toward a functional theory of text organization. *Text* 8 (3), 243–281.

Manning, C. D., and H. Schuetze. 2000. *Foundations of statistical natural language processing*. Cambridge, MA: MIT Press.

Marcu, D. 2000. *The theory and practice of discourse parsing and summarization*. Cambridge, MA: MIT Press.

Marcus, M., G. Kim, M. A. Marcinkiewicz, R. MacIntyre, A. Bies, M. Ferguson, K. Katz, and B. Schasberger. 1994. The Penn Treebank: Annotating predicate argument structure. Paper presented at the ARPA Human Language Technology Workshop, San Francisco, CA.

Martin, J. 1992. *English text: Systems and structure*. Amsterdam: Benjamins.

McKeown, K. R. 1985. *Text generation: Using discourse strategies and focus constraints to generate natural language text*. Cambridge: Cambridge Univ. Press.

Mihalcea, R. 2004. Graph-based ranking algorithms for sentence extraction, applied to text summarization. Paper presented at the 42nd annual meeting of the Association for Computational Linguistics, Barcelona, Spain.

Mitra, M., A. Singhal, and C. Buckley. 1997. Automatic text summarization by paragraph extraction. Paper presented at the ACL/EACL-97 Workshop on Intelligent Scalable Text Summarization, Madrid, Spain.

Moore, J. D., and M. E. Pollack. 1992. A problem for RST: The need for multi-level discourse analysis. *Computational Linguistics* 18 (4): 537–544.

Moser, M., and J. D. Moore. 1996. Toward a synthesis of two accounts of discourse structure. *Computational Linguistics* 22 (3): 409–419.

Nakatani, C. H., B. J. Grosz, and D. D. Ahn. 1995. *Instructions for annotating discourse*. Cambridge, MA: Harvard Univ. Press.

Nestle, W., ed. 1977. *Aristotles: Hauptwerke*. Berlin: Kroener Verlag.

Ono, K., K. Sumita, and S. Miike. 1994. Abstract generation based on rhetorical structure extraction. Paper presented at the COLING-94, Kyoto, Japan.

Page, L., S. Brin, R. Motwani, and T. Winograd. 1998. *The PageRank citation ranking: Bringing order to the web*. Stanford, CA: Stanford Digital Libraries.

Penstein Rose, C., B. Di Eugenio, L. S. Levin, and C. Van Ess-Dykema. 1995. Discourse processing of dialogues with multiple threads. Paper presented at the 33rd annual meeting of the Association for Computational Linguistics, Cambridge, MA.

Polanyi, L. 1996. *The linguistic structure of discourse.* Center for the Study of Language and Information Technical Report 96-198. Stanford, CA: CSLI Publications.

Polanyi, L., C. Culy, M. van den Berg, G. L. Thione, and D. Ahn. 2004. A rule based approach to discourse parsing. Paper presented at the SigDIAL 2004, Cambridge, MA.

Polanyi, L., and R. Scha. 1984. A syntactic approach to discourse semantics. Paper presented at the 10th International Conference on Computational Linguistics, Stanford, CA.

Radev, D. R., E. Hovy, and K. R. McKeown. 2002. Introduction to the special issue on summarization. *Computational Linguistics* 28 (4): 399–408.

Raghavan, S., and H. Garcia-Molina. 2001. Crawling the hidden web. Paper presented at the 27th International Conference on Very Large Databases, Rome.

Reichman, R. 1985. *Getting computers to talk like you and me.* Cambridge, MA: MIT Press.

Salton, G., and C. Buckley. 1988. Term-weighting approaches in automatic text retrieval. *Information Processing and Management* 24 (5): 513–523.

Sanford, A. J., and S. C. Garrod. 1989. What, when, and how: Questions of immediacy in anaphoric reference resolution. *Language and Cognitive Processes* 4 (3/4): 235–262.

Schauer, H. 2000. Referential structure and coherence structure. Paper presented at the TALN 2000, Lausanne, Switzerland.

Shieber, S. M. 1986. *An introduction to unification-based approaches to grammar.* Center for the Study of Language and Information Lecture Notes 4. Stanford, CA: CSLI Publications.

Skut, W., B. Krenn, T. Brants, and H. Uszkoreit. 1997. An annotation scheme for free word order languages. Paper presented at the 5th Conference on Applied Natural Language Processing (ANLP-97), Washington, DC.

Smyth, R. H. 1994. Grammatical determinants of ambiguous pronoun resolution. *Journal of Psycholinguistic Research* 23: 197–229.

Sparck-Jones, K. 1993. What might be in a summary? In *Information retrieval 93: Von der Modellierung zur Anwendung,* ed. J. Krause and C. Womser-Hacker, 9–26. Konstanz, Germany: Universitaetsverlag.

Sparck-Jones, K., and T. Sakai. 2001. Generic summaries for indexing in IR. Paper presented at the ACM SIGIR-2001, New Orleans, LA.

Stewart, A. J., M. J. Pickering, and A. J. Sanford. 2000. The role of implicit causality in language comprehension: Focus versus integration accounts. *Journal of Memory and Language* 42: 423–443.

Tanenhaus, M. K., and J. C. Trueswell. 1995. Sentence comprehension. In *Handbook of perception and cognition,* vol. 11, *Speech, language, and communication,* ed. P. Eimas and J. Miller, 217–262. New York: Academic Press.

van Dijk, T. A., and W. Kintsch. 1983. *Strategies of discourse comprehension.* New York: Academic Press.

Vogel, C., U. Hahn, and H. Branigan. 1996. Cross-serial dependencies are not hard to process. Paper presented at the 16th International Conference on Computational Linguistics, Copenhagen, Denmark.

Walker, M. A. 1998. Centering, anaphora resolution, and discourse structure. In *Centering Theory in discourse,* ed. E. Prince, A. K. Joshi, and M. Walker, 401–435. Oxford: Oxford Univ. Press.

Webber, B. L., A. Knott, and A. K. Joshi. 1999. Multiple discourse connectives in a lexicalized grammar for discourse. Paper presented at the 3rd International Workshop on Computational Semantics, Tilburg, Netherlands.

Webber, B. L., A. Knott, M. Stone, and A. K. Joshi. 1999. Discourse relations: A structural and presuppositional account using lexicalized TAG. Paper presented at the 37th annual meeting of the Association for Computational Linguistics (ACL-99), College Park, MD.

Webber, B. L., M. Stone, A. K. Joshi, and A. Knott. 2003. Anaphora and discourse structure. *Computational Linguistics* 29 (4): 545–587.

Winograd, T. 1972. *Understanding natural language.* New York: Academic Press.

Wolf, F., and E. Gibson. 2004. Paragraph-, word-, and coherence-based approaches to sentence ranking: A comparison of algorithm and human performance. Paper presented at the 42nd annual meeting of the Association for Computational Linguistics, Barcelona, Spain.

Wolf, F., and E. Gibson. 2005. Representing discourse coherence: A corpus-based analysis. *Computational Linguistics* 31 (2): 249–287.

Wolf, F., E. Gibson, A. Fisher, and M. Knight. 2003. A procedure for collecting a database of texts annotated with coherence relations. Unpublished manuscript, Department of Brain and Cognitive Sciences, Massachusetts Institute of Technology.

Wundt, W. 1911. *Völkerspsychologie.* Leipzig, Germany: Engelmann Verlag.

Zechner, K. 1996. Fast generation of abstracts from general domain text corpora by extracting relevant sentences. Paper presented at the COLING-96, Copenhagen, Denmark.

Zukerman, I., and R. McConachy. 1995. Generating discourse across several user modules: Maximizing belief while avoiding boredom and overload. Paper presented at the International Joint Conference on Artificial Intelligence (IJCAI-95), Montreal, Canada.

Index